Observations

Most memorable individuals become revered in the eyes of history. Maurice Warshaw received the honor while yet living. History writes songs and tells stories of the past, but when Maurice Warshaw died in 1979, only four years after his biography was published, he received more honor than often given those long after passing. A bust was made and displayed in the state capital rotunda, an original musical score and production was performed in the Promise Valley Playhouse in Salt Lake City—all based upon his colorful life. His story equaled that of a Broadway production, but certainly not equal to a Broadway performance.

Who receives such honor before they die? In contrast, you will find only a handful in 2015 that would even remember him. There is nothing left of his enterprise still standing or anything that bares his name. Many of the locals laughed at him when he spoke, but U.S. presidents and world leaders honored him and almost every service organization depended upon him. Many life-long employees served him. Few however understood that his buffoon style simply covered his concern for those far less than society ever seemed to consider. For this reason Vision Impact Publishing has chosen to publish this second edition. Whether any will read in under such troubling times, it is still story and a dream out of history never to be forgotten.

Ron Kelsch – editor for Vision Impact Publishing

Dedication

To my wife Inez,
my daughters Marge and Pat,
my son Keith, and their families.
They are the part of this story I do not know how to tell.

They are the most important story of my life.

Appreciation

My grateful appreciation to Rhoda and Clarence Kelsch for the three years they worked with me in the, research, compiling, editing, and preparation of this book for publication.

© Maurice Warshaw with Rhoda Kelsch 1975

First Publication in Salt Lake City by C.O. Kelsch &: Associates

Publisher Clarence Kelsch, Associates: Maurice Warshaw and Ronald Kelsch

First printing by The Quality Press
Original illustrations by Mike Nelson

Second publication by - Vision Impact Publications

ISBN 978-0-9827313-4-5

Second Edition Preface and observations by Ronald Kelsch

Life more sweet than bitter

Maurice Warshaw
with Rhoda Kelsch

Preface to this addition

Maurice Warsaw was a gifted man. He was perhaps my first mentor beyond that of my mother and father. It was the three of them that undeniably colored my life to such an extent that every bit of success I owe to them. Although Maurice was not a writer nor did he have the formal education sufficiently to communicate eloquently with words, his mind was quick, perceptive, with more understanding than anyone I have ever known. His self-important style was a bluff and his anger a tease to few that really understood him.

My first confrontation with Maurice was the summer of 1954 at the age of 15. It was my first relationship when it came to my my first employer. I already had a run in with my grandfather, a bit older than Maurice, but also an immigrant from the old country. This generation had a special flare about them that is rarely seen today. It is that confidant look and attitude that says, "I am going to succeed." To that generation, this book was certainly written. I knew how my father could show his temper and I often was a scared little man. Maurice stood taller than my father and his voice would certainly carry. If it was not for my father's previously smiling reactions I have thought I would come to my end.

Maurice had a special phrase that I still use to this day at the age of 75. Upon a grand entrance into the very small advertising department, Maurice would project as if from a Shakespearian stage, "Where is it?" I knew the voice from before, but this time I would be the recipient of this classic alarm. I was on my knees giving the last coats of paint to a retail display. As a child with a hearing disorder, I did not pay any attention until I was painting near this giant shoe holding down my work. I looked up into the face of a giant. I was not the beauty, but rather the beast. His scowl mimicked disapproval that something was not finished. I do not know what came over me, but I smiled as a neglected child would smile when his father would finely pay attention to a youth's artwork. Despite Maurice's sternness, I treaded the incident as if someone cared. I never forgot that incident. I learned that to do a good job you may not get praise, but you can still see in the eyes of a good mentor giving his approval. I saw over the years every one of his devoted employees gave their all. Maurice built and enterprise that a typical Walmart of to day can only come close to. In the 1960's Maurice had super stores that were larger or better than we might see in the twenty-first-century. Maurice had a classic method that does not survive with the political ramifications of today. No matter how hard I tried to preserve his true and inspiring method every business that I would council over the years would eventually fall into the hands of political vultures. So many great things have come and gone and almost in every case we fail to preserve the spirit of these great men.

For this reason I have resurrected something out of the past for those who what to read the story of life most bitter, but demonstrates a faith in his God that is treated with distain in our troubling times. It was my mother that wrote this work while she worked with Maurice starting eight years before his death. I have few corrections, but essentially remains the same. Maurice and my mother were working on a novel about modern Israel. It was called *Ben Arron*. If God permits something may come of it. Out of respect for the man and to those who still might remember him, I give you again this publication.

Ronald Kelsch

The Jewish community was our world

How it began

In the shadows of the onion-spired churches of mighty Russia, the Jews lived quietly, Families were organized into communities, both religious and civil in character, and their towns flourished.

Introduction

I was born in 1898 in Dubossar, Russia. It was the year that Czar Nicholas II called upon the world powers to renounce war and disband their armies. For years the events of that time were still so fresh in people's minds that they continued to be the main topic of conversation. Certain things became indelibly stamped on my mind. Even today I can almost reconstruct the history of those years, for as a child I lay on our sleeping bench in the evenings listening to the adults talk about their lives. We were Russian citizens, but Jews as well. Everything which happened to the country doubly affected us.

My father had hoped that 1898 was to be the year of blessings. First, a son was born to him, and that same year Czar Nicholas not only surprised the world with his peace proposal, but with an order to cease the persecution of Russia's Jews.

Gathered around the samovar, family and visitors used to talk about the magnificent coronation of Nicholas. It had taken place just two years before I was born - a splendid ceremony in the Cathedral of the Ascension in Moscow. Of course Jews did not have the same religious beliefs as the Christians; but since the church and state were as one body, all citizens felt they had a vicarious part in the celebrations.

Nicholas II has since been portrayed variously as benevolent and good, or as selfish and wicked. My father placed great hope in the young Czar's proposal for permanent world peace which stated that "To continue to arm for war would create an ever increasing financial burden that would attack prosperity at the roots and weaken the physical and intellectual strength of the people. War causes heavy tax burdens that accomplish nothing and leave only misery in their wake."

The *London Times*, August 29, 1898, commented upon this proposal:

> The state paper which was by direct order of the Czar had addressed to representatives of the powers accredited to the Court of St. Petersburg a very remarkable and most unexpected document. On the eve of inaugurating a memorial to his grandfather as the Czar Liberator, the present autocrat of all Russia seizes the opportunity to appeal to the civilized world in the still more lofty capacity of the Czar Peacemaker. The proposal, in which the views and aspirations of the Czar are expounded, breathes a spirit of generous humanity, a spirit with which we have long been familiar in visionaries and enthusiasts, but have been so seldom privileged to find in the utterances of great sovereigns and responsible statesmen. Never perhaps in modern history have the aspirations which good men in all ages have regarded as ideal and unattainable found so responsive an echo in the counsel of one of the greatest and most powerful of the world's rulers.

The plan included a great conference to consolidate the efforts of all countries that sincerely wished to realize the triumph of universal peace. Nicholas pledged the support of his empire and cooperation with other nations in disbanding their armies. A circular was sent to various governments setting forth the points for discussion at the proposed conference. When the points of disarmament were published, however, people all over the world began to protest that they were impractical.

Nevertheless the appointed delegates met; but it soon became evident that no country would take seriously any real plan for disarmament. As a substitute, the United States and Great Britain proposed the establishment of an international court of arbitration to settle disputes among nations. This instance in history is but a glimpse into the never ending cycle of wars and attempts at peace, but it did mark modern man's first attempt to negotiate peace by talking it over rather than slugging it out.

After the approval of the basic idea of peace, each of the powers waited to see what the others would do, and how a disarmament proposal would affect the prospects of the political parties controlling their governments. Each expressed its favor in such a manner as to make practical endorsement possible if the tide should turn in that direction, yet to allow a graceful way out should the measure fail. During these negotiations, sad to note, the United States was preoccupied in a war with Spain. One is tempted to muse upon what wonderful results might have come about had America embraced the proposal for peace, thus spreading the enthusiasm of a young democracy among the many countries that looked up to us.

It has always saddened me that all the participants did not heartily join in this first plan to abolish war. Instead, history proved once more that man remains more concerned about power, land and trade than about the most vital issues with which he is faced at any given period of time. Maybe the tragedies in the years since could have been averted, maybe not. It does seem that the delights and advantages of war, the splendor of military pageantry and the power of governments and their armed forces overcome any serious considerations of peace. One can only ask, "Do countries actually prefer war as the principal means of displaying political strength and so-called national glory? Do peace proposals fail because the basic instincts that lie beneath the surface of the human personality allow man to carry his country into war?" Perhaps the answer can only be found within ourselves.

From the different pulpits we are admonished to respect God, to love our neighbors, to be tolerant and to "tum the other cheek." But even Nicholas II, a devout Christian who could speak in glowing terms of the lofty ideals of peace, changed when his autocracy was threatened. He fought for survival with the same basic instinct of any man and become instrumental in the slaughter of many of his own people, at the same time averting his eyes from the terrible plight of the Jews.

It is doubtful that peace can be found in either ideologies or plans for Utopia. My own life tells me that the answer will be found in learning to cope with that strongest and most fundamental of all instincts, survival—the struggle which stimulates the competitiveness that causes one human to fight against another. Paradoxically, the desire for peace seems as deeply rooted in us as the instinct for fighting to survive. In my travels around the world I have never met a man who did not have, within himself, this longing for peace. I can only speak for myself. I was fiercely competitive in building my business and I believe that the competitive instinct is in every man, whatever his age. It is with him to the very end. But the years themselves soften the edges of competitiveness as wisdom brings an awareness of others. In my own case, the desire has grown to unite this spirit of competition with the fight against hunger and disaster and disease—to join with others in order to move further toward the ultimate goal of freedom of spirit and the universal regard for the worldwide good of man.

My parents told me as a child about a horrifying incident in May, 1896, during the celebrations of the magnificent coronation of Nicholas II. Fifteen hundred people were trampled to death when the masses stampeded in their frantic efforts to get hold of the food being distributed among them. This tragedy cast a gloom over Russia that was not lessened by the payment of 1000 rubles plus burial money to each family to sustain its loss. The nature of the incident made it impossible to fix the blame on anyone, but it was evidence of the disastrous potential of uncontrolled crowds of hungry and desperate people. A few short years later I myself watched our Christian neighbors, some of the most easy going and gentle people in the world, become so agitated by their conditions and the propaganda fed them as a substitute for easing their plight that they actually went out and killed others for their possessions. This mob violence, with the Jews its principal victims, forced us to leave Russia. This madness continue in that unhappy land long after we left.

I have seen repeated wars ever since. Yet I know that opportunities for peace continue to be offered us, not only in formal proposals between nations, but in our everyday life. I know this because during these same years the greatest social and technological changes in history were taking place, changes which produced much for the advancement of mankind and enhanced our potential for peaceful coexistence. It is this period of history that, having lived through it myself, I would like to write about. By now I have had a whole lifetime to subdue my angers and hostilities. I hope now to present a clear picture of my life experiences at a time when my own wrongdoings have fallen into proper perspective. I want to leave as a legacy for my children and others who may wish to share them, the positive lessons learned in the recaptured cross section of those years of the twentieth century that I have known.

Maurice Warshaw

Salt Lake City, Utah 1975

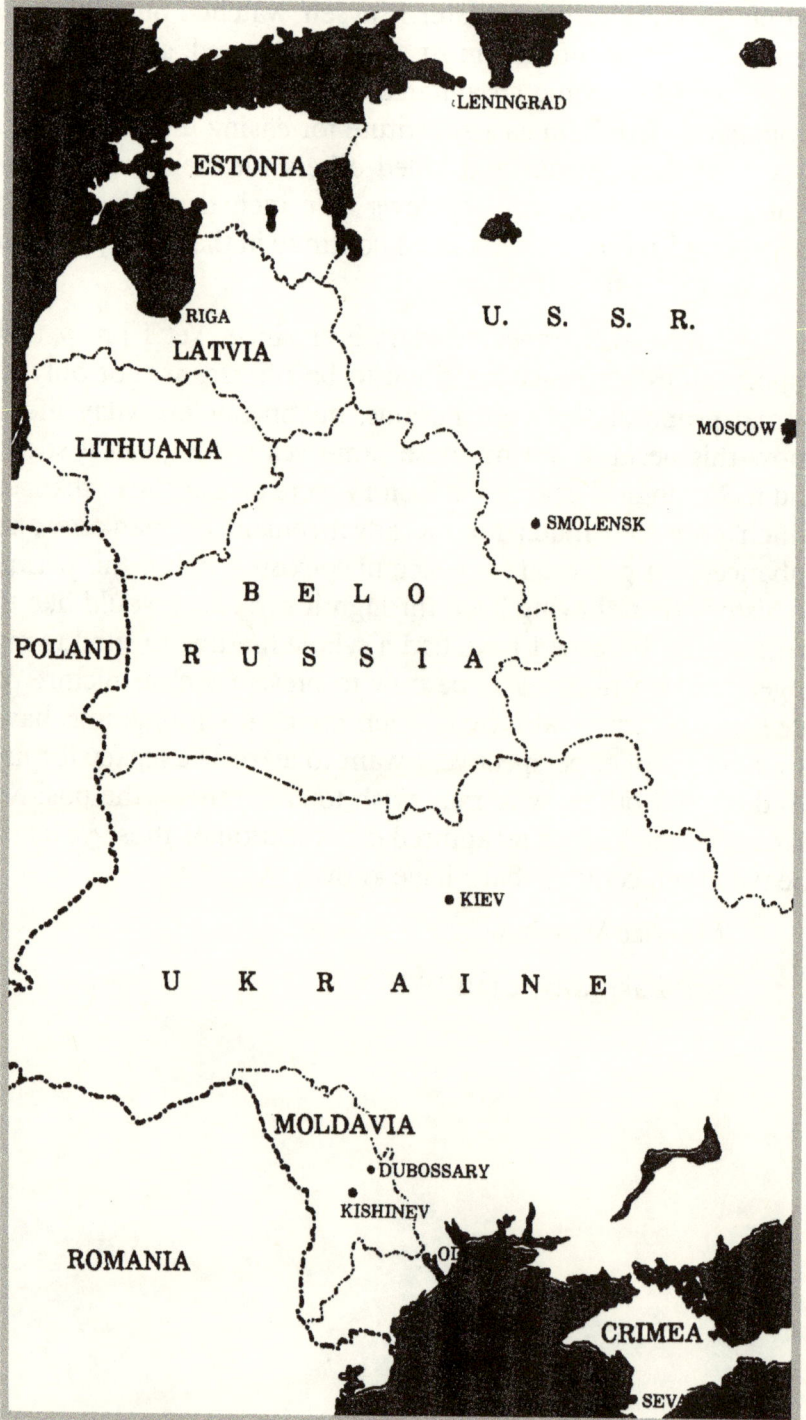

ontents

At Cheder (Hebrew school)

*D*ubossar

*I sat on the bench, the open Torah on
the table before me. Under the strict eye
of the Rabbi I learned that we should not
hate.*

1.

Dubossar

Some of the events of my early childhood which merge
into my conscious memory are vague, others sharply clear.
Some are quite bitter, but some are very sweet. The name given
me at birth was Samuel Warshawsky. As a very young child I
could dart around so fast by crawling on my hands and knees,
that my family called me "Little Mieche," or "Little Mouse."
When we immigrated to the United States the closest name in
English was Maurice. Eventually we dropped the last syllable on
Warshawsky and I became Maurice Warshaw.

My early memories are of a happy and prosperous
Jewish family living in the little village of Dubossar on the
Dniester River in czarist Russia. Dubossar was populated by
Russian Christian peasants who worked the surrounding lands,
and by Jews who for the most part had businesses in the city of
Kishinev twenty-four miles away. My father was a successful
food broker and owned a warehouse in Kishinev, which was
reached by crossing the river on a ferry and going the rest of the
way by horse and wagon.

Ours was one of the best houses in the village - very well built of lumber with stout shutters against the storms. I can still remember the fragrance of the summer flowers that grew in every yard.

The largest building in town was the police station. There was one *cheder* (Jewish school), one synagogue, and a few Christian churches. There was also a high school, which only those whose parents could pay tuition were allowed to attend. Joe, Eva, and Julie attended. There was also a school for the elementary grades which Phillip and I went to. Little Eda was not yet school age. There were both Jewish and gentile stores. Every house had lanterns in case people wanted to go out at night, as street lamps were few. The town's only public recreation was sleigh-riding in the winter, but we Jews had more: the Jewish community life with all its traditions.

A fiddler would sometimes play in the village square. His haunting music entranced the children who followed him around wherever he went, like the Pied Piper. Parents watching the joy on the children's faces would toss him a few coins. The fiddler was always invited to play at weddings and parties, but I think he loved playing for the children best.

It was up to the older children to keep the water barrels in our house filled from the well in our yard. A rope was securely fastened to a cross piece above the well around which the rope coiled when the water was drawn up by turning the handle. We were warned so often of the danger of falling into the well that I had nightmares about it and, as adventuresome a child as I was, would never climb the four-foot rock walls that surrounded it.

The family of my friend Bola, who lived on our street, had no well and had to carry water from the town pump. We would go with Bola's father to get water. He wore a harness over his shoulders with a bucket on each end, and it was fascinating to watch him carry the water home without spilling any from the swinging buckets. Bola and I would each take a bucketful and whoever spilled the least water on the way home was the champion.

My father's friend, Aaron, was the cooper—a good one, according to my father. Aaron made the barrels for Father's herring and other pickled items. Father greatly admired good workmanship. One day when I saw Aaron the cooper all dressed up at the synagogue I almost laughed aloud because he was growing so stout he was beginning to look like a barrel himself.

Our family kept horses and cows and over the stable were the living quarters for the servants. A couple named Hanka and Yvon, very religious Christians, lived with their little boy Dominic. The children of servants rarely went to school, so Dominic would help his father with the animals and other chores and especially with the harvest. Dominic's mother would work in our house. Even though Dominic was only a little older than I, there was a great barrier between us because of religion. Our mothers would not allow us to play together.

As long as I could remember we would walk across the street to avoid the police station. In a similar ritual whenever we passed a Christian church we would always turn and spit three times. Somehow it got to me early that gentiles didn't like Jews.

Because of these religious differences would never invite our servants into our home as guests and they never invited us to their quarters. One day while delivering a message to Hanka, I noticed through the half-open door a square center table covered by a red velvet cloth with exceptionally long fringe knotted into tassels. On the table were some figures like the ones on the stained glass windows of the Christian churches and the big statues along the road to Kishinev. I had often seen people kneeling down before these. One day I asked Hanka, "Why do you make that sign with your hands across your shoulders? Yvon stops many times during the day and does the same" she replied, "It is a means to keep the evil spirits away." That answer didn't satisfy me and I was still puzzled, but I didn't want to ask any more questions.

I also have memories of lice and bedbugs. There were lice all over our bodies and in every part of our clothing. They were in our hair and behind our ears. They even hid in our collars and cuffs. Mothers were always fighting them with kerosene and using a fine-tooth comb on our hair to get them out. These lice were no respecters of Jew or gentile, servant or master, rich or poor, young or old.

The unpaved streets of Dubossar and the dusty summers that came after the muddy spring. In some ways we would look to the cold winters for a change. The snow outside was often piled higher than my head and there was a good deal of sickness.

One winter typhus took my mother's life. I remember the morning I woke up and they told me she was dead. It made a very deep impression on me, though I was only four years old and scarcely knew the meaning of death. Outside the house people were crying and telling the neighbors who came to see what was going on, "Rivka Rample Warshawsky is dead!" I remember thinking, "I will soon be ready for cheder. Won't Mother be here?" I sensed that something terrible had happened, but my mother still seemed real to me and I expected, at any time, to see her familiar figure bustling about the house taking care of us. I cannot remember crying.

We took her to the bath house later that morning, for it was the Jewish custom to take the dead, accompanied by the whole family, to be washed and ritually cleansed. I think that it was the dramatic and traumatic experience of this solemn rite that made me realize that my mother wouldn't be there anymore.

My mother, whom Father always described as "wonderful," had worked side-by-side with him to build up the family fortune. We were well off financially, but lonely without her, especially me. I knew she wasn't coming back but I didn't know where she had gone. Eva and Julie were thirteen and fifteen and very much needed some womanly guidance. Joe was older and soon could take care of himself. Phillip was almost nine and my little sister Eda was almost three. The girls did what they could to keep the house going, but it wasn't the same without our mother. Jews believe it is not good for man to be alone, so Father decided to marry again.

Father was considered a great catch and every matchmaker was anxious to match him up with someone. They were always trying to make a match for my older sisters, too, but Julie and Eva only laughed about this old custom. Julie already had her eye on someone, but my brother Joe liked the matchmaking way of doing things, and our neighbor's daughter Sadie had already been promised to him.

I don't know how much negotiating took place to arrange for Father's marriage. One matchmaker had already come to our house several times, always consulting his little book with a smile, but Father only shook his head at every name presented to him. One afternoon when the matchmaker came I could tell he had some special news. Through the gossip that went on between towns he had heard about a certain special lady. She was a widow and her only son was married. The matchmaker had a long list of her qualities and education: She was sweet, lovely, beautifully built, a good manager, perhaps rich, would not object to a large family, and could play the piano. Her name was Rebecca. This time Father seemed not only satisfied, but happy with the choice. We were all happy, for a large family desperately needed a mother.

The day my father married this beautiful lady was memorable. We had arrived in Kishinev four days before the wedding to visit with her family and get acquainted. She and my father had not yet met. This new mother also wanted to look us children over and get acquainted. She was taking on a great responsibility with six children, but I think she was lonely for a family. We must have pleased her too, because she seemed so happy about the arrangement.

The marriage took place at the new bride's home in Kishinev. We children were impressed by the aristocratic feeling surrounding her, the fine china, silver and linens, the house with enough bedrooms for everybody, and all the evidences of her Russian education. We were amazed and delighted at the modern plumbing. She had one of the few flush toilets in Kishinev—the first we had ever seen. Fascinated by the sight of its flushing, I pulled the chain again and again until someone came to intercept my childish behavior.

The dowry was always an important part of a Jewish marriage arrangement. I don't know just how this was settled when Father married because I later learned that Rebecca had been running out of money and, soon after she was married, sold her house and some of its furnishings. Most of the lovely things were moved to our home. Father used to joke with her about how he thought he had married for money.

According to custom, everyone was invited to the wedding—every friend, relative, and neighbor. They all came, even from surrounding towns and villages. Even a few gentile friends were invited. Not to come would have been unthinkable in our culture. Many people from Kishinev that I had never seen before were there, as Rebecca had many friends among whom she was obviously popular. Everyone loved her.

A Jewish wedding was always a time of festivity and rejoicing. Great amounts of food were prepared for the feast following the ceremony, but on the wedding day both the bride and the groom fasted. (On that day all their sins were forgiven.) The *badkhen* (jester) acted as master of ceremonies. He stayed with the musicians, and as each guest arrived, they played a little fanfare and as he announced the name and the *yikhus* (title or status) at their arrival. My father didn't regard it particularly important to go through every detail, but it was the Jewish custom and he did love tradition.

The ceremony was held in Rebecca's garden rather than in the synagogue—probably because the spring air was so wonderful. The guests came bearing lighted candles. There was much laughter among them and much crying, too. I remember how bright the stars were shining that warm night and how the colorful embroidery on the *khupa* (wedding canopy) glowed in the candlelight. It made an unforgettable scene.

Father stood under the canopy and our mother-to-be joined him. The guests were all seated, the women on one side and the men on the other. We children sat down in front. The rabbi said some words over a goblet of wine, then my father and new mother took a sip. Even though I had been to weddings before, it startled me to see Father throw the goblet onto the floor and stamp it into splinters. "Mazeltov!" the crowd shouted. "Good luck!" Then the rabbi read something from a paper and they both signed it.

These were just the preliminaries. The real marriage took place when Father placed a ring on Rebecca's finger and recited: "Behold, thou are consecrated unto me, according to the Law of Moses and Israel." Then it was real and legal. By the warm look with which they regarded one another it was clear the couple would know love for all the years to come. It was a joyous occasion.

The next morning, before all of us went home to Dubossar, Phillip and I watched some Russian horse soldiers at sword practice in the street near the house. They marked branches on the trees, then rode their horses past at breakneck speed trying to slash through the mark with their swords. For some reason we boys imagined that they were practicing to kill Jews, an impression that was to last a long time, even though our new mother tried to discourage us from thinking such things.

Rebecca did a wonderful job of helping us function as a happy family again. She was an intelligent and loving woman with a fine sense of humor. I remember her walking in late afternoon among the flowers in our garden, and the gracious thing she made of morning chores as she moved, calm and erect, in her long red cape, showering feed from the basket on her arm upon the chickens, turkeys, geese and ducks that followed close behind her. She was a great organizer, and in no time at all had the household running smoothly. She was kind to us younger children and understanding with the older ones. My teenage sisters especially had needed someone like her. We took her to our hearts and started calling her "Mother" right away. She never wanted us to think of her as a stepmother. She always spoke to others as equals - even children - frankly and with real interest. Gentiles seemed drawn to her, and although she was very orthodox in her own beliefs she never had a mean or fearful thought about Christians like many Jewish women. When I grew up I often wondered how those gentiles who had treated her as a friend could have changed so at the end. In every way she was a wonderful mother to me.

My new Mother and Father usually made two trips to the market each week. We children could go along if we promised to behave. Yvon would hitch the wagon up to two of our horses (feed had to be hauled home for our livestock) and we would all climb in. On Monday and Thursday, the regular market days, the whole town turned out to buy food for the middle of the week and for the Sabbath.

While most women looked drab, especially at the market—assuming it easier to "haggle" if they did not look so prosperous. My new Mother always dressed up for these occasions with gloves and a parasol. I think a little of the Russian aristocratic manner had rubbed off on her. When we went to market it was like Cinderella going to the ball in her golden coach.

I loved the colorful activity of the market. The cobblestoned square at the juncture of several streets was crowded with people meeting acquaintances and exchanging gossip. We always had to wait for Mother to finish shopping, as she took great pains to select the very best of everything for our family. That's why the refreshments were the best part of the trip—making the waiting pleasant. Little booths were set up so we could stop and eat cookies and drink tea sweetened with sugar cubes, which we held between our teeth as we sipped.

Proprietors of the produce stalls would save special things for Mother. She always knew who had the best vegetables and fruits, and was a favorite customer, liked by all the merchants. She never used angry words or insults, and because she loved everyone, she would buy extra sacks of carrots or beets to distribute among our needy neighbors—both Jew and gentile. When the wagon was finally loaded, we children would scramble for a place among the produce and bags of feed, singing to the rhythm of the wagon wheels as they rolled along the road home.

Mother kept a strictly kosher house. The Sabbath chicken had to be killed in a certain manner. Mother would catch one in the yard and take it to the *shoket* (ritual slaughterer) who killed it with one swift stroke, using a knife so sharp no flesh would be torn. Mercy for the animal was very important. The hygienic laws of the Jews laid great stress upon freshness, and our fish were always selected from those swimming around in a big tub of water at the market.

Mother kept the cooking and eating utensils for meat separate from those for dairy foods out of respect for the Biblical injunctions. There were especially beautiful dishes set aside for the occasion such as the Passover Feast when once a year all Jews recalled the Exodus from Egypt and the freedom from slavery. There were many small observances which elevated ordinary housekeeping chores to an expression of worship by Jewish women.

Borscht was our staple food during the week, but the Sabbath meal was always special. My father was not very orthodox in his thinking, nor was he a religious man in the strictest sense of the word. Having a strong emotional attachment to Jewish tradition, however, he was strict about keeping the Sabbath and delighted in the Sabbath meal.

The Sabbath was the "queen of days." Even the poorest Jews in our village felt like royalty when celebrating it. My father always wore his prayer shawl and made us boys put on ours. I had to wear one when still so small my shawl was only a miniature of Father's. Before sunset my mother and sisters would scrub every inch of the house and bring out the best linens and dishes. Together with the Sabbath chicken, they baked little cookies with poppy seeds and other delicious things reserved for Friday. Like gefilte fish, chicken soup with noodles, and the beautiful, white, braided *hallah* (Sabbath bread made with eggs) we enjoyed the Sabbath. We always had *kugel* for dessert.

Before each Sabbath meal the men of the family all went to the bath house to scrub and put on fresh clothes. We would return home to find the table laid with the white cloth. It was then Mother's joy to greet the Sabbath with a prayer as she lit the candles with a special, tender reverence. And for a moment, her eyes catching the flickering light, she cast a loving glance around the table which embraced us all. Father's deep voice then sounded in thanks for the wine and bread, and we sat down to our feast.

Father delighted in bringing home guests and there was usually at least one for the Sabbath meal. It was considered a privilege to be invited to share the Sabbath with us, knowing that the man at the head of the table would also be giving them food for thought. Guests furnished a very attentive audience while Father expounded the Torah. I loved to listen.

The meal over and dishes washed and put away by the maid, guests sat around the fireplace telling stories and singing Russian songs and songs from Jewish folklore. Father had a sonorous baritone voice and my sister Julie a beautiful soprano. Father loved singing and probably went to the synagogue mainly to be part of the musical chanting. I carried the tunes in my head and hummed them to myself all week.

Father was my childhood hero—a warm, friendly man with a great sense of humor who loved to tell his children stories. One favorite story was about a couple of horse thieves who had their eye on the prince's horse.

One day when the prince went for his daily ride, the thieves followed him into the woods. He stopped his carriage by a tree and, after absorbing the beauty of the scenery, fell asleep, whereupon the thieves crept up and unharnessed his horse. While one took the horse to the next town and sold it, his companion harnessed himself to the carriage in the horse's place, and waited. When the prince awakened he cried, "What's this?" The thief explained, "Your Honor, Prince, you see, twenty years ago I sinned and God punished me by making me become a horse for twenty years. My time is up today and I have become a man again." "Oh my, oh my," said the prince, "I am highly honored that you have been redeemed while in my possession!" He unharnessed the thief, gave him a few rubles, and walked to the next town to look for another horse. There in the town stable stood his own white horse. "Oh, my Yonkel!" exclaimed the prince. "You couldn't hold out. You've sinned again!"

Father's ability to read the Torah and to speak Yiddish and Russian enhanced his social standing in our little village. He was often called upon to participate in the various ceremonies of the Jewish community; and because he knew a great deal about gentile customs, too, men came from all around to consult him on social and political problems.

Once he was asked to go with a committee to plead with a government official for better treatment for the Jews. He was well prepared to show that the Jews were an asset to the country and should be welcomed as citizens rather than discriminated against. "The Jews stimulated business and industry wherever they lived and their skills enabled them to produce many items needed for the everyday life of the nation. Far from being troublemakers, they lived in peace, educated their children to the fullest extent possible, and were industrious."

The plea got no response. At that uneasy time the Russian ruling classes, both secular and religious, were strongly influenced by fortune tellers, astrologers, magicians, and soothsayers who had great power at court. Séances were held at the Czar's palace for divine guidance of the nobles.

This was strange behavior indeed to the Jews, for our way was to speak directly to God without any intermediary and to accept the Ten Commandments as the disciplinary code for ourselves and our community. Inasmuch as Jews were not allowed self-government and were still subject to Russian whim, committees such as this were assigned to plead the Jewish cause from time to time. A threatened autocracy which sought "other-worldly" solutions to its very real problems was of course deaf to rational suggestions from its subject lower classes.

Father gained most of his knowledge by reading. It is ironical that in the great vastness of late 19th century Russia almost no one but the nobility and the Jews could read and write. Between these two worlds the masses of the population were illiterate. I can see now that part of my father lived in the world of orthodox Jewish tradition and part of him comprehended a world outside his own community.

Being so proud of my father I liked to think I was sometimes his favorite son. I pretended to be his favorite when I rode in the wagon seat beside him or when he looked so impressive at the Sabbath meal.

In his food brokerage business Father was a real expert in China tea. In his stocks he carried sardines and other delicacies in cans, as well as barrels of pickles, tomatoes, olives, lump sugar, poppy seeds, raisins, dried prunes, dried mushrooms, dried corn, candies like Halva and toffies bought from Mr. Kolosky, the candy maker in Kishinev. Food from the surrounding countryside was stored in Father's Kishinev warehouse and from here it was transported directly to stores in villages like Dubossar, or to our basement where it was kept until delivery to customers. Nearly everything had to be eaten fresh in the summer or dried, canned or pickled for winter.

During the summer peasants came to market with their great harvest of many kinds of fruit and vegetables, potatoes, onions, mushrooms, barley, wheat and much more. Those who could afford it canned fruits and vegetables, and canning time was hectic—people running around the house with steam all over the place. The smell of pickles and onions brought tears to our eyes. Many of our neighbors joined in the production. In addition, we hired people to help "stock the basement." Afterward, if certain pans or broken ladles were missing, my sisters would be furious, but Mother would say, "Perhaps they needed what they stole more than we do." This usually ended the argument, but I could hear my sisters saying under their breath, "Why did they take them when we paid for them?" Julie and Eva based all their conclusions on a strong sense of Jewish justice.

Fresh meat and fish were scarce except for carp and herring, which for us were generally available from the Rumanian fisheries just across the nearby border. In the fall at butchering time meats were koshered and smoked to preserve them (We never ate ham or shell fish). Our favorite condiment was horseradish—a must in every Jewish garden, as were beets for pickling and cabbage for the sauerkraut Mother stored away in crocks.

Mother often used cornmeal, which she cooked and made into bricks. She sliced the bricks with a wire and poured in chicken fat to give it a good taste.

Our breakfast was a roll and tea. The tea we drank had to be made fresh in a small pot several times a day. A samovar was kept going all the time to heat the water, and Mother saw to it that the taste was just right to please my father. The big meal of the day was eaten at noon, when the whole family gathered. Father took a little *schnopp* of straight whiskey before the meal, joined by Mother to be sociable. Adults and children alike stopped many times during the day for tea and cookies—little sweet biscuits without frosting.

The Jewish holidays furnished our childhood with drama and social life. Our favorite was Rosh Hashana, the beginning of the Jewish New Year—the birthday of the world. Determined by the lunar calendar, it always fell in late September or early October and opened the Ten Days of Atonement, which ended with the solemn day of Yom Kippur. The most exciting part of Rosh Hashana was blowing the *shofar* (ram's horn) as in the days of our ancestors to celebrate that God was our king and we were His subjects and children.

To me as a young child such ceremonies were of course far more dramatic than meaningful, but I appreciated the glorious festivities and the happy family times the holidays brought. My father followed the tradition of dipping an apple in honey to demonstrate hopes for a good year ahead. Everything was renewed with the New Year. For instance, a hole was dug in the ground and filled with boiling water in which to sterilize all the silverware.

We learned early why we celebrated the Feast of the Passover. Each year Father would ask the boys questions: "Why do we eat *matzos* (unleavened bread) at this time?" We memorized the answers: "To commemorate the children of Israel passing out of Egypt in such a hurry that they did not have time to let the bread rise." And Father would say, "That is why we eat the *matzos,* to remember what our fathers did, and we eat the bitter herbs to remember the bitterness of slavery."

Despite the complex traditions and rituals customary at the Jewish Holidays, we children had a wonderful time. Friends and relatives gathered from all directions on these occasions. The feasting was the best part of all, but the fasting times seemed endless and when still young I would get so hungry I would snitch a little food here and there. I eventually decided that the guilt was worse than the hunger.

I was attending cheder (Hebrew school) at the same time I was attending Russian school. Cheder was strictly for teaching the Torah - " the laws of God to man," in order for Jewish boys to enter into God's divine presence. To know the Law was a Jew's highest ambition—a wonderful concept zealously guarded, for only to Israel had the revelation been given. To be a scholar was greater than to be a king. Parents were so proud and happy that their little boys were learning that they would come stand at the schoolroom window and watch us at our lessons. To learn our Hebrew alphabet we used to sing a little song that sounded like this:

> *On a little stove burns a little fire*
> *And in the house it is warm*
> *And the rabbi teaches little children*
> *The alphabet.*
> > *A.B.C., Aleph, Bet, Gimel*

For Jews there is both the written Law and the oral tradition. We could always tell a rabbi if we passed him on the street by the way he did every little thing according to tradition and followed every little law. I am not sure that even the rabbi fully understood these traditions, but he followed them. A rabbi wore a long beard and *payas* (side curls). He never used a handkerchief or touched his face and therefore wiped his nose on his sleeve or on a handkerchief tied around his sleeve.

As children we could see the different rabbis' little quirks and flaws and would name them accordingly. If one were nearsighted or a little deaf we called him in Yiddish "Mortacha der Blinder (Blindey) or "Ershil der Tuber" (Deaf Ears).

Although the rabbi who taught us followed all the laws to the letter, he did not teach by their spirit. He took advantage of his authority to beat us, and for this we hated him. He also told us what I considered to be tall tales, such as, "When the Messiah comes, for the Messiah is sure to come, he will give wooden boats to the Jews, but to the gentiles he will give metal boats. If a flood comes to the earth again, the Jews will stay afloat in their wooden boats, but the metal ones of the gentiles will sink."

One day the rabbi stood at the back of the room and told us to look straight ahead because God was going to shower candy down on us as a particular favor. I was not so easily duped. "The candy is coming down from heaven," he said, but I noticed it coming overhead in a horizontal line. I turned just in time to see the rabbi himself throwing the candy in our direction. This was like a gentile child learning there is no Santa Claus. It was my first disappointment in religion and created my first doubts about God. I don't know what I thought God was like, except that He was someone in the sky who always stayed behind the clouds and rewarded the good people and punished the bad.

Even my friends who were poor somehow managed to go to *cheder*. Not all of them went to the Russian school, however, for this was not compulsory and required a tuition fee. In the morning we went to the Russian school, where we learned to read and spell and do our figures. After Russian school let out in the afternoon we went to the rabbi's house for *cheder.*

In winter it was dark when school ended for the day as there were no street lights. A familiar sight in Dubossar was that of children winding their way to their homes, holding glowing lanterns to light the early evening hours.

There can be no end to childhood memories. Each day a new one comes to the fore. I am sure, though, that my conscious memories could not have had any more influence on me than the unconscious ones. Even though the rabbi could not communicate the true spiritual meaning of the law to us, life in the *shtetel* (Jewish village) had meaning in itself and it had an atmosphere of its own whose lessons all who lived there could not help but absorb, such as proverbs teaching such concepts as giving and receiving and the everyday emphasis of our particular culture.

We children were happy, sheltered, and generally unaware of the problems outside the *shtetel,* which were growing in force to change things for all of Russia and for us.

Observation:

When one reads the life of another, there is a sense of pleasure when we recognize something we have forgotten. With this is often a consciousness of terror. When we are confronted with this dread, we either want to joy in the lessons we learn or become a goliath and do everything in our power to see that others thereafter are forced ta accept a path of obedience in order to avoid the learning. The thing that made the Jewish people great was the persecution they suffered. Perhaps we can learn to accept the burden of another's prejudice so as to joy in the quality of life we learn.

Ronald Kelsch

Father anticipated the pogroms would break out again

Troubled days

The origin of the Jewish pogroms (and non-Jewish) was clearly traceable to the Russian Government, who used them as a means of combating any revolution against them.

2.

Troubled Days

My happy home life in those childhood years must have been fringed with uneasy feelings not obvious to me at that time. Though my parents did everything they could to keep the ripples of political events from disturbing our lives, they began to show feelings of anxiety. Father didn't sing much anymore. Instead he talked a lot about the fate of the Jews in Russia since our ancestors had first come here and the new problems besetting us. Gradually I became aware that things were not going so well with the Jews in Russia as I had supposed. I learned that the "May Laws" passed in 1882 forbade Jews to live in any part of the Russian Empire other than certain designated places known together as "The Pale of Settlement." Jews were limited as to education, denied the right to engage in agriculture, and participation in the trades and crafts was highly circumscribed. Overall, even a youngster could realize that we were lucky to have the home where we had always lived.

Perhaps we were ourselves little affected at first because our village was small and insignificant. Certainly, we were more fortunate than Jews placed into big city ghettos. However, the realization came that our luck so far was no guarantee against some new official order, which would render us homeless and ruin my father financially.

In 1904, Russia went to war with Japan. Father had always talked about the suffering of the Russian people caused by the Czar's constant involvement in military struggles. He was very upset when this latest war was declared.

For years, Russia's historic ambition had been to extend her empire eastward in order to gain an outlet to the navigable seas. Japan was aware that if Russia established herself in Manchuria she would have control of the Yellow Sea, then Korea, which was then menacing Japan itself. While Russia was fighting for a dream, Japan was fighting for existence.

The Russians seized the Liaotung Peninsula and Korea, and pressured China into permitting the extension of the Trans-Siberian Railway to Port Arthur. Japan became alarmed, and the smoldering fire became the raging flames of war.

Government authority shipped trainloads of Russian peasants on the long journey across Siberia, meagerly armed and thrown into battle against fresh Japanese troops just arrived from Korea and Port Arthur. They slaughtered the peasants. The Russian Baltic fleet made the long voyage around Africa, Arabia, India and up the east coast of China, only to meet utter destruction by the Japanese.

Father had talked about going to America quite often, but now he talked about it all the time. America was a "land of milk and honey," a ray of hope amidst the gathering dark clouds of political and social storms. My brother Joe had already started planning with a friend who was a conductor on a train between Kishinev and Rumania to smuggle him onto the train, so that he could then make his way by boat to America.

Joe could plan, for he was without adult responsibilities, but with the war on no one could leave the country. He had been able to stay out of the army so far, but it was impossible to hold out much longer. We all thought, "Maybe the war will soon be over and we can all go to America," but in the meantime the family did not want to leave Joe behind, because if he were wounded someone had to take care of him.

Many of the drafting of Dubossar's young men sometimes received news that one would not return. Occasionally a wounded soldier came home who would describe the nightmarish hell and bloody slaughter of the war. Each returning lad felt he was only a pawn in the senseless struggle of a losing battle.

My father used to watch the war news anxiously. The only source of information was the village bulletin board, but it was so full of distortions and lies that no one bothered to read it. If things went well for Russia, the government was loud in her claims of victory when the battles did not go well.

One day some news appeared on the bulletin board. It had no connection with the war. The Czarina had given birth to a son. The Czar thought this was an occasion for all Russia to rejoice, but the people were more concerned about the terrible ongoing tragedy and devastation than they could possibly be about the birth of an heir to the throne.

We knew there was real trouble at the front when the food shortages began. No longer used to store food, the warehouses held only ammunition and guns. We heard rumors that army food supplies lay rotting at railroad sidings because of congested traffic on the lines. The Japanese captured many provisions. As the war went on, the great amount of army supplies needed created a terrific shortage of civilian supplies. Half a million soldiers were dependent on the Trans Siberian Railway to transport these supplies—an extremely difficult logistical problem under any circumstances.

The poor now faced a real struggle. The market place in our little town had always displayed an abundance of food in peacetime, but now it was almost empty. Priced so high, hardly anyone could by the food needed. Our family had a great many things stored in our cellar and could get along well for a while, but my parents could not stand to see our neighbors go hungry, especially those with children, so our cellar supplies became so depleted we could no longer help our neighbors. Both Jews and gentiles suffered and prayed to God for help. As a child, I used to wonder why everyone had no anger with God. No matter how much people prayed, He did not seem to be listening. In later years, my father could never forget the poor people who died of starvation at that time.

Our happy life was fading now, and worst of all, the hope of ever remaining was fading. Father said there would be little hope for Russia's Jews unless the present government changed its policies. He was afraid that anti-Semitism, one of the great fears that haunted our family. The fear of blame for the whole catastrophe cause fear among the Jews.

We heard rumors of anti-Semitism in the Russian army. It was difficult enough for an orthodox Jewish boy forced to eat food that was not kosher, but reports said that the soldiers' food was not even edible. The army treated Jews badly. Forced to act as servants and do many menial tasks, every time we heard a rumor of this sort we would think more and more about Joe's escape.

One afternoon a horse and wagon pulled up in front of our neighbor's house. Frightened and curious, someone helped a soldier down from the wagon. We did not know him at first. It was Solomon, our neighbor's boy. Mother paced the floor, wringing her hands and saying repeatedly, "A nice boy like that had to go to war! Just a few short months and we don't even recognize him!" Father went over the next morning to offer his help, but after returning his eyes showed greater anxiety than before.

Solomon reported that conditions at the front were even worse than rumored. Other than those rescued, men wounded and left to die on the battlefield received no medical help. In addition, there was as much hostility among the Russian soldiers as there was between the fighting countries.

One time I peeked through the lace curtain and saw our sister, Julie, bidding goodbye to her boyfriend, Lazer, a man none of us liked, never looked directly at people when he was talking to them. Julie could not see me watching her. She had a strange look on her face as she came up the path to the house, opened the door quietly and walked toward her room without the usual greeting to the family. Father called her back, wanting to know what was making her coat pocket bulge. Slowly she took some pamphlets from her pocket and handed them over to him. Glancing at the titles, he paled and shouted "Anarchist!" I had no doubt that whatever this word meant, it was something dangerous.

By that time, there were rumors of riots and strikes in the industrial and merchandising centers, a crisis potentially as great as the military one. It was a yoke of "double trouble" for the country. There would be double trouble in our home, too.

Father and my sisters argued a great deal in the months that followed. I began to piece together more of the true situation of the Jews. Things simply were not the way they had looked through the rose-colored glasses of childhood.

Father often pleaded with Eva and Julie, "How can I make you understand that any revolutionary movement will only meet with a counter-revolutionary one? The Czars have always suppressed any organizing by discontented people. Their spy systems know instantly when murmuring among the people arises. No revolutionary reforms can ever take place! The autocrats will divert people's attention from their injustices by throwing the blame on the Jews!"

Father anticipated that pogroms would break out again, and I gradually began to understand what the pogroms were like. *Pogrom* was the Russian word for *massacre*.

I soon learned why the threat of domestic revolution might be blamed on the Jews. The government held the socialists responsible for stirring up the peasants to revolt. The socialists were a group of intellectuals who tried to convince the masses to fight for their rights. Many of them were Jewish.

Father had become somewhat disillusioned with Nicholas II. He could not understand why a man could abandon his former energetic approach to peace. Survival is the most dominating force in man; however, Nicholas had come to the position of having to defend his rule. He claimed to be not only absolute sovereign of all Russia, but also head of the Orthodox Church. The Czar's conviction of his divine right was so complete that anyone who showed the slightest inclination against him represented enemies against the government and against God.

One morning while Russia was still in the war, I went with my mother to the market place in hopes of finding something to buy. There was Julie's boyfriend again, this time talking to three strangers who were gentiles. He now looked like a Gentile with his Jewish pay trimmed to mimick his simpler clothes. Mother spotted him, too, and at first I thought she was annoyed, but then realized that she was frightened as she hurried us off in a different direction. That night she told Father she had seen him, and Father immediately cautioned Eva and Julie to be wary of the revolutionary movement. He seemed to sympathize with my sisters' feelings, but all too well, he understood the dangers that we all faced if they were caught. He did not even want them to talk loudly for fear of the revolutionary's overhearing. He especially wanted them to avoid their friends, because their friends were very careless about letting others overhear them. I think the hardest thing for him to make them understand was that the situation of the Jews was much more precarious than that of their other Russian friends. To begin with, our god was not the Christian god and those who did not accept the Christian god was *ipso facto* against the government. We did not receive a denial of the rights of Russian citizens because of being Jews, but for being non-Christians. We could remedy this at any time by receiving baptism into the Russian Orthodox faith. If we refused, not only would we be without protection, but also our persecution would be permitted and even promoted and authorized by the government itself.

This didn't seem to dampen anyone's enthusiasm for the socialist movements which were being organized. My sisters kept attending the secret meetings. The organization they belonged to was now collecting money to buy guns. Eva boasted that the guns would be used in the riots against the police and other government officials.

Soon we were hearing of strikes everywhere. Businesses closed down for lack of money. The police no longer concerned themselves with justice. The socialists wanted to fight against these conditions, but anyone that rose up against the government was considered a traitor and was ruthlessly dealt with.

Father decided that Joe must leave at once and make his way to America, no matter what the danger. The family enlisted the help of a friend that Joe had brought to the house several times. Father didn't especially like him, but he knew all the police at the stations along the way to the Rumanian border. Each one had to be bought off and I've wondered many times since just how much it cost. (As near as I can figure out, it must have been the equivalent of ten dollars for each policeman.) The plans called for short train rides and the conductor would require a fee to pass Joe through.

There was no time to lose. Joe's escape was arranged for in a single day. Father counted out the money and Joe put it in a belt around his waist. He left that very night. We hated to see him leave, yet we knew that there might be a better hope for him in America. After he left, Mother constantly prayed for his safe journey, talking to God as though He were standing next to her. Father was quiet, but his eyes were misty. I sought to console myself at my fears for my beloved big brother, by saying over and over, "Joe will get to America. Then he'll be able to come right back."

The Russian people were sick of the war. The families of the front-line soldiers and the new conscripts at home, shocked by the remote and reasonless massacre of their kin, rebelled, forcing the Czar to withdraw his forces from Korea and Manchuria.

In the summer of 1905 when Russia was obviously losing the war, President Theodore Roosevelt of the United States proposed a peace parley. Sending identical notes to Japan and Russia, he called upon both countries, in the name of humanity, to meet and discuss peace terms at Washington, D.C. For the success of this meeting, "Teddy" Roosevelt was hailed as the benefactor of humanity. My father's admiration of him and of America soared, and he began to talk more about going there.

The Czar tried to mollify the people by granting a constitution and a parliament (Duma). This may have only been a pretense at reform, for the government soon began to turn the hostility of the Russian people from the Czar toward the Jews. Was history going to repeat itself?

Father told us he had hoped for awhile that the Czar was going to institute a new policy in Russian government, but he said that the Russian pogrom system will flare up time and again because the Czar is so obsessed with his own autocratic rule that he will let nothing that grants the people freedom stand for long. All is hopeless. Even the autocratic rule is becoming a despotism. To listen to the people would only be destroying itself. There is just no means of reasoning between the people and a despot.

Years later, upon reading the history of the Russo-Japanese War, I learned what had happened militarily and politically during those boyhood years when our family was under such terrible stress. It was many more years before I could fully comprehend the deep-rooted causes of the conflict that eventually changed our lives.

Terribly worried now, Father was afraid that my sisters would throw themselves completely into the revolutionary movement which was sweeping up the Russian youth "in the name of liberty," who thought that their own enthusiasm could be spread among the illiterate masses through lectures and rallies. Father knew better. He had no doubt that the reactionaries were already stirring up anti-Semitism and the Jews would be in real trouble. It was a pattern.

Opposition groups all had to meet in secret. The slightest suspicion of any such movement detected by the secret police would mean instant death to the participants. Father pleaded with my sisters not to endanger the Jewish community. He stopped giving them money in order to avoid falling into the hands of the socialists to acquire guns and other equipment, but it was too late. Eva and Julie each had a gun hidden in their room. When Father found out, he ordered them to get rid of them. Rumor indicated the government remained unsatisfied until they could eliminate every Jew. He especially did not want anything around traceable to our family. Eva and Julie refused to part with the guns, but promised to be extremely careful.

They planned to participate in the peaceful demonstration about to take place—a bloodless revolution to force the Czar to an act of self-abnegation along with the proclamation of civil liberties. As Father had predicted, the Czar's army got wind of it and had already planned a counter attack that would end in bloody slaughter. The socialists heard of this in time to cancel the demonstration, but even Eva and Julie became frightened, and they buried all the literature they had, together with the red flag and the two guns, in our back yard.

I can still remember the hurried and huddled nighttime consultations between my parents, the whispered rumors, the refusal to let us children go anywhere alone, the daily mounting fear and uncertainty in my parents' eyes.

Then the police made a routine search of our house. Father remained outwardly calm, but after the police left, he broke out in a cold sweat. All of us thought about what might remain underground in the backyard.

All their throats had been cut

If we went out into the streets, there was danger and the Gentile children started calling us "Kristo provgatsi," (Christ sellers) at school, so Father made the whole family stay close to the house. One time I looked out on the street and saw terrible devastation, but I still didn't comprehend the extent of the trouble.

One terrible incident etched forever into my young mind the stark reality of that fateful year. Worried sick about my best friend Bola, I slipped out one morning to see him. A man came running from his house, leaving the door open and crying out in hoarse terror. I ran to the open door and peered through. Lying in grotesque positions, like so many rag dolls, were Bola's mother, father and all the children. The man had cut all their throats. When I first saw my playmate and his family lying there with blood all over them I was stunned, then ran screaming home. It disturbed me so that the family watched over me for some time. After my hysteria subsided, they told me the neighborhood men had organized a committee and traced the murderers. It had not been difficult. They were renegade peasants stirred up to believing that it was not only forgivable, but also patriotic to kill Jews. They had gone straight to a local tavern and, under the influence of vodka, had boasted freely and in detail about their black deed. My father attended the funeral of the victims. He said it was the saddest he had ever attended. He burst out crying when he told us about it.

There was a great commotion in the street next day. I ran out and hid under a wagon, huddling behind the back wheel and looking through the spokes. Wide-eyed I watched my kinsmen gather to take justice into their hands, executing the three murderers in the old Israelite mode of trampling. The three men stripped of their clothing and flung full length on the ground, the crazy with anger and frustration over their helplessness as Jews, the men and women gathered and ritualistically, kicked, jumped and walked on the murderers while cursing and swearing out their revenge. It was the first and only time I had witnessed the old Mosaic law of an eye for an eye and a tooth for a tooth, and

I watched my kinsmen take justice into their own hands

They ritualistically kicked and jumped on the murderers

a life for a life. I still have mental glimpses of three torn, naked bodies beaten into the dirt by dozens of trampling, kicking feet.

I stayed in the house after that. News came of many incidents of rioting in Dubossar, and there was little hope these would decrease in number or intensity. When we heard that the Rabbi, whom we knew so well, and all his family were murdered, we knew that no one would be safe. Father decided that the family should go to Kishinev until trouble would either blow over or get so bad that it would be impossible to stay anywhere in Russia.

It was important to leave in haste, without advance notice to any gentile who might prevent our going. Still, the move was fraught with delays. Mother clung, as women do, to her household treasures, but photographs of us children, group pictures of happier times, her favorite books and music all had to be left behind. The chickens and geese of course had to stay, but Father found a Jewish neighbor to take care of them. We took only what was necessary and all the jewelry converted into cash. The only possession I could take with me from   Dubossar was my slate and slate pencil, but I carried in my mind the vivid picture of my young friends being slaughtered.

At first, my sisters refused to go. They wanted to fight with the rest of the socialist party members, insisting this would all die down and the impending revolution would make things easier for us. Father was kind but adamant that the family was going to Kishinev and the girls would go, too, though he did offer them hope that they might return soon. I just kept wondering how certain gentiles who had been so good to us could have been incited against us.

Father hated to leave the good business he had built. Mother wanted to get in touch with her married son, but was afraid. Julie's boyfriend arrived as we were preparing to leave. We could tell she almost decided to stay with him when Father sent her a warning glance.

We left at night, quietly putting our bundles into the wagon with Father's help, because he was tall and could let them down over the side of the wagon. Then he helped us in. Even though it was dark, we could see a great deal of property damage from the riots. We noted sadly that one of our Jewish neighbors had placed an icon in his window to save the household from the pogroms. Further, down the street we passed a cart with four bodies in it. There was a big sign painted in white on the cart saying, "Kill the Jews." We passed the market place, where everything was upset and ransacked. We knew to whom each stand belonged, for here was where we had bought our fish and poultry and produce.

How we got to Kishinev safely, I will never know, because just after we crossed the river the barge was destroyed and swimming became the only means of escape. When we heard this, we began to lose hope of ever going back.

Father told us on the way that he heard the plenty of advice for the last two weeks to get out because we were Jews and sure to be in trouble. He particularly, because of his wealth and influence, was a target. For one thing, friends had told him, we would not be able to get any food. Even our gentile friends had warned that the government would not stop the pogroms until every Jew, especially every male, was eliminated.

As we approached Kishinev, which had been so peaceful on our last visit, the scene was worse than that in Dubossar. Sacked shops and evidence of riots appeared everywhere. We saw a Torah ripped and thrown into the street, and a prayer shawl trampled on. We could see at a glance that there would be little safety here. Father was nervous and surprised us by driving straight to the house of Mr. Kolosky the candy maker. Mr. Kolosky was a Christian, but he had not only been a good customer, but a great and valued friend. Luckily it was getting dark and we weren't too conspicuous. We waited in the wagon while Father went up to the door. Mrs. Kolosky answered, then Mr. Kolosky came. Surprised and frightened, he nevertheless motioned for the rest of us to come in at once. We entered their living room and waited while Father hurriedly explained our situation, and begged them to let us stay. Mr. Kolosky consulted with his wife, then they darkened the house and continued talking. We were to remain.

The danger in Kishinev was as bad as in Dubossar. After much discussion it was decided that we should hide out in the Kolosky cellar until further arrangements could be made. We were also lucky that Mr. Kolosky was optimistic that the pogroms would only last a short time.

Our wagon and horses had to be taken away from the Kolosky place for fear of drawing too much suspicion. Father decided to drive them to the livery stable away from the house, where he gave a fictitious name. We knew he took his life in his hands when he ventured out, so everyone sat in fear until he returned.

Observation:

Few realize that the socialist revolution, persecution of the Jews by government edict, and the warring of Japan existed in Russia prior to World War I. The culmination of the above continued through World War II. We often neglect what happened in Russia starting in the late 1800's. In the United States we also had a civil war carried with prejudice.

Christian prophecy knows well of the scattering and persecution of Jews and their eventual redemption, but non Christians deny this prophecy. About thirty years before the Civil War, Joseph smith gave a prophecy indicating the precise location where the Civil War would begin. After it's beginning, his record indicated war would then spread throughout the world. We have experienced wars and rumors of wars to this date.

War caused Maurice to carry a sense of humor as did his father. He avoided political serious remarks except in family, business, and service. I never discussed with him the Mormon prophecy regarding war and the Jews. Long after his death, I have since felt that might have been interesting to him, if I only understood the full concept at the time.

Ronald Kelsch

Hiding Out

the Cellar

Enough! Enough! Of the irritation.
Enough! Enough! Of the punishment.
I cannot take it any more.
The eight day they start to spill my blood.
The eight day refers to the day of circumcision
wherein the blood is spilt, in which manner
the Jews, through persecution have also
spilt their blood.

3.

The Cellar

The Koloskys had a typical cellar with earthen walls dug under the house for the storage of food. It could be reached from the outside by lifting two doors which slanted against the foundation and opened upon eight dirt steps. There was also a door cut into the kitchen floor giving access from the inside down a wooden staircase. I remembered what a strange feeling we had going through the darkened house and down into the cellar, knowing we could not come up whenever we wished. We took candles down with us.

We turned over an empty barrel for a table. One of the plates Mrs. Kolosky brought us served as a candle base. We could only use it when there was real need, as light escaped through the crack of the outside door. Mrs. Kolosky gathered all her small rugs and spread them out among the barrels in the cellar for us to sleep on, then brought some extra blankets to cover us. Fortunately it was early fall and the cold weather had not yet arrived.

No plans were made that night. We lay down in our clothes, and it was not until the next day that we began to figure how to keep alive. None of us slept well that night because of the terrible fear.

The cellar was windowless. During the day all our activity had to be carried on with just the slit of daylight coming through the space between the outside doors. No matter how dismal it was, Mother did not doubt that God would see us through.

The cellar was well stocked with barrels of herring, smoked meats, and all kinds of pickled and otherwise preserved foods. Mr. Kolosky had a lot of grain stored there, too, the indication of a rich man. A poor man could have put aside only meager supplies.

There was not much room for seven people to turn around in, but I could keep little Eda amused and quiet by playing hide and seek with her among the barrels. We were only allowed upstairs twice a day to use the bathroom, which was now shared by the nine of us. Luckily the Kolosky home had inside plumbing. In addition Mother went up to fix us something to eat twice a day. Those trips upstairs made our situation endurable, but we had to be very quiet and constantly alert. Mrs. Kolosky was always correcting us children if we made any noise. At the slightest suspicion of someone in the street she would send us immediately to the cellar. The first morning her husband had gone to tell their married daughters not to come with their families to visit while we were there, for fear the children would innocently give us away.

As we passed through the kitchen and hall on the way to the bathroom we could sometimes see into the other rooms. It was a glimpse into the Christian world. The crucifixes with the figures of Jesus Christ looking down upon us, bleeding from his wounds, frightened little Eda and me, and made Mother and my older sisters shudder. There were pictures of unsmiling saints everywhere. Portraits of the Czar and Czarina in coronation robes hung in the parlor. The Koloskys did not dress differently from my parents, as Father was clean shaven and Mother was stylish like a gentile merchant's wife. Today I know, too, that, other than the religious artifacts, there must have been a basic sameness in the way homes in Russia were furnished. Yet memory tells me that the atmosphere of the place was for us wholly alien and Christian.

The smallest of us were confused to see that it was the gentiles that drove us out of Dubossar, yet it was now gentiles that were helping us. We were being shown that there were some Christians who were not against us. In fact the Koloskys considered it their Christian duty to help us. It seemed a little strange to me when Mrs. Kolosky told Mother that she prayed for us every morning and night. I knew she didn't pray to the Jewish god. Two people were praying to different gods. Which one would be heard?

Mr. Kolosky's friendship was shown by his deep concern for our safety. He and Father obviously admired each other. All consultation between the two men took place in the cellar, with every sentence punctuated with fear. "Nathan, they will be searching for you," Mr. Kolosky said anxiously. "You must get out of the country as soon as possible." They spent four days planning Father's escape and the disposal of our property if it became necessary. The only thing we had brought from Dubossar besides the clothes we wore was our jewelry, which Mr. Kolosky would somehow convert to the cash needed for Father's journey to America.

Father spent the last day before he left giving us instructions: "If the pogroms subside, go back to Dubossar until you hear from me," he said; "But if things continue this bad, you must find a way to get out of Kishinev and make your way to Joe and me in the United States." It was hard for him to keep Mother's attention. "What about our things in Dubossar?" she asked, but we knew she was really most concerned about her son and his family. Father made it emphatic that we would have to forget about the house and belongings, and that to contact her son would only endanger them all.

Then he and Mr. Kolosky made out a predated bill of sale for our property if it had to be sold. Father could do nothing about his business inventory. Nor would he dare touch the bank account which contained the bulk of his fortune. It was doubtless being watched for information of his whereabouts. An attempt to draw on it would bring catastrophe upon us. We would just have to manage on what came from disposal of the belongings we had with us. It was impossible to get full value for anything, because any sale had to be quick and of such a nature as to protect our identity. All we could realize from it was a price that would enable us to flee.

As his departure neared, Father turned to Eva and Julie and said earnestly, "Daughters, please try to help Mother in whatever must be done, and be very considerate of Mr. and Mrs. Kolosky." Then he put on the boots, big hat and baggy outfit of a *mujik* (peasant soldier). We all exclaimed that the disguise made his chances of escape very good, but we worried. He hugged and kissed us one at a time, promising he would somehow get word to us of his whereabouts. For one thing, he would send a letter to us at the German seaport of Bremen upon his arrival in America, and we could pick it up at General Delivery if we, too, had to flee that way. "Remember," he warned, "Don't try to communicate with our relatives in Dubossar." Then he and Mother clung to each other with tears in their eyes. I am sure they wondered if they would ever see one another again. We doused the candle and he carefully went up the muddy steps of the outside entrance into the darkness and the first rains of the late fall season where Mr. Kolosky was waiting.

With Father gone we directed all our questions and fears toward Mother, who assured us that God was "looking after us every minute." Within a few days after Father's escape, however, the danger from the mobs increased so much that Mr. Kolosky restricted our trips upstairs to once a day. Young as I was, I thought a great deal of all these events there in the darkness. There was little to do except think. Anything else made a noise. Sometimes the sound of the cow moving outside or the scurrying of mice behind the barrels would wake me with a start. Staring into the blackness I imagined we were caught, and pictured our slain playmates lying in their blood, or our dead rabbi and my old schoolroom with the classroom furniture smashed and scattered about.

The hostility against the Jews was incomprehensible to us younger ones, who asked Mother about this over and over, until the day she looked at us sadly as though she were going to cry, then murmured, as though trying to convince herself more than us, "God is Israel's lucky star." Jews uttered proverbs as often as Christians crossed themselves. "Our identity will always be preserved," she said. "God has promised." She was always talking about God as though she knew him personally.

The smell of pork hung in the air the first night we had arrived, but out of kindness to us Mrs. Kolosky never cooked it again while we were there. Mother was constantly fearful our food would be tainted by being prepared in a *trafe* (non-kosher) kitchen. It was a great worry and trouble to keep meat and milk products apart, and especially to avoid any contact with pigs. For example, she was in constant fear of inadvertently getting lard in something like the noodles Mrs. Kolosky liked to share with us, so we ate mostly herring and potatoes. Mother was frantically worried that God, who looked down upon her, would find her at fault for breaking the rules of *kashrut* (the code for food preparation). She did her best, but it was difficult in a house that was not organized for cooking in the prescribed way. Once Julie reported with horror that she saw some meat and cheese on the same dish on a sideboard upstairs and Mother, equally horrified, nevertheless had to explain to us that in times of great danger we would have to compromise. Furthermore, we must not cause more trouble to Mrs. Kolosky, who was helping to save our lives. In the end, of course, Mother had to close her eyes to a lot of things.

Mr. Kolosky brought us the latest report: Jews killed in the Kishinev area, many severely injured, hundreds of shops sacked, houses demolished, thousands of men, women and children homeless and, worst of all, many women and girls raped—the implications of which I was too young to understand, but which made my mother and sisters pale and tremble. From then on, nobody was allowed upstairs for any reason except to empty our waste pot. Since we could no longer go to the bathroom privacy became an awful problem. It was not so bad for us youngsters, and it was dark most of the time; but for the three grown women and with the shyness of those days, it must have been painful, indeed. They tried to put up a sheet to hide behind. We all had to learn to turn our heads at the right times.

Toward the last of our stay the air got terribly stale and smelly. Mother was constantly remarking about it. For a woman ordinarily so clean and well-dressed, and for the young women, too, having no change of clothing or adequate washing facilities was torture. The space now seemed even smaller because we could never leave it.

Mrs. Kolosky's friendship with Mother bloomed here in these conditions, for one of the kindest things she did was, after bringing us our food, to sit down at the top of the stairs, despite the foul air, and talk to Mother. She not only brought the news of the outside world, but gave Mother the friendship of another woman in her time of trial and responsibility. Her ample figure was silhouetted against the light of the kitchen lamp. Once, after she had scolded me during the day for making a noise near the top of the stairs, she stood in the doorway above and whispered down sweetly to me, "I can see where you are, Little Mouse. The lamplight shines on your golden hair!" I believed her, because I looked at Julie, also blond, whose scarf had fallen down. There *was* a golden glimmer there.

But when Mrs. Kolosky closed the door and said goodnight, we were left alone, crouching together, silent in the dark, knowing each others' identity only by feel or whispered words. Somehow I knew when Mother unbound and combed her rich dark hair. The women kept their hair braided and covered against the dirt and dust of the earthen walls.

Mother customarily went into a corner and prayed. Sometimes during the day we could see her by the little ray of sunlight coming from between the doors as she fervently mumbled her entreaties to God for the safety of all of us. One day, when the news was particularly bad, she prayed alone, then rejoined us, saying, "The Jews have always been persecuted and driven from place to place, hoping to find refuge. Yet Russia and other Christian countries allow these massacres." Just then Mrs. Kolosky came downstairs with the herring and potatoes. We children were glad for the interruption of this sad recital. Philip and I went back to carry on our whispered conversation among the pickle barrels.

What was the god of the Christians like?

My sisters were always saying that religion divides people and, although our mother never agreed with them, I wondered if they were right. The gentiles seemed to hate the Jews. The Jewish tradition and the conditions forced upon our community made it hard for me to think any differently. For years afterward any symbol of the cross would give me anguish. One thing I made my mind up to, even at that young age: religion does not stop conflicts.

The endless days in that cellar began to make even a dangerous escape look good. The smell of pickles mingled with the stale, acrid air remains with me till now. Then one morning Mrs. Kolosky came to the top of the stairs and softly called down to us, "My husband has made the final plans for you to leave. You will soon be on your way to join your father and brother in America! To avert suspicion you will leave on the Sabbath. No one would suspect of traveling then.

Two hours past midnight, on the seventeenth day of our stay in the cellar, Mother gently roused us from sleep. "We must be ready and on our way before dawn comes," she whispered urgently. She and Mrs. Kolosky had readied everything we were to take along, including the gift by Mrs. Kolosky of two of her quilts. We each had a small bundle to carry, even tiny little Eda. We dressed and waited for the wagon to come.

Mr. Kolosky was very agitated and anxious for us to go, fearing that by now a search for us was already under way which might include his house. He chose Saturday because nobody would think that Jews would travel on the Sabbath.

The wagon came so quietly we heard nothing until the cellar door to the kitchen creaked as it opened. I thought, "I will soon be breathing fresh air."

We climbed the wooden stairs in silence and moved through the house and through the sweet-smelling candy shop, hurrying so as not to keep the wagon waiting in front of the house. "Here," Mrs. Kolosky whispered, pressing a parcel into Mother's hands. "Take this bit of cheese. I put in a sausage, too, and some cookies." She had spent the day before baking. Phil and I had smelled the aroma coming down from her kitchen.

She kissed Eva, Julie and us boys. Then she hugged and kissed little Eda with all her heart. At last she and Mother embraced like the good friends they had become. We and the Koloskys all embraced again, and even Julie and Eva thanked them for saving our lives. While they were sorry to part, I'm sure our friends gave a sigh of relief when we had all climbed into the wagon. The strain on them had been great, and our presence in their home had endangered their whole family. Mr. Kolosky had planned to accompany us to the border, but at the last moment his wife was too frightened to let him go.

The driver flicked the reins over the horses' backs and we started off.

Observation:

Comparing the gentile God with the Jewish God should not make a child question if God only listens to one or the other. This is the result of religious prejudice ingrained in one's culture.

When a Jew suffers small quarters in contrast to a gentile friend helping them, will overcome their prejudice grater than any modern law requiring political correctness.

Does one understand why one such as Maurice would help those in need throughout his life? Those who were cynical in talking about the nature of Maurice, I observed were also lacking a life of difficulties they could not recall. Their complaints were prejudicial and often sought retribution from wrongs they manufactured. I saw jealousy of Maurice in others rather than the appreciation I came to gain from his mentorship. Perhaps it was because I could recall my suffering from childhood peers and could always remember the few who helped me throughout my life.

Ronald Kelsch

Almost to the border

the **Escape**

*We were taking two things with us:
memories of violence and persecution,
and of a beloved home and a happy life.*

4.

The Escape

The fresh air and space of the outdoors were exhilarating. Once released from that prison-like cellar, all of us, including four-year-old Eda, caught the spirit of determination to make it through to Joe and Father. Nevertheless, we began to shiver more with fear than with the cold night air. I clutched my sole personal possessions, the cap Mrs. Kolosky had given me and my slate and slate pencil, for comfort. Mother felt in her petticoat pocket for the money and slip of paper bearing the name and address of the Koloskys' friends we were to find in Poland. We were terribly anxious to go from there to the German seaport of Bremen where, we were almost sure, Father's letter would await us.

In the silent streets the clopping sound of the horses' hooves and the squeaking of the wooden wheels seemed loud enough to rouse the town, but no one stirred, not even a dog barked anywhere. Eva cuddled Eda as we all shifted around trying to find space enough to be comfortable. Mother patted a rolled-up blanket into a pillow for me, but I was too excited to sleep.

Soon the shadowed light of dawn began to reveal the terrible destruction that had taken place. Many houses had been battered or burned down.

"Look!" Philip whispered excitedly. "Mr. Rubenstein's store and art gallery are all wrecked!"

"Shush, children," Mother whispered, leaning across to touch our knees. From then on we silently pointed out one terrible sight after another, imagining that somebody was watching us from every door left standing. As we made our way to the outskirts of the city, we could hardly believe that we had gotten by without incident. All was quiet, as though the city was exhausted by the wild nights of destruction. By the time the sun came out we were well on our way out into the countryside.

The streets soon became mere country roads. The horses seemed to plod along and the driver spoke only to issue instructions. "We will stop by this stream to rest and feed the horses," he would say. "The children may get out if they stay near the wagon." We drank from the stream with cupped hands. We had just enough food for two days so it was rationed. During the morning Mother gave us each some cheese and one cookie. "Let's let people think we're just on an outing," Mother said to us, and with our new freedom we could almost feel it was true. To our delight Mrs. Kolosky had also included some candy.

The sun pouring down upon us in the open countryside made me drowsy, but I vaguely heard the driver tell Mother, "We must take the long way, down the back roads to avoid the big towns." There were some villages we could not avoid, however. At one a man stopped us.

"Do you have room in the wagon to take me to the next town?" he wanted to know. Fear brought me alert. We all held our breaths while our driver told him, "Nyet, nyet. We are only going a short distance."

At one town we stopped to send the driver for some bread and sour cream. He came back with the bread, but couldn't get the sour cream because he had no container. He made us happy, though, because to avoid suspicion he had bought three herring wrapped in paper, a cabbage, and four onions so as to appear a normal shopper. Whenever we passed through a village my mouth became dry and my heart pumped faster.

"Mother! Will we be killed or put in jail?" piped little Eda in fright.

"No, *Bubale* (Little Doll), not if you say what I tell you," Mother answered. Even though we hurried through populated areas, our hearts were pounding.

To rest the horses several times a day the driver always chose an isolated place with a good view down the road. We especially enjoyed stopping near a stream so the horses could drink and we could play in the water.

In the middle of the next morning I was wakened from a nap when the wagon stopped with a jolt. The driver turned to Mother saying, "This is as far as I dare to go." He gestured up the road. "The border is just a few miles straight ahead." Then he gave her detailed instructions about landmarks that would indicate when we had reached the Polish border. After helping us to unload our few belongings and receiving some money from Mother, he turned the cumbersome wagon and team around and started back the way we had come. We were left quite alone on the road. There was nothing in sight but fields stretching to the horizon, and no sound but the humming of bees and the occasional song of a lark. As we began walking we moved closer together, a lonely little band clutching our bundles and moving cautiously toward freedom.

We took turns carrying Eda when she whimpered with exhaustion. By noon we were all tired, and Mother let us stop at the side of the road to rest and eat a ration of the food. We tried to get some shade from the tall, dry amber-colored grass. Mother took off her blue kerchief and used it to shield Eda's face from the overhead sun. We were terribly thirsty. It took real effort to get started again, but with Mother's urging we picked up our bundles and started to walk. Ordinarily Mother would have encouraged us by having us sing along the way; but we didn't dare do anything but go forward quietly.

As the day passed and the sun lowered in the sky our feet began to drag and Mother's manner with us became sharp. Instead of coddling us she spoke firmly, even harshly, to keep us moving. Later on I could understand that the kindness and love she would have preferred to give would not have kept us on our feet. We were hobbling forward on blistered feet when Mother suddenly rasped, "Children! This way. Past the big ditch!"

Her change of voice frightened us. "Will the police prevent our crossing?" I asked her.

"There are no police," Mother assured us. "We have left Russia. Now we are on Polish soil." She then thanked God for our safety.

My older sisters looked surprised at what had been accomplished, in amazement they exclaimed at the same time: "We have stolen the border!" Of course a child like me could see no difference between Russia and Poland, but Mother must have read the landmarks. We were well over the border before she had let us stop. Then she sat down on the ground and burst into tears. We all clustered around her, anxious to give comfort, but when she saw our dismay she wiped her eyes on her petticoat and forced a smile. While she took out the name and address of the Kolosky's friends and studied them, we drank and washed our faces in a pond and brought her water in our cupped hands. Then she parceled out the remainder of the food. As soon as we had eaten and rested a little, she helped us to our feet.

We passed a huge crucifix on the road, mounted on a pole with the figure of Jesus in agony. Too weary to run past, we simply stared at it in awe, and Eda clung to my arm. A cluster of small, dilapidated cottages appeared ahead in the dusk. Mother knocked at one door and a man dressed in shabby working clothes appeared. He seemed to understand Mother's request for directions to the town where we were going. As he scratched his head in thought a bunch of peaked little children began peering at us around the doorjamb. Finally he motioned ahead, "About eight miles," he said in Polish, holding up eight fingers. It seemed like a thousand miles! A cart stood in the yard, but no horse or wagon was in sight.

"Will you take us there?" Mother asked with gestures?

"Nyet, nyet," he said in Russian for emphasis. Then Mother turned away and reached into her petticoats.

Facing him again, she extended a handful of coins and said "Da, da." Without a word he went over to the small, weather beaten bam, led out a very thin horse, and surprised us by hitching it to the cart. Since we could not all fit into it, we took turns riding and walking alongside.

The peasant took us just to the edge of the town we wanted. Darkness had fallen and he wanted to get back. Mother paid him, nodding her head in thanks. He turned and went away without a word.

I no longer recall the names of the people the Koloskys told us to find, nor the name of their town, but the warmth and cheer of their house is always with me.

"Welcome! Welcome!" they said in Russian when they heard the Kolosky name. They hurried us in out of the dark and the mother of the house motioned the daughter to bring us glasses of scalding tea and some black bread with honey on it. Then they showed us where to wash and the boys brought us buckets of water. They even helped us to brush the dust off our clothes before we sat down to a good dinner of chicken with dumplings and sweetened red cabbage. They were obviously poor but they shared with us wholeheartedly. As Mother related the recent happenings in Russia they sighed with sympathy for us. They spoke of their mutual friends the Koloskys with great affection.

"Poland is not free of anti-Semitism, either" said the father, showing an obvious sense of shame. "Many Polish Jews are living in ghettos." While the grownups talked we children looked around the room at all the Christian pictures of saints, priests and famous Polish churches, without the former distress. We were beginning to see the difference between good Christians and bad.

At the end of the evening Mother collapsed. Perhaps knowing we were safe she was able to let herself go. Thankful to be among good-hearted people, she allowed herself to be put to bed. They made beds for the rest of us on the floor along the walls of the main room where we'd be together and keep nice and warm. They even gave the older girls candles so that when the lamps were out we need not be without light if we younger children got frightened.

They watched over mother for two days, and drew fresh milk every day from the cow to nourish her. On the third morning the father brought around his horse, hitched it to his neighbor's wagon, and took us to the railway station for our journey to Bremen.

To children the pogroms seemed to be a fight among grownups. On the train going across Poland in to Germany, however, we got an insight into what prejudice against us really meant. Some German soldiers were playing cards in our car. Curious, I walked up and down the aisle, then stopped to watch the card game. When one soldier would apparently lose, the other would laugh uproariously, pointing to him and shouting, "judicherl judicherl" Thus I learned the word Jew to be an indication of scorn in any language.

As soon as we got off the train at Bremen we bought our steamship tickets and checked our bundles with the agent. Then we went to the post office General Delivery window. We held our breath while Julie asked for a letter. The postmaster disappeared, and we were overjoyed when he returned with not one, but three envelopes addressed to Mother - one from Joe and two from Father. We knew without seeing the contents that they had arrived safely in America. We presumed they both had good jobs already in that fabulous country. The five of us crowded around Mother in excitement as she read Father's instructions as to where we should go upon our arrival in the United States. But the most glorious news for Mother was that he told her that her son and family had escaped to England.

Next Mother marched us straight to the public baths, used so widely in those days. As we boys separated from her and the girls at the entrance, she warned us to take our time and not to *come* out until *we* were soaked and scrubbed clean of the dirt from all our past weeks' ordeal. Inside the bath house were hundreds of men, mostly speaking German, but many speaking Yiddish, Russian and Polish. By the way they worked at getting themselves clean it was obvious *we* were not the only emigrants who had found the place. When we came out we felt like new people, with new skins. We complimented each other when we *met* again outside. It was strange to put our dirty, shabby clothes back on, but Mother promised us new ones before we met Father. *We* all stood up a little taller. Mother and the girls all looked beautiful with their long hair washed and brushed to a sheen.

We did not have money enough for a hotel, but we learned to our relief that those purchasing steamship tickets were allowed to sleep on the floor of the steamship company waiting rooms and mattresses were provided for that purpose. There was even a little room for changing clothes beside each bathroom.

Mother constantly worried about money, counting it over and over, with Julie trying to help and assure her we had enough, even after paying for the steamship tickets. They cost the equivalent of twelve dollars for adults and somewhat less for children. Rubles were accepted, but for shopping in Germany marks were required so we went to the money changer.

We wanted to eat kosher food again, and wandered around until *we* found a delicatessen with a Star of David on it. We didn't dare spend much for food, but Mother reminded us that we were better off than the majority of the emigrants who crowded with us in the waiting rooms. Most of them were penniless and waited every day in long lines at soup kitchens, even though many were well dressed and obviously newly poor.

Bremen was a beautiful city with much *more* cultural development than we had *ever* experienced. People were clean and fashionably dressed, the stores beautiful and well kept. There were lots of streetcars, wagons and buggies. It was busy. Workmen of all types were hard at it everywhere we went. It was a wonderland. There were parks and art galleries and museums, all for the people, not just the aristocrats! Philip and I rode the streetcars for a pittance until Mother became afraid we would get lost.

Eva and Julie sought out the bookstores to get material for learning English, while Mother shopped for some needed items of clothing. Our shoes and stockings were worn out and we needed new underwear. She bought knitting needles to make a new shawl. She took us down to the park every day so we could play on the grass while she knitted. She had even bought a little doll for Eda, debating a long time over the purchase. But Eda's eyes were shiny with joy as she held it in her arms, and she knew it was worth it.

Though less evident than in Poland, anti-Semitism in Germany was brewing. Fellow passengers who spoke German had picked it up in conversations with local Jews. German Jews had even more freedom than Russian Jews; however, we grew to be at ease when we saw a soldier or a policeman, and began to feel we were now in a less hostile world.

In those three weeks my mother and sisters made friends among the other passengers waiting for the ship. Eda stayed close to Mother while Philip and I played together at the dock.

Every passenger seemed to be studying some little book or other and each day new refugees joined the crowd waiting for the boat's departure. We didn't know any of the Jews who came in from Russia, but as we spoke together it became clear that there was not one who had not lost some member of the family from pogroms. "Maybe God was watching over us," Mother observed gratefully.

Most of the refugees could speak and read only Russian or Yiddish, so the English language was very strange to them. Using the Russian-English dictionary, Eva and Julie would help others to learn as much as they could. In this way they earned a little money to buy more books to study on the ocean voyage. It was interesting to see husbands trying to help their wives and vice versa. Just looking at the printed page of the new language seemed to frighten them.

Pictures have a universal message though that everyone can understand. Some of the passengers had gotten hold of some books with pictures of how they dressed in America and everyone was curious to look at them. One thing they seemed most anxious to learn was how to order a meal in English, especially a kosher one. One of the greatest fears of the immigrants was of changing their diets. Rumors were flying all over the place about the food and clothes in the United States. My mother and sisters could act knowledgeable on this subject because they had read the letters from Father and Joe giving a glimpse of how things were in the new world. Everybody listened.

I clearly remember that though we were all timid and frightened of the new adventure, all who were going to America thought they were going to heaven.

The crossing seemed endless

O the cean voyage

When we reached America, all our troubles would be over. We children could be raised in a more relaxed situation, have a better education and forget all our problems.

5.

The Ocean Voyage

It was 1905, the year of greatest influx from Europe to America. Thousands of people boarded the S. S. *Bremen* at the time we did. Teeming masses of them, mostly Jewish fleeing the pogroms. There were others speaking different languages such as Bulgarian, Rumanian, German—each language wearing different clothes we were not familiar with. From whatever country the Jews came, we could nearly always tell they were Jews. It was their facial characteristics, their mannerisms, the hats on the men and wigs on the more religious women and in many other ways.

"Why are these people all going to America?" I wondered. "Are they fleeing the pogroms too? Did they have to run, like Joe, to escape being drafted into the last raging battle of the Japanese war?" As we were acquainted on the ship, we learned a variety of other motives for people to leave the land of their birth, such as perennial food scarcity and unemployment. We all believed America would be different. Everyone would have plenty of everything and wonderful opportunities to earn money. "But," I wondered looking at the huge crowds of passengers, "How could so many find jobs?"

We were shown to our quarters down in steerage, where mattresses were laid end-to-end the full length of the deck, accessible through aisles between the long rows. We hurried to find places where we could all be together. I saw the other passengers had put their belongings either on the comers of their beds or along the aisles.

"Hey, Phil!" I shouted. "Let's use our bundles for pillows!" Delighted with this ingenious solution, Phillip and I left Mother and the girls to explore the rest of the ship. It was hard to get through the crowds. Some people knew what to do, but many milled around looking bewildered. Some had already mislaid their possessions and even their youngsters. I clearly recall the long ropes and the huge pulley for letting the full lifeboats into the water if the ship should sink. I could not see how everybody on board could possibly fit into that small number of boats. I worried that if such a catastrophe occurred, members of our family might get separated, and that we might float forever without being rescued.

The sleeping quarters were awful. Small children fretted and babies cried. Everything was hectic. At the call, "All aboard!" Phillip and I rushed out to from the deck as the ship moved away from the shore. Slowly the land disappeared. "Are we going away from here forever?" I wondered. Then I turned my thoughts to Father and Joe and the new land on the other side of the ocean.

Conversation among the passengers changed from one mood to another, from homesickness for the life we were leaving to hope of a better one in the new country. We younger children looked for places to play, but soon had to give up. My older sisters quickly found a more or less secluded spot where they could study English. They were good for each other. Mother tried to help the rest of us keep occupied.

"Draw us some pictures on your slate," she urged. "Draw me, for a start."

I did as instructed and spent many hours sketching Mother in her different moods, both smiling and frowning, and other people and things on the ship.

Toilet and shower facilities were inadequate and after one day out a terrific stench arose in our quarters. So much quarreling developed among the passengers that as time went on nerves grew frayed. Nineteen days were too much for strangers to tolerate each other under such circumstances. Seasickness became so prevalent we could hardly breathe. People began to accuse each other of pilfering. It seemed that open hostilities would break out any moment. Especially on stormy days, we had to stay huddled together and could not go out on the deck.

We had to stand in long lines to use the toilets and showers. I figured out when they were least in use—mostly after meals. Breakfast was always mush in a tin plate. The ship furnished meals with the passage, but they were not kosher and sometimes so greasy or spoiled we felt lucky to be seasick so we would not be hungry. Even a well person might turn it down. We all lost weight and we children took turns coaxing Mother to eat a little something.

Even on the ship the Jews never failed to gather to pray. They *dovenned,*[1] which meant to sway or bow up and down as if praying with all their body, their heart and their soul. Standing separate from the men, Mother and other women always participated in those prayers. I am sure this helped her through the hard times.

On day, I found a place to sit on a big coil of rope at the stem. Here I could idle away the time by watching the sailors at work or dreaming of Father and Joe and the wonderful meeting that was going to unite us all. One chilly afternoon I went back to our quarters and found it unusually quiet there. Mother was

---

1 To *doven* means to sway or bow up and down in prayer. Orthodox Jews perform this rhythmical movement in order to maintain their mental alertness and to overcome the tension and severe fatigue that inevitably accompany long sessions of prayer in scripture reading.

obviously frightened. Some of the passengers had become very ill with what was evidently no ordinary seasickness. The old couple on the mattresses near Mother were both ill. "What if it is cholera?" people were whispering. Terrified of quarantine, the whole ship was on the verge of panic.

With no more cases reported, that acute fear subsided, but we could tell Mother was still very much worried, even though she tried to conceal her fears from us. She worried about what might happen when we landed. "What if any of us were sent back by the health inspectors? To have the family separated now would be a tragedy!" Scantily covered at night, she worried about us catching cold. She checked us constantly for lice with her fine-tooth comb and became alarmed by every little cough. She worried about our eyes because of a rumor of a strange eye disease breaking out. Though she depended upon God, Mother was afraid of reality in our fast-changing lives. With five children to shepherd to the other side of the world, she also worried about herself. 'What would we do if *she* were the one to be refused admittance? Could she ask us to go back with her? Who would care for us? She was afraid the luck we had so far was too good to last.

We tried to play with other children, though there was so much seasickness that friendships for us younger ones never seemed to blossom. Mother kept me quite busy with errands and taking care of Eda, whom I took with me to my place on the coil of ropes. She could draw on my slate, or we would watch the ocean waves together.

All kinds of rumors covered the ship, both encouraging and discouraging. "America is a heaven on earth, a country friendly and eager to help immigrants," or "There are plenty of jobs and the pay is wonderful." The only discouraging rumors were those, which could prevent us from reaching our destination.

Philip and I would lie awake nights discussing how wonderful it would be when we got there. Our older sisters did not quite share our enthusiasm. Julie kept thinking of Lazer, her boyfriend. Torn between going back to him and figuring some way to bring him to America continually occupied her mind.

"Oh, how I wish I could go back," Julie often said, "and fight with him in the revolution!" Consequently, Eva was also ambivalent about the trip.

"If you go back I will go, too," said Eva. "We can't be separated."

The crossing seemed endless. So much water was incomprehensible. "Mother, we are lost," I told her once. "The captain is going in circles." She told me that other people on ships sometimes thought the same thing.

"Father and Joe reached America safely," she assured me. "God watched over them and He will watch over us. Besides," she would add, "You have your sisters and brother right here with you. Have you noticed how many passengers are without family or friends?" Despite her assurances, I used to go up and anxiously watch for land.

Everything frightened us. Rather than toughen us, our experiences thus far seemed to have worn our nerves thin. We were physically tired and uncomfortable, as well. Some children huddled together in corners with their parents like frightened little animals. The crowded, tense passengers were always noisy, but one day a terrible hush came over them all. Two had died within the space of two days and suffered a quick burial at sea. They lowered the wrapped bodies over the side without even the cleansing ritual of the bathhouse. The ship's doctor had come down to steerage and pronounced them dead, returning without another word. This scared us more than ever.

One day a strong ocean breeze blew away the cap Mrs. Kolosky had given to me. I suffered a great loss as I helplessly watched it disappear into the water, because for men and boys to wear a hat was a religious imperative with Jews. I was so upset that Julie convinced a steward to find me another, an old, frayed one, but it made me feel secure and I hung onto it as if it was a great treasure.

The great lady welcomed us

Occasionally a friendly passenger would come down from the higher-class decks. One such man took a shinning to me and showed me my first American coin—a nickel with a buffalo on one side and an Indian on the other. He was returning to America from a trip to his native Poland and could speak Yiddish. He would tell everyone about America, always drawing a crowd.

The suspense mounted day by day. "Is this the day we will see America?" I would ask Mother each day.

"No, not today," she would answer.

It would be four more days, three more days. Then it was only one. On the last morning, I stood at the rail for hours watching for a sign of land, trying to keep from blinking for fear of missing the very first glimpse of the fabulous new country. There were only waves and ocean fog. Perhaps Mother was mistaken about our reaching New York that day. Then the fog suddenly lifted a bit and I spied the dim outline of land! My heart pounded with excitement. We began to hear whistles from other ships and small boats, each with a different tone.

Soon the fog lifted completely, revealing a beautiful day. I could see all around me, ships big and small, tugboats chugging about among them. Then, remembering the family, I flew down the steps crying, "We are here! We are here!" My brother and sisters rushed up to see, while Mother went quietly about gathering our things together, worrying about admission through Immigration. The girls went back to help her and we all took up our belongings. We were all dressed in the best we had.

We were all together on deck when the most impressive sight of the day came into view. "Look! Off to the left!" someone shouted, and there she stood—the Statue of Liberty. She stood proudly against the skyline with skyscrapers that looked like castles commanding our attention. The man who had shown me the coin came down to relive his own first view of America with us. With misty eyes, he translated the inscription on the statue into Yiddish for the crowd.

They began to dance in the Jewish way

Give me your tired, your poor,
Your huddled masses yearning to breathe free,
The wretched refuse of your teeming shore.
Send these, the homeless, tempest tossed to me.

People were thronging the decks. Suddenly we all started celebrating our arrival in America - singing, shouting, and hugging. The men on our deck formed circles and began to dance in the old Jewish way and then the women joined arms and danced, too. It was a wonderful sight to see Jews from different countries dancing because they were so elated and thankful to God.

There had been so much sickness and misery on board and then things burst into life. The crew had a hard job with us on the crossing, but now they showed their good will. The cooks brought tea and cakes out on deck and surprised us by joining in the dancing. A steward grabbed Julie and me and whirled us around. Another clapped Philip on the shoulder and shouted in German "Good luck, boy!" Smiling first the second-class passengers leaned over the railings while watching us, and some even came down. Shortly forgetting her great fear that something might go wrong at the last moment, Mother entered into the spirit of things and in her dignified way, started to dance. We enjoyed watching a change come over her from being so serious with worry and responsibility, to having almost a light-hearted air. She must have been enormously relieved after our family safely arrived. No doubt, she was longing to see Father, and realizing the union gave her great confidence. The worry fell away from her demeanor like an old cloak.

The Jews kept dancing until the ship reached the wharf. Then everybody ran for his belongings.

After all the excitement, we had a long wait, but we were patient, because there was not one on board who was not grateful to have come. Standing around on deck or sitting on our bundles, we waited quietly to disembark at Ellis Island. Each had his own thoughts about the new land.

"Grandma, will Daddy be there to meet us?" asked a small girl looking up to the old woman holding her hand.

One woman told her twin boys, "We must write Father in Warsaw right away."

Officials gave us each a number, and we disembarked in turn. Two old people were sobbing with joy as they went ashore. Children were quiet and obedient as we all waited in suspense for the greatest step in the journey: admittance to the United States. The thought of rejection terrified some, like Mother. Others were confident and in high spirits.

The Immigration building is a clear memory to this day, with its four towers and strange flag flying. Why should we be afraid? We are about to enter the land of the free! As we edged toward the railings that formed contiguous stalls, a door opened and we caught a glimpse of some dejected people. Were they the ones that must return from which they came?

The lines seemed endless. Authorities wanted to know where we were born, why we left, and all kinds of questions frightened us. Julie and Eva gamely tried their English words on everyone in uniform we met, but no one understood them.

Bribing officials in Russia was such a common, indeed a necessary practice, that Mother had put money aside for this. She began trying to give out coins to each inspector we encountered. She was terrified that each refusal meant it was not enough money or that we were not going to pass.

As time wore on and people tired of standing in lines, babies began to fret and cry and people pushed. Finally, we reached the man who questioned us about our money. We were terrified, because we heard that each immigrant needed to have twenty-five dollars. Mother carefully untied her handkerchief and counted out her money. Since it was not yet changed into dollars, she did not know how much there really was. Looking hopefully at him, she told him through the interpreter about Father and Joe, they dispatched a telegram while we waited to one side. "At least Father and Joe will know we're here," I said. We all relaxed a little.

A pleasant woman in a uniform beckoned us into a large, clean dining room where the multitude of immigrants were being fed free soup, sausage, bread, milk and tea. America was just as people said it was. We even got food we liked.

Then an officer summoned us back into the line. The reply had come from Father and we now were to go on for the health inspection. A doctor and nurse in white uniforms took great pains to examine us for bedbugs, lice, skin disease, coughs or other signs of illness. It was our first experience with a stethoscope.

"Eda! Stop crying." Mother whispered in a frightened tone. "If they think you're sick we'll all be in trouble!"

Eda stopped at once. The doctor who had been so serious about his work gave Eda a big smile and turned to the next family in line. Mother must have misunderstood, because she gathered us close around her, took a big breath, and bypassing the interpreter, began to tell the medical officer in rapid-fire Russian what a good, healthy family we were. The interpreter quieted her down and beckoned us into another room. Then we were fumigated and immunized.

We were detained just one last time in order to receive a lecture on the greatness of the land we were about to call our home, and how to enjoy it. The lecturer did not have misty eyes like the man who had read us the Statue of Liberty poem. Maybe he did not know how it was to come from tyranny to freedom. The interpreter was looking Julie and Eva over, and he seemed to want to detain us later in order to be a little more acquainted with such beautiful girls.

Herded onto the ferry and taken to New York, groups of us continued as instructed. Someone must have kindly shown us how to get to the railway station, I cannot remember; but no immigrant can forget the utterly staggering impact on him of the noise, traffic, and structures of that great city. The streets were great yawning canyons of cement and stone. Horse-drawn carriages, cabs, buggies, freight wagons and streetcars jammed the streets. Right in front of the railroad station a uniformed chauffeur waited with a car, explaining its parts to a crowd around it. When a man in a silk hat and white moustache got in the driver started up, the horses all around reared and skittered with fright.

Observation:

We have forgotten the stories of immigration and how many had suffered coming from devastation and poverty. Our emigration policy had become so difficult over the years that that illegal alien has become the new norm. Once we had an open border restricted by identification and health with a minimal fee. Now we have chaos. I cannot see the difference in the human nature of immigrants. Why we do not use modern technological knowledge to catalog each entry with less physical restrictions in order to limit the illegal and encourage honest entry, is beyond human understanding. Human nature finds a way.

The paradox is we have become a polarized nation of greater restrictions on one side and over tolerant attitudes on the other. Despite our modern technology, we play political games that do not foster solutions.

Ronald Kelsch

I could always say "look in the basket"

the New land

It was four blocks from Fourth Street to Front Street along the Delaware River. As you walked along you passed tenement houses, warehouses, bad houses, shops and saloons, and came to the wharf where you could watch the ships being loaded and unloaded.

6.

The Ocean Voyage

By late afternoon we boarded the train for Philadelphia. Little Eda fell asleep immediately, with her head on Julie's lap. The anticipation of seeing Father and Joe again turned Eva and Philip into different people. They were alert to everything about us.

It was getting dusk. The small towns we passed along the beautiful countryside were a far cry from those back in Dubossar. Many more people had little houses with gardens. Even the trees looked different.

"Look, Mieche," Philip remarked. "There are telegraph poles connecting every community." He had started counting them, but gave up because there were too many. Then he counted the towns. The people in these towns seemed to be going about different activities than we knew in Dubossar. Our eyes drank in everything.

As night fell, we turned from the windows to watch and listen to the people on the train speaking the new language. Julie and Eva were wide-eyed at the clothing women wore on the train and how much more casual they were than on the trains of Europe. We began to feel that there was something wrong with our clothes and shoes, which always squeaked. We now stood out as being different.

I asked Julie, "Do you think Father and Joe look like Americans already?" She didn't answer. She was deep in thought. My heart pounded when I thought of our meeting. "Will we have the same amount of servants as we had in Dubossar?" I enquired of Mother. She did not hear me, either.

We kept pointing out the different things to each other. A man in uniform came down the aisle who gave us each a large bar of chocolate and some fruit. The conversation among the immigrants rose to an excited pitch. "What a country, America!" Then the letdown: The man was soon back to collect. My mother grabbed what was left of the chocolate and fruit from us children and gave it back to him. In Russian she said, "This is what we have not eaten!" Then she paid for the rest. Mother later told me that I cried out in a loud and articulate voice in Russian, "My, what a gimmick!" Sensing our disappointment she promised that when we got to our father he would give us candy and fruit. This was the first introduction to the disenchantments we were to experience in the Promised Land.

Finally, the conductor, who had punched our tickets, came through again and announced in a loud voice a word I already knew: "Philadelphia!"

The train slowed. I strained to see the station platform, but there were too many cars ahead of ours. It wasn't until we came to a complete stop that I spotted Father. Then I saw Joe running along the platform trying to see which car we were in. Russia was forgotten. In another moment I flung myself into Father's arms.

That first meeting at the railroad station in Philadelphia is never to be forgotten. Father and Mother embraced each other with tears of joy running down their faces. Then Father and Joe embraced and kissed us all in turn. Everybody screamed with the gladness of the glorious reunion. Our load of troubles seemed to drop away all of a sudden.

Our joy was marred only by the sad appearance of those lone immigrants who had made the journey with us, who stood there as though clinging together in pairs or groups of three or four seeming not to know which way to turn. "What will happen to them, Mother?" Eva anxiously inquired.

"God has seen us through," Mother answered her. "He will care for them, too." Nineteen days together gets people pretty well acquainted. We were concerned about them as if they were good friends.

The street car took us part way to our new home. We walked the rest, a jaunty little band of pilgrims walking down the cobblestone street, each loaded with bundles. Father carried Eda on his shoulders with great joy. Everyone was so happy that our burdens seemed light. The street lamps gave a romantic glow and a cheerful welcome.

Our new neighborhood was not what I imagined it would be. The people were unmistakably Jewish, but with many different languages and costumes. One could only guess whether they were Russian, Polish or German Jews. Some were already "Americanized" in their dress. The dim light showed some old Jewish men still wearing their caps and beards, but now and then we were surprised by seeing clean-shaven men, especially the younger ones.

Joe and Father looked funny in their derby hats. Since they never took them off, they seemed like part of their bodies. They wore shoes now, too, rather than their Russian boots.

Ours was the third house from the corner of Front and Carpenter Streets. I couldn't read the street sign then, but I soon learned to pronounce Car-pen-ter. We stood on the steps and waited for Father to unlock the door. The inside was nothing like our house in Dubossar. The rooms were unventilated, though this didn't seem important at the time because we were so glad to be together again as a family. We children quickly explored the small rooms and were surprised to find there was only one stove in the whole house and that was in the kitchen. There was no friendly sleeping bench to curl up on by a warm fire. In cold weather we would just have to stay as close to the stove as we could.

Small vents in the ceiling let a little of the heat go through to the bedrooms above. The stove would serve for cooking as well as for heat, and in the days to come my mother would be spending almost all her time right by the kitchen stove where all the meals would be prepared. This meant cold beds in winter. We would just have to heat some bricks to take to bed with us. There was a kitchen sink with a skirt around it and two spigots for water. I was glad to see water inside the house. The bathroom had running water in it, too. Father said a fire in the little "monkey stove" attached to the water tank would give us hot water. But most people went down to the public baths, since those little stoves could not heat enough to fill the tubs.

Father and Joe had bought plenty of things for our dinner. Mother started hustling around right away and the girls pitched in to help prepare for this wonderful occasion. To show love for his family Father had splurged and bought steaks at ten cents a pound, one of the rare times we had tasted beef. The steaks were so tough we could hardly chew them and Father was terribly disappointed. Mother saved the day by making a kugel with brown sugar and nuts.

We all talked at once about what had happened since we last were together. Joe drank a little too much wine and began to tell jokes. The wine only served to make him more enthusiastic about America, its street cars, the lighted store fronts, the drug stores, and the ice cream parlors. He acted as though he had been here forever and said he was going to ask his boss for a day off work to show us around to see for ourselves how exciting the city of Philadelphia was. He would take us to see the statue of William Penn on top of City Hall, where we could walk around the rim of William Penn's hat, five hundred feet above the ground! Everything would look small when we looked down at the street. Joe said he would put on his best suit and show us the town. We would visit the great market places and Fairmount Park, which was a world in itself.

Mother let us children tell about our scary experiences on the way to America. Then it was Father's turn. When he spoke we had a sense of breathing free air.

"There is no Czar here," he said. "No bayonets to cut you down, no spies to watch your every move." Over and over again he repeated: "I never knew what freedom was like until I came to America." He assured us we could say whatever we wanted without fear. We stayed up late making plans for the next day. Joe had gotten a job as a tuck maker in the needle trades industry. He would take Julie and Eva out tomorrow to places where they could find daytime jobs. At night they could attend school. Philip and I would have to start the public school right away. The whole thing sounded exciting to me that night, but within the next few months I was to learn a great deal that was dismaying about the tenement district of Philadelphia where we found ourselves living.

Visualize, if you can, a sudden influx of over a million poor immigrants into any large city—all of them competing to live. The results would be inevitable, overcrowded slums.

Fortunately, Father had an acquaintance from the old country who had already been living in our house. When better things came his way he offered to let Father take it over before anyone else knew it was going to be vacant. Even then Father had worried about paying money out for empty rooms before we got there. So he had rented it and moved in with Joe, meantime looking for second-hand furniture, which would always be a good investment because any extra rooms could be rented out. Once in our house, Father tried hard to make things as nice as possible for Mother. At least she would now have a bathroom inside the house like she did in Kishinev.

Others were not so fortunate. Most people considered themselves lucky if they could get a room or even a part of a room. Even fire escapes were used as sleeping space, and in summers every fire escape was in use. Very often a single man would sleep in a furnace room in exchange for tending the furnace during the cold months. The circumstances in which we lived then were in some ways terrible. Roofs leaked, pipes froze in winter and the plumbing was never in good shape. The immigrants seemed to get used to it. We all learned to "do it yourself" fast, sometimes paying dearly for our lessons. I poured a pail of soapy water onto the floor to surprise Mother with a clean hallway. For the remainder of our stay in that house we had to walk over warped boards and be careful to keep them covered when the landlord was around.

If we were not crowded to begin with, we crowded ourselves up to rent out "living space" for a little extra income. Even then life could be humorous. There was a joke about some people that lived in the slums. Four families lived in a shabby old building on the sixteenth floor. They all lived in one room divided by chalk marks on the floor. When asked by one of their visitors how they got along with so many in one room, someone answered, "Oh, we were getting along fine until one of the families started taking in boarders."

How I longed to be a real child that first year, and join in with the others. Mother worried that we kids could not get out to play, but there was no time for play. Every moment had to be spent earning a livelihood. Family conversations were centered around lack of money. Someone always needed shoes, socks or underwear. Most of the money went for food and rent. The future looked bleak. What little credit was allowed at the grocer's upon our arrival was used up right after the first of every month, but we paid promptly and gained a good reputation. I smiled when I remembered my expectations of the servants we would be having in Philadelphia. How innocent I was.

Our daily life was put askew right away because our main meal of the day in Europe had been at noon, after which everybody had a chance to rest, even the servants. Here we grabbed our customary piece of bread and drank some coffee or milk and ran to our jobs or school. We worked on more or less empty stomachs till noon, when we ate the lunches Mother had packed for everybody. Each morning Mother made a kettle of soup. This formed the main part of what had become the main meal of the day, when all the family gathered for supper.

Mother started right in working hard, making every penny count. She was ambitious for us and obsessed with making the money last. She really tried hard. We began taking in boarders right away. Somewhere Father had gotten a little wagon, which I used to run errands for Mother, such as bringing home coal and groceries. With a house in primitive condition, a family of eight and boarders to see after, Mother always had things for me to do and I took pride that she counted on me most of the time.

I already had a job delivering newspapers after school and Saturdays. This gave me the chance to see what the inside of most buildings looked like. There were no real apartments in the tenements. There were "housekeeping rooms," where the tenants lived by day and slept by night. Sometimes the doors were ajar and I caught glimpses of beds where several people must have slept. Sometimes chairs were put together to form beds for children. There were very few closets. Most of the family clothing was hanging from nails in the doors or walls. Cooking was done mostly on hot plates in chipped granite pans. Any curtains were so skimpy they barely covered the windows. The only table covers I ever saw were oilcloth.

Many rooms had no water. People filled pails and dishpans from taps in the hallways, which were always gloomy and dark. Cracked walls and clutter were everywhere. This, then, was my introduction to our new world.

We felt very fortunate to live across the street from a synagogue. A friend of Father's knew a rabbi who taught Jewish boys at *cheder* for a dollar and a half a month. The regular fee was three dollars, but this particular rabbi was so anxious to preserve Jewish learning among the immigrant children that he was willing to teach at a reduced rate.

"Unless the children learn the things written in the Holy Tongue," he said, "all will be lost in the generations to come."

It is hard for a gentile to understand why a free-thinker like my father, who cared little for religion itself, would be so anxious for us to be in Hebrew school. The Jewish culture and traditions, thousands of years old, was so dear to parents that they accepted the expense of cheder as a normal obligation. In the months which followed, learning from the rabbi was the one thing that kept me from loneliness, at least for a short period of the day, for it would transport me back into the old familiar atmosphere of my native surroundings. I don't think any other people in America spent the time or cared about the preservation of their traditions like the Jews did.

The public school was free and very large, but at recess time the playground was a regular bedlam, with all the children laughing, shouting and screaming in all the languages of the immigrants as well as English. When the bell rang out to warn that school was going to start or that recess was over, its clanging tongue called in magic tones, transforming chaos into order. The girls would quickly line up in one row, the boys in another and we marched straight to our classes like little soldiers in an army.

The bell hung in a little cubicle with its rope hanging down where the students could take turns ringing it—either a husky fellow or two little boys.

My first few months at school were the most lonesome in my life. To make myself more at home I turned my long trousers up inside to the knees trying to make them look like knickers. At recess the boys would be playing ball. I had to stand on the sidelines and watch, being unable to understand what they were saying. Sometimes I saw Philip at recess but we were in different grades and he couldn't understand any better than I. Finally I made friends with a boy named Solomon who came from Russia, though a different area than we. We could communicate, and he helped to take the place of Bola. The problem was that neither of us could speak English. Not even my teacher could understand what we said. We both had to learn.

The one bright note in my whole school experience was the kind face of my American teacher instead of a stern-faced *melamed* (Jewish teacher). If one cannot speak the language one has to resort to facial expressions and gestures. I am sure my teacher understood my feelings from the frightened look on my face when she seated me near two colored boys. I had never seen a person of another race before and I cried "Nyet! Nyet!" and ran toward the door. She gently pulled me back and put me in another seat.

One day I was watching the boys play ball when the ball accidently came my way. I caught it and threw it back. There was a fleeting glance of communication on their faces. I wanted desperately to communicate. I thought, "Somehow I must learn this language."

I kept listening to the English gibberish they were speaking and occasionally a word here and a phrase there would come out of the dark cloud of confusion and suddenly its meaning would appear like a sparkling gem in the sunshine. Soon people seemed to make out what I was saying. Each new word learned gave me confidence to learn another. At first looking at the shop signs was bewildering, but I slowly began to associate the words on the signs with what was sold inside, and the trade symbols, such as the mortar and pestle for an apothecary.

After the initial months of struggle the language came more easily. Being young makes it easier. Even so I recall the period of non-communication as being acutely lonely. I had to struggle to change nyet to no, and da to yes. Once the teacher told me to tell the class about the massacres in Russian. Then she told them that although she didn't understand the Russian, I had been trying to tell them about our escape. This helped them to know I was a child with problems, just as they had problems.

Joe had it much harder with the language. He called our mantelpiece a masterpiece. We would get into arguments. He was determined to prove me wrong because he had been here longer. I enjoyed winning. My Mother encouraged us to learn and speak English, insisting that we explain every word. If she spoke the wrong name for something she would bring out her small pad and write it down in Yiddish. Sometimes she would call the iceman "Mr. Icebox." She never did learn the difference between "kitchen" and "chicken."

Somewhere she had read that one who was going to live in America must give up talking Russian or Yiddish. At school we children were gradually forced to speak English as best we could, so we learned faster than Joe, Eva and Julie, who worked among fellow immigrants speaking Yiddish or Russian most of the time. Even their work instructions were in those tongues.

Everything was strange to us, everywhere we turned. "Joe, tell me quick," gasped Philip, rushing in to supper one night. "Why does a baseball need to wear a glove?"

The strangeness was as overwhelming as the ocean we had crossed, but I never wanted to tell my parents how I felt, so when we all shared our experiences of the day, I would invent stories rather than relate my true daytime activities. Once I told my father I saw a horse with a wooden leg which I hit with a stick. He was disturbed to hear me lying and gave me a licking. I was laughing and crying when I finally told him it was a wooden horse.

I was full of practical jokes, like putting an "out of order" sign on the bathroom so I wouldn't be disturbed by all the people wanting to get in. I took the sign away with me afterward and hid it. Once on April First I told a woman her husband was arriving from Russia on the boat, and the poor thing went all the way to the docks in great excitement. Father gave me a licking for that.

We all ached for Father because he could not get work truly worthy of him; but as intelligent as he was, he just could not get a working knowledge of English. He was always known for being unusually honorable, and it is to his credit that he did not entertain false pride. He put support of his family first and took on any job he could get.

It was somebody else's practical (and profitable) joke that landed him his job as attendant in the local bath house. The former attendant had bored holes in the walls of the ladies' section and was selling "peeks" to the men on the other side. The man was fired and the holes plugged up.

One of the great discoveries in America for the Jewish immigrants was the Jewish Forward, a newspaper printed in Yiddish. Mother would read the "Bintele Briefs," a kind of advice to the lovelorn column, except that these cases were extremely sad and sometimes the writers' situations were desperate. There were things for us children to read in that paper, a continuing love story for the romantic members of the family and, of course, the news. We children listened to Mother read the love stories and Father tell us about the news. He said the pogroms were still going on and many were being killed.

One day a reporter came to our house with a photographer. They took a picture of our whole family together and wrote down the story of our escape, which later came out in the papers. Big headlines read, "Whole Family Escapes Kishinev Massacre." After that many people came to see us and talked for a long time asking Father and Mother questions in hopes of finding clues to the whereabouts of their own relatives.

There was an organization under way to protest the massacres that were going on over there. One day some people came to our house and told us about a large protest parade arranged for New York and a smaller one to march down Broad Street in Philadelphia. On the day of the parade we gathered early in the morning and put on arm bands. We were given banners to carry and Philip got to carry the American flag. It seemed strange to see that in place of the Russian flag, but it gave us a great sense of pride and identity. Mounted police and a band playing for the marchers gave the event a lot of color. Mother tired before the end and had to drop out.

Haggling was the Jewish way

Struggle for existence

Beyond the financial necessity that compelled us, there was a willing heart and love of family which liberated a force within us to push beyond our external circumstances.

7.

Struggle for Existence

My first job of delivering papers lasted only a few months, because one day I came home and told Mother that I had seen a neighbor man coming out of one of my lady customers' houses. She consulted with Father and they decided that a route which included the red light district was not the proper place for a boy to work.

My next job was on a milk wagon helping to deliver the milk, or holding the horses' reins while the milkman delivered the milk to the shops. The horse knew exactly where to stop. I thought it was a great job, even though I had to take my pay in milk every day, which amounted to eight cents in merchandise. My only problem was that I had to get up at four o'clock in the morning. Once in awhile I would get an extra bottle and I would take it to my teacher. At first she refused the milk, but then she must have seen how great was my need to give, for she graciously accepted my offering.

My schooling, meantime, was suffering. I was always falling asleep in school and something had to be done about it. My parents were called in to the superintendent's office and my teacher went with me to meet with them. The principal had difficulty understanding them when they told him they were so sorry and promised I would not go on that job again. My teacher, who seemed to understand things beyond words, explained it to him. I will always remember her. She taught me to say "please" and "thank you" and "excuse me." Somehow in those days I missed childhood, a dog, a toy, swimming, or playing with other children after school. Sometimes I envied other children, even the black ones, who could play in the street. It wasn't that the language held me back continually, nor did my parents make me work; but that while the family was so hard pressed we children wanted to share the responsibility. It was hard to compare myself with the average boy of ten or eleven because, between school and working, my life was made up of long, tedious hours.

My next part-time job was operating a machine in a cardboard box factory. I would push down a foot pedal to cut the cardboard into about twelve pieces, then push one to cut out the corners. Afterward I folded them by hand into chocolate boxes. When things were slow there I would work in a factory varnishing furniture.

Many of the Jewish immigrants began to rise in business and industry through the free enterprise system, but many fell into the old familiar talk of socialism. American working conditions at the time furnished a fertile field for this. To understand how this strange paradox could have occurred, one would have to understand the poverty and struggle, hopes and disillusionment of the great influx of Jewish immigrants of that time.

Years later, when there was less poverty and hunger, socialism would be less attractive; but during that difficult early period it had a great deal of vitality in the slums. It had fed on the revolutionary spirit in the old country more than anything else, and need for secrecy added to its intrigue there and gave to it an impetus that would grow weaker in a free country. Still, it maintained sufficient strength to create a significant impact on the American scene.

Eva and Julie were working in the garment industry or "needle trade" as it was known. The sweat shop system relied upon contracting most of the work outside the factory to subcontractors in small shops, factories or people's homes. When it was carried on in the homes, the wife, the children, the neighbors and every immigrant that could be pressed into service were used. A home would be a cutting room, pressing room and sewing room. Even the youngest children would be threading needles, sewing on buttons and taking out bastings. The hours were long—ten to twelve hours a day, six days a week, and the pay was small. Children could earn about a dollar a week and adults could earn around three to six dollars a week.

Actually no one was making any money in "sweating." The margin for any contractor was minimal and amounted to little more than the workers' wages. If there was any compensation it was in a slight independence for the contractor, yet he worked as hard as anyone. He did not live in luxury as he might have done in czarist Russia. He worked right alongside the workers. To exist in the business, it was necessary to meet the lowest price possible and therefore to use the very cheapest labor.

Being forced into the situation of hiring themselves out as cheap labor was too much for Eva and Julie to accept. In Russia they had never worked except at home. Now they felt no better off than the people in Russia, and they wanted to fight their exploiters with the same zeal they had directed against the czarist regime.

Life was more than just running needles through one's fingers in the sweat shops, however. The newcomers eagerly grasped any opportunities to better themselves and became part of the social-revolutionary forces quickening among them. They eagerly attended lectures, concerts, plays, classes, union meetings and theater groups. Unions were then the expression of idealistic, daring among the intellectually eager youth. Julie became involved in the theater sponsored by the Union and was in a play depicting the terrible working conditions. Mother made me get dressed up and attend out of family spirit, but I would rather have gone to the vaudeville or the penny arcade.

Eva and Julie nearly lost their lives in a fire at their factory. The place was a firetrap that burned fast, but the firemen caught it in time to keep it from being completely destroyed with the workers in it. My sisters were out of work four days before it got cleared up. I remember how frantic they were to pick up some work so as not to miss any money.

A fire in those days in the tenements and factory district was a horrible sight. Bystanders collected not so much as spectators, but to see whether any of their own family members were dead or hurt. Knowing the flimsy firetraps the buildings were, they always expected the worst. Horse-drawn fire wagons often had a hard time getting through the narrow alleys, and through the people milling around. The firemen were fearless, but their equipment was nothing like what we know today, and sometimes a fire was almost brought under control when the water supply failed, leaving life and property to the flames. The loss of a job in the family when a factory burned was almost as bad as the loss of a life, because people were so desperately dependent upon every hand to keep the family alive.

Julie had never forgotten the boy back home. She didn't talk so much about him lately as when we were coming over on the ship. She had been determined to get enough money saved in America to send for him to join her, but that hope had long since dwindled, especially since they had not been able to communicate. Letters had not gotten through and she had given up wondering why she didn't hear. When she finally did get a letter it was not from him but from a Russian girl she had known in Dubossar:

Dear Julie,

Our mutual comrade in the cause, Lazar Goldberg, is dead. It happened right after you left, but I never knew where to reach you until they finally let the mail through.

He was so fully intent on aiding the revolution that one day he and his companions were trying to blow up the police station and were caught. He defied a Russian soldier and was shot down in the square. We are not only thinking of ourselves, but all the Jews in Russia must find their place, too.

The revolution will get underway soon. That is all we think about. It is hard to think of any pleasures or fun anymore. We are becoming better organized all the time. I work for the cause every moment I have. I married Arie in December. You remember, he was a comrade, too.

I wish you were still here to help us with our cause against the autocracy and to share the victory with us when it is over. We are preparing for the day when we have to fight so the workers of the country will have their chance. Maybe you have already found peace and prosperity. If this is the first time you have heard about Lazar, I am sorry to be the one to break the news, but remember, he died for the cause.

Your Comrade,

Anna.

By the sparks in Julie's eyes you could tell that, had we remained in Russia, she would certainly have continued to espouse "the cause." She was always telling us that nothing could be more defeating than standing over a hot pressing board, or bending over a sewing machine for endless hours with her head filled with the ceaseless whirring noise. She would have had a greater sense of real living in Russia doing battle with her comrades against the government. Father reminded her of the fear our family had known when the Russian soldiers came to search our house and barely missed finding the red flag in our back yard.

There were a lot of quarrels and fights resulting from the strikes in America, because the big companies had strike breakers in those days. Joe came home bloody and battered more than once. Once I even went with Eva, Julie and Joe to the Union Hall to see the Union Leader, who was depicted as a kind, but rigorous father who would lead them out of the bondage of working for practically nothing. The union boss was leaning against a stand, wearing a derby hat and smoking a cigar. Banners hung all over the place. The heroes of the Union halls in those days were Eugene Debs, anarchist; Joe Hall, union organizer; Big Bill Haywood, the IWW organizer; Emma Goldman, socialist; Joe Hill, union organizer; Upton Sinclair, socialist whose famous novel of the Chicago stockyards, "Jungle," appeared in 1906; and Theodore Dreiser, whose "Sister Carrie": was then illicit literature.

Many parents backed their young people in their frequent strikes for humane working conditions, but my father never felt that way. At the dinner table each night Julie or Eva would talk about the middle man, the villain of the production shops and factories who pounced on the profits of the workers. My father knew that wages were low and times were hard, but he felt it was like many other problems, something that time would cure. He felt there should be no talk of socialism in this country with its free enterprise system and opportunities for development.

He would ask them if they had forgotten the seventeen days we spent in the cellar, and reminded them of the pogroms and the situation of the Jews in Russia where they had been nonentities without citizenship without the right to vote. Here in America they had the opportunity of becoming citizens with full rights and would be equal, at least on a political level, with every other person in the United States. Here they would count as individuals and live in a country they could be proud of as their homeland.

Father's point of view seemed most reasonable to me. He always gave one the feeling he would rather be poor in America than rich in Russia, knowing that his children and grandchildren were to benefit greatly from our coming here. He studied constantly to qualify for U.S. citizenship.

Father was still a great admirer of Theodore Roosevelt, then President of the United States and who now advocated the "Square Deal." He would beam with pride that we all lived in such a progressive nation. Julie, Eva and Joe never saw it that way. They joined the Working Circle and attended their union meetings and, since they didn't have to hide things in America, they brought literature home and left it lying around the house. Father looked defeated when he tried to communicate with them, and couldn't understand why they didn't see this as a wonderful land where every citizen could vote.

My sisters' and brothers' attitude never kept them from partaking of the centuries-old culture of the European Jews. The Jewish theater had been established before we came to Philadelphia. No matter how menial a person's job, he could attend and be comforted to know that there was so much Jewish culture here.

One night when Julie came home from some kind of a socialist meeting she brought a new boarder home with her. His name was Sam.

I hated to see Mother take in a new boarder because she was already working so hard. It pained my heart to have her standing over the stove so much of the day, trying to prepare enough food out of the little she had for the family and our boarders. Occasionally a boarder wouldn't have enough work and would be unable to pay board. Mother would always be good about it, never making him uncomfortable, and would wait until he found some work. The hard physical work and the strain of adjustment to this new life took its toll. She seemed to be losing her youthful good looks, and I reflected upon the marketing days in Dubossar when her beauty and great style made everyone proud of her.

As the months went by a romance developed between Sam and Julie which eventually led to marriage. Eva was only fifteen when she was working in the dress factory and met another girl just a few months younger. Sasha Ostrowsky was making buttonholes. They became good friends and Sasha took Eva home to meet her family of mother, father and five brothers. The oldest brother, Emanuel was very attracted to her, but shy before his sister's beautiful new friend.

Spring came and my father gave up his job in the bath house where he had worked for a pittance. He had worked on his English, but when spring came he still had not learned it well enough to find the kind of job that would pay more. He decided to peddle things and I wanted to help him. I could speak the language better than he could.

We must have been quite a sight, father and son going to the market. Each morning we rented pushcarts for ten cents per day and pushed them to the wholesale market where we loaded up with any kind of produce that was a good buy. Then we were off to the Market Row to find our place amidst the throngs of people. The more produce we had, the harder it was to push the carts. By the time we arrived almost every space was taken and we could hardly ever get a place side by side. Sometimes I would be around the corner from my father. What made me so happy was the pride he took in me. He thought I was a nice looking boy who would attract lots of customers.

It would be hard to explain about market row in those days. The noise and the smell and outselling each other became an adventure of its own. There were a lot of fish and chickens sold there because Jews loved fish and chicken and they could make a great meal at low cost from them.

To the housewife it was an adventure to find enough food to feed a family on such a little money and to the peddler it was a challenge to sell an ear of corn already cooked for one cent and still make a profit.

I was always tempted to cut the prices down. Father kept warning me not to give all my profit away. Sometimes it would be lessened when a policeman would stroll by and help himself to a piece of fruit as policemen used to do in those days, and you couldn't say anything about it.

There were always a lot of disputes among the peddlers and the customers in the market, mostly over minor things such as a rotten apple slipped in, or suspicion of a penny over, but Father was a peace maker. He spent a lot of time calming people down who argued about price.

Haggling was the Jewish way. It was in those days that I got my first, and perhaps my best insight into the real Jewish world of business. I think I have seen every market in the many countries I have visited, but none can compare, in local color, to the market in our tenement district in Philadelphia.

Friday was our busy day because this was the day Jewish people bought for the Sabbath. Our business started early because everyone had to shop and prepare the food before the first evening star came out. We always sold out early on Fridays and there was never anything left. The immigrants were so poor they would buy anything, even the poorest quality. In fact, all peddlers sold out every day, because when only spoiled food was left the Negroes from another part of town would come down to buy it.

I think the thing I missed most about Dubossar were the gardens. One hardly ever saw growing things in Philadelphia where the good earth was buried under what seemed to be acres of cobblestones. Only the market place with its produce made me feel close to the earth again, with its array of colorful fruit and vegetables against the drabness of the tenement houses.

I kept my pushcart very tidy and never let anything spill over on the ground. Philip, who worked at a small store near our home, would come to see me on his lunch hour and eat something off my cart. I tried to be fair with people and measured very carefully with my container that was separated into peck and a half-peck measurements which looked very much like a reversible cone with a small measure at one end, and a large one at the other end, separated in the middle. You just turned it upside down when you wanted to change the measurement.

Produce was not all that was sold on Market Row. One could buy anything there, from bits of lace to all kinds of clothing; pots and pans and treasures from the old country people had to part with, like a samovar or a piece of silver— almost anything that would fit in a pushcart or stall.

One day I looked around at my fellow peddlers, who did as they knew in the old country? Many of them were now old. The scene remains unforgettable: men with long beards and the poorest clothes, standing all day in one spot calling out their wares. They never seemed to be getting anywhere. I decided to look for a better way. I went into a business only slightly better than the push cart business, but it was a step up.

Philip quit his job and we became partners, with him being "general manager" and I his assistant. We got ourselves a basket, fitted it with a rope to put over our shoulders so we could carry it around and filled it with all kinds of notions, such a shoelaces, match boxes, hairpins, safety pins, needles and thread, fly paper, celluloid collars and cuffs, buttons, visors, and sleeve covers. We even tried to sell medicine and hair restorers. The baskets were very heavy and I often sat down to rest because my shoulder would get so sore from the strap. Philip reported to Father that I was lazy. I felt guilty and told Father I was sitting down to figure out ways to sell my stock sooner and lighten the weight of the basket.

Even without sufficient English to give a fast sales talk I could always say, "Look in the basket." I found the shoe shine boys and sold them supplies, looked at people's hair to determine potential comb customers, watched for those who smoked and sold them matches, went from house to house, demonstrating to the bewildered housewives just how many flies they could catch when the roll of sticky fly paper was unrolled. Many times this demonstration gave me trouble. They didn't like to see the dead flies.

On the way home each evening I would stop on the cobble stone streets and, under the street lamps, count again the coins I had earned that day, happy because when the family pooled their earnings I would be able to contribute as much as any member. We were finally forced out of this business because the fee for peddling on the street was twenty-five dollars a year. We could never pay it. After about eight months of dodging the police we finally gave it up.

Julie received more letters from Anna. When translated into English we had a good picture of what was going on in our old home.

Dear Julie,

As you know when you were here we had already started to organize ourselves to combat the power of the Czar. At first we thought we might weaken his position by causing division between the State and the Christian church. I am afraid this will not work now because things are taking a strange turn. The young prince is suffering from a rare inherited disease. In her great anguish the Czarina has been seeking even something more tangible than the usual séances at court. She has the monk Rasputin at the palace now and he is supposed to be a great healer. She has absolute faith he will be able to cure their son.

Rasputin has been able to make great inroads into the Royal Family, not only in a religious way but in a political one also. He is an unsavory character who makes his own laws and seems to have the power to enforce them. Because the family is so hypnotized by him I think he is going to gain even greater power. He also hates the Jews and you know what that means.

Little can be done now, but we are biding our time, hoping to find a chance to get things underway.

Anna

Dear Julie:

We are starting to make headway now by using another approach to organize the people in trying to transfer them from the grip of religion to socialism.

I think it is going to be easy because those same people who were so easily stirred up during the pogroms can be just as apathetic. For this reason it should be easy to make the transfer with almost total unawareness to them of what is happening.

Our first claim to them is: a Christian community is supposed to be a social one. The workers are to be fed and lodged from a common supply, by a common authority, where all things are provided for all in common.

At the head of every bed we allow these workers to hang a sacred image and for the time being the atmosphere will remain a religious one. This is bound to fade away and gradually things will become secular. It will be easy then to change Moscow, the Holy City to a socialistic one.

How are things going in America? How are the socialists doing there? I hope you will be as victorious there as we plan to be here.

Anna

Not having my business anymore I had to find something else. I decided to sell papers again until I could find something more productive.

Not wanting to just stand on a corner and yell "paper," I walked down the street to figure out a new approach, and looking inside a saloon window, saw, besides those playing pool, a lot of men just talking to each other. I went inside with a stack of papers under my arm. The bartender spotted me first thing. I was too young to enter a saloon, and to avoid having any trouble over minors, he yelled at me to get out. Some guy in a derby hat, big cigar in his mouth, pool stick in his hand poised to hit the cue ball, calmly cocked his eye and said, "Ah, let him be. Why don't you let the kid sell his papers?" The manager gave in, grumbling to himself, and I had a bunch of new customers. The saloon not only afforded a short refuge from the bitter cold each afternoon, but I could watch the fascinating procedure of men spitting the remains of their chewing tobacco into the spittoons.

Besides the spitting exhibition, there were sure to be some interesting snatches of conversation, perhaps a heated political argument. Of course I wouldn't ever stay long enough to hear much of it because the policeman, wearing his coat with nine shiny buttons down the front and his high-crowned derby hat, would be sauntering by. The badge and the long slender club that hung from the waist, which would sometimes be swung around in a circle, were enough to cause a state of hysteria in me. It would be years before I would be able to associate a policeman with law, order, and protection.

I shall never forget the saloon, though, with its wooden floors, the dark, bold-patterned wall paper behind the heavily framed picture of nude ladies. The big mirror behind the bar was lit up by clear glass light globes in the center of fluted shades. The whole thing hung from a cord attached to the ceiling. I can still remember the dull-colored wainscoting around the walls, the brass railing that ran around the bar a foot from the floor. Behind this were several spittoons, set several feet apart, for the customers at the bar. There was a side door where ladies could bring buckets for beer. Inside there was a counter spread with cold cuts and pickles and bread and butter to eat with the beer. I always looked at the food, but none was ever offered to me.

The barber shop down the street was almost as fascinating and less of a problem to get into. I could always sell an evening paper to the barber for his customers to read, and often two or three men, waiting their turn, would buy one to take home with them, as well.

I have never seen, even among the most expensive places of today, a shop that could compare for glamour with that barber shop. Sometimes four barbers would be busy at one time, each at his own leather-upholstered swivel chair with carved metal frame and foot rest, which could be converted into a recliner with the push of a lever. A man could relax even while the barber was manipulating a sharp-edged razor across his face. Before shaving a customer the barber would sharpen his razor on a strap hanging from the cabinet. Using one hand to hold the strap out in a horizontal position, and the other to hold the handle of the razor, he would run the blade full length of the strap, turning it to the other side as it moved back and forth. So swiftly did he do this that it took me a long time to understand just how it was done.

One side of the barber shop was a wall of open shelves divided into cubby holes, each just large enough to hold a customer's shaving mug and brush. Each mug had a man's name on it. My father and Joe, clean shaven Jews, kept their mugs there. It was a masculine world, where a man could sit in the chair in front of the fancy marble-topped cabinet, facing a mirror with a gilded, carved frame. After his hair was cut he was shifted to a reclining position for a shave and had a steaming towel placed over his newly-shaved face. Sometimes the bay rum used on the customers' face smelled stronger than the cigar smoke circling the room. Outside, the revolving striped candy-stick standard invited customers to have a "Shave and Haircut - Two Bits."

Safety razors were just coming in and Joe became interested in selling those. He carried his little stand by the strap around his shoulder and to demonstrate he chose a young man to have the side of his face shaved. He bought ten razors at a time at a dollar twenty each, then sold them for two dollars, but he himself still liked to go to the barber shop. I could hardly ever afford the fifteen cents they charged for kids, so most of the time my hair fell on my forehead or in my eyes.

One day I found a twenty-dollar gold piece in the street. I couldn't believe my eyes. It could buy a whole winter's supply of coal or clothing for the whole family. As usual, my first impulse was to run to my father and lay the fortune in his hands, envisioning in my mind the joy on his face when he saw it.

My second impulse was far from noble, but it opened up a glorious picture in my mind. I imagined myself as captain of the baseball team that played in the park almost every day since. Through the magic of the gold piece, the old ragged clothes the team members wore disappeared and new uniforms took their place. When I made my dream known to the team they readily, if not enthusiastically, let me play on the team. I soon realized that I would not be captain, but at least I would be part of the gang.

The "Nationals" could not have been more proud of their uniforms than we were. We strutted around like peacocks. Besides, after the uniforms had been paid for with the gold coin there was enough money left over to buy a new glove and mit and enough popcorn and candy to stuff the pocket of every member besides stuffing ourselves.

It's sad that such quickly-won glory can fade just as quickly. I still had to deliver my papers every night and, no matter how I hurried, I nearly always arrived at the "park" too late for practice. Also, thoughts of what could have been done for my family tormented me, and when Father told me about his best friend losing a twenty-dollar gold piece I swore myself and my teammates to eternal secrecy.

I was thirteen when I put my application in for the Jewish run National Farm School. My bar mitzvah (age of responsibility) had passed almost without notice. Since we took our synagogue duties so much for granted, and no one had money to make any celebration out of it, I still realized a great source of pride to the family when each boy "became a man."

The Farm School was established to teach young Jewish men the art of farming as part of the Jewish "back to the soil" movement. The required age for entry was sixteen, but I looked big for my age and our rabbi gave me a very good recommendation, so they made an exception. (Maybe they were also short of pupils.) They sent me a list of what a student would need, including underwear, pajamas, various work clothes, sweaters, coats and dress clothes. My folks couldn't even afford a pair of socks for me, but they beamed with pride at my going.

Philip was working as an orderly at the University of Pennsylvania Hospital and had a little money which he happily spent on a pair of canvas shoes for me at some bargain place, guessing at the size. They soon started to pinch and I had to take them off. I entered school with practically none of the clothing specified except what I was wearing. The school furnished every student with a pair of boots for use in the stables. I would clean these up and wear them to class, as well.

The school was supported by wealthy Jews, so board and room were furnished, but we worked hard for our tuition by currying horses, cleaning stables, feeding cows and picking produce. My clothes started falling apart and I had to have some money. So I waited on tables three times a day for a dollar fifty per month; picked tomatoes by moonlight for five cents a row; made beds for three rich kids at five cents a week, and sold candy for the Athletic Association (I ate up all that profit). How I envied the other boys when they would receive money from home every month. My parents just didn't have money to send me.

I was not only the poorest kid to enter the school, but the youngest. The headmaster overlooked many of my shortcomings.

"You excel everybody in arithmetic, Maurice," he said, "but beyond that you know less than anybody here."

He did noticed I was good at the farm jobs and working the ground. That ground was so hard it couldn't be broken with a plow, so we were taught to bore holes in the ground, put in dynamite sticks and set them off.

The older boys were nice to me and tried to help me with my classwork, but they had fun at my expense, like sending me for a bucket of "cold steam," or "hard rocks," or a "paper stretcher." They made us freshmen paint a building with our toothbrushes. I had to use the only one I had. When they decided to initiate me into their group they painted my body all over with house paint and marched me through the school grounds. This prank nearly cost me my life, since it closed up all the pores and before long I was overheated, unable to breathe, and delirious, then in a coma. I was in bed a long time, but it made many friends for me. They were so sorry for what they'd done they gave me constant attention.

"Gee, Maurie, we didn't mean any harm, honest," the leader said with genuine remorse the first day they came to see me.

"Maurie, how'd you like to be on the football team? The guys have decided to let you play," one told me. This was repentance at its height, because my being so young precluded their even considering me for anything more than a little practice in the past.

There were a lot of tragi-comic episodes in my life. One was the day I ate a couple of sandwiches after waiting tables at lunch and ran down to watch the team practice, not knowing members weren't supposed to eat before a game. That was the day they decided to let me play. The sandwiches ended up all over the field.

The Board members were always coming around to lecture us on how to become "good men." I didn't have a chance to be anything else—first because I was too young that the guys wouldn't take me with them when they went off the campus, and second, because I never got the time or money to get into any mischief worth mentioning. The older boys were sixteen and seventeen and taking out girls, if they could find any. The biggest excursion I had was with another boy down to the little town nearby to get a pair of socks.

I learned some wonderful things at the agricultural school: about the soil, seed, and green living things. I knew the joy of watching them grow and the value of water for the thirsty earth; how to make a furrow and feed the animals. It was the classwork I couldn't keep up with, no matter how I tried.

I seemed to be running all the time. Doing all the extra jobs to make money made me so tired at night that I would fall into bed with my clothes on without studying, and have to be out early to milk the cows. I wrote a letter to my father trying to explain my predicament without making him disappointed in me.

Maybe if a letter had come from home just then, when I needed the bolstering of their pride in me, I might not have given up, but I must have done too good a job of covering my desperation. A letter never came.

I went to the headmaster and poured my heart out to him. He was a non-Jew with a big belly and plenty of knowledge about agriculture and boys, as well.

"I understand what you're up against, Maurice," he told me, "and I admire you for putting everything right on the table. How would you like to get some experience on a real farm?"

I nodded, not knowing what else to do. I had given up on myself at the school, as much as I was ashamed to disappoint my family. So it was settled. In a few days he had a job for me with a farmer in Georgia. He even paid my fare to get there. When I told the other boys some of them sat on my bed with me, not knowing what to say. Then they walked me to the barn; the headmaster let one of the boys take me down to the bus on the plough horse.

That Georgia farmer really wanted to get his money's worth out of the five dollars a month he paid me. He was a bachelor, about forty-five years old, and a stern, hard taskmaster. At night we would eat together and talk in his poor little farmhouse. He was trying hard to make a go of that place and needed somebody badly. But under his hard-bitten, work-worshipping exterior he was a human being who understood that the loneliness out there was intolerable for a kid.

"You're homesick, boy," he said after three weeks. "You'll never be any good to me here. You'd better get started back to your folks." I knew he liked me then, because he had already told me I was a good worker. He paid for my ticket back to Philadelphia.

It was a wonderful feeling to be home again. I hated being separated from my family. Philip still had his hospital job and got me on as an orderly. That was another dramatic change for me. One day a gust of wind blew the window curtains into the flame of the heated sterilizer. They caught fire and everybody panicked except a nurse who ran over and yanked the curtains down. Her starched uniform caught fire. Without thinking, I threw her down on the floor and smothered the flames with the matting. Putting that fire out naturally made me hero of the day.

Once when a patient jumped from a third story window another orderly and I had to take his mangled body into our small morgue on a stretcher. We were directed to "get him ready" by stuffing his openings with cotton so the fluid would not escape. I was horrified. Nothing in my life had prepared me for such a thing, and I was ready to run away from that job; but we did what we were told. Jobs were scarce.

In general the job of orderly was terrible for a youngster. I worked hard to get promoted to the operating room, and as soon as I was transferred, I began to learn the name of every instrument. Soon I knew them all, and could be a big help to the nurses and doctors. Their only acknowledgement of my age, now fourteen, was when they nicknamed me "Babe."

I also made great headway with the patients, because, while getting them ready for surgery, I made an extra effort to ease their tension and make them comfortable. I allowed them as much time as possible to be free before strapping down their limbs, and speaking very kindly to them in my broken English, explained what I was doing and why. They used to give me nice tips when they recovered. Father saved every penny of these tips for me and the savings came in handy for my future venture.

Surgery at University Hospital took place in an amphitheater for the benefit of the medical students. Normally the overworked, underpaid nurses had their hands full administering the ether onto a gauze mask over the patient's face from a can, and assisting the doctors in a hundred different ways. In those days, however, not only were there almost no women doctors to speak of, but for "certain" operations the nurses weren't permitted in the theater because they were women. At those times the surgeons relied quite heavily on me for handling the equipment and of course presenting the right tools at the right time.

It seems incredible today that a fourteen-year-old would be entrusted with this kind of duties, but they never seemed to have enough help at the hospital, and medical work anyway wasn't a popular thing. I made a dollar a day on that job, and lunch.

I grew up fast there and began to look older than my age. The heavy responsibility, the confrontation with the different ailments and the experience with people facing death in the operating room or dying violently matured me overnight. Suddenly it was too much for me. I began to dislike the ill people and, while I couldn't tell my father about it, I reasoned it out with myself that the honest thing to do was to quit.

Just then the night switchboard operator's job opened up at Mt. Sinai Hospital, close enough to our home for me to walk and save the ten cents a day carfare. I took it; but soon I became sort of an all-round man. It started when a contagious disease was discovered on the top floor and for some days the entire hospital was quarantined, allowing no one in or out. They had me doing everything: serving food to the doctors, replacing light bulbs, trouble shooting on the floors—everything.

Once I was sent up to deal with a deranged man in the isolation ward who was dissatisfied with his food. He tried to kill me by throwing me down the stairs, but I was able to grab hold of a heavy cart full of trays of dishes and hang on. He struggled to get me loose and there were dishes crashing and rolling in every direction. None of the hospital staff appeared, but some of the patients came running out of their rooms to help me. We got him strapped down, but not long afterward he somehow got a razor blade, cut himself loose and came looking for me. I just happened to have gone to a little room in an odd comer for a nap, so he couldn't find me before they took him away to the insane asylum.

The hospital's alcohol supply was disappearing and it was obvious somebody was drinking it. The new head matron confronted me with it, but the nurses just laughed. One look at my face told them I was too dumb to steal and too innocent to hide the truth. The orderly who took it was found drunk in a storeroom and confessed.

The hospital now had a motorized ambulance made by putting a new body on a second-hand chassis. Those were the days when the chauffeur had a lot to do to keep a car running, including mixing the oil and gas, which slowed things down. One night there was such a bad fire downtown this wasn't adequate. The casualties were so heavy the hospital drafted every possible person and conveyance such as when the stable man brought the horse-drawn ambulance around front.

"Get behind that horse, boy!" the doctor in charge of Emergency hollered, "and get down to that fire!"

I had never driven through the narrow city streets before and the horse got up onto a sidewalk and actually pulled away some wooden stairs; but I got the rig down there and, with the help of the police, through the crowds of bystanders without hurting anybody. Many people had been trapped and burned to death. I had to pick up two moaning victims so badly burned I couldn't look at them and, with the help of the firemen, put them into the ambulance. By now I was so nervous from the excitement of the fire and not being able to handle the horse in all the commotion that I asked a man from the crowd to drive us back to the hospital.

One pleasure among the many miseries of tenement life was the wonderful days at the city's enormous Fairmount Park, which offered so many things to see and do. On Sundays the park was full of people of every sort—newcomers and old timers; nursemaids watching children play on the grass while policemen watched the nursemaids; working families picnicking; teenagers and lovers boating on the lake; and fashionable ladies and gentlemen promenading along the garden walks.

One of the most rewarding events of the week would be the performance of John Philip Sousa's Band. His stirring music in that beautiful outdoor setting seemed to bring people together. All the varied types and classes of Philadelphia would be drawn to the band stand area by strains of music, and we would all be joined as Americans while the performance lasted.

Sousa's music has probably had more influence on American public life than any composer or band leader since.

He was, in fact, so important a part of the more enriching facet of our lives in Philadelphia that the working people complimented him with a rather fond series of jokes, such as

" ... Sousa played 'Down by the Old Mill Stream,' and then fell in."

Our humor was simple then, partly so the immigrants could understand, and partly because pleasures in general were simple. The working people, exhausted a good deal of time, were grateful for anything that would bring them an easy smile.

We younger children absorbed our father's attitude and enjoyed the freedom of America for its own sake. Julie and Eva, on the other hand, became more disheartened every day about working conditions. The terror of the pogroms and the fact that we barely escaped with our lives neither compensated for all the present hardships nor made them grateful for America. Five or six dollars a week can hardly be considered a living wage, and they had, after all, to put in a sixty-hour work week with a long streetcar ride to and from work every day except Sunday. My older sisters could not see how even a decent wage could ever elevate them from their slavery in buildings that were overcrowded, unventilated and dimly lighted, where the perspiration ran down their faces in the hot, humid summers of Philadelphia, or when they froze in winter.

Yet I don't remember that our family ever really looked at ourselves as typical immigrants or in dire poverty—only "down on our luck." Had it not been for the pooling of all our meager earnings (Eva would come in with three dollars, Julie with two and a half, I'd give my share and so would the others) and Mother's careful stretching of the meals with lima beans and noodles, we could never have survived at all. Mother never let the struggle get her down, nor did she ever refer to the days she had servants and every convenience and all the luxuries of the times. Nobody could wait on her like I did, and I took special pride in anticipating her needs and wishes.

Little Eda was growing up and giving us a lot of pleasure, especially father, who would hoist her up on his shoulder and sing with her as they danced around the kitchen until Mother shooed them out. Very pretty Eda now spoke the best English of us all. She stayed close to Mother as a rule, came straight home from school, and took special pride in her homework. Her mannerisms and the way she carried her head and smiled made her appear sometimes very much like Mother, even though she was her step-daughter.

After all we had been through together, with Mother as our guiding light, we were so close we never thought of her as anything less than the best possible mother. Our natural mother would be very happy if she knew how wonderfully we children had been treated.

When the older ones came home after a long day's work, exhausted and irritable, Mother and Father both understood their anguish at being young and tied to jobs they despised, in conditions to which they could never adjust. Mother offered her sympathy in the way of a little snack or a loving touch of her hand, or a piece of new ribbon—whatever simple gesture she could make. Father tried to soften their arguments against the "capitalist exploiters" by listening and then counseling patience and patriotism.

"Conditions in this country are impossible," they would say vehemently. "They must be changed!" Julie and Eva never stopped trying to convert people to socialism. Later, Eva had a little daughter who was so influenced by her mother's fire that she was arrested before she was twelve for substituting the word "communism" for the word "Jesus" on the "Jesus Saves" signs. She grew out of it, though, and ended up a fine artist in capitalistic New York City.

My sisters were not alone in feeling that freedom by itself could not compensate for all their burdens. Many of our friends were overcome by discouragement and returned to their homelands, as bad as they were. Father hated to see them go. He could not deny that poverty dimmed the brightness of freedom, but he was in continuous dispute with those who were uncertain about the choice they had made and who argued that the American dream was a false one. I cannot recall my father ever letting his gratefulness be outweighed by the hardships he was to face for the rest of his life. He and Mother both seemed always to be cheerful and satisfied with the knowledge that at least the children would receive the opportunities America had to offer.

During those hard times we were very grateful for any extra money. We were especially happy when Joe came home one day and told us he had a job in Gimbals department store. Actually, a group of managers had offered him a job in Chicago to manage a warehouse at a good salary, but, unknown to him, it was only a front for a crooked scheme. Joe's English was still not very good, and they used this to their advantage. Putting him in charge of the warehouse gave them a perfect outlet for the stolen merchandise that was coming from Gimbals as though the warehouse was a legitimate branch of their firm. How they managed to cover up the invoices I do not remember, but Joe kept writing glowing reports of how business was in Chicago. He was selling furniture, sewing machines and even piece goods, and begging them to send more merchandise so he would not run out. Every letter from Joe bore a glowing report filled with his increasing confidence in himself until one day the family received a letter saying that Joe was in prison, where he remained until the end of the trial. He had been duped, but he had kept track of every transaction in Russian, which not only cleared his name, but helped to trap the crooks as well, and after everything was over, he went back to his job in Philadelphia.

Life in the slums had its humorous side too. Mother used to read stories that made her chuckle. For instance: A Jewish man gave his old suit away because it looked so bad, ("It must really have been in bad shape for that!" she commented). Needing another suit before the next Sabbath, he went down to the secondhand shop. Finally, after looking a long time, he found one he could afford and went home to try it on so his wife could see what it looked like. "Oh, Sol!" she exclaimed. "That's the suit you threw away!"

Shopping was a real experience in those days. I remember walking down the street counting at least fifteen second-hand stores. The shopkeepers would stand outside their doors and call out to the passersby about "how great and fine" they could make us look in their suits, hats or coats. A prospective customer would stand in front of a mirror trying on a coat . If the coat was too big, the shopkeeper would take the slack up in back with his hand so it would have a nice, smooth look in front.

Today, a person might take an hour trying to decide whether to pay the list price, but in those days haggling was an everyday part of living. Whenever my mother got a dime or any little extra money she would put it in a special box. When we desperately needed something she would take that precious money and go shopping and surely would haggle.

In retrospect, it is comical to remember how the seller tried to get as much out of the customer as he possibly could, while the customer tried to get the smallest price she could. My first lesson in psychology was from watching customers start walking out when they couldn't agree on the price. Rarely did one make it to the door without the shopkeeper taking after him and coming down just enough, and no more, to make a sale. The majority of sales were completed about half way between the asking price and the first offer. I suspect both parties enjoyed the haggling. My mother never went haggling for second-hand clothes for me because I always wore my older brother's hand-me-downs.

Being poor and ragged didn't keep the peddlers and shopkeepers from sending their children to schools and sometimes even to universities. I think most Jews would have sent their kids to school if they had to starve to do it. We all had to plan and scheme over every nickel to make both ends meet, and most families lived on "bargain foods" like soft tomatoes, "utility" potatoes and cabbage, turnips, parsnips and carrots. It was amazing how many ways Mother could cook carrots, even for dessert. I have to look back on those immigrant days with philosophical eyes to see that those struggles were not in vain. I am sure that it was the struggling and hard work of the immigrants that helped this nation to progress. They operated on the old adage "necessity is the mother of invention" because they had to think up short cuts to save hard, endure tedious labor, and to make their lives tolerable at home.

The invention of machines was bound to replace much of the manual labor and those who had begun as unskilled laborers now entered the industrial revolution with real trades. In my lifetime I have seen this simple foundation of the needle trades industry spawn a thousand related businesses from the manufacturing of clothing and fabric to all the different fields of color and design for better homes and better lives. Every generation seems to be a little better off than the last one, but only because the last generation handed over so much to the next one.

It was important to the immigrant to get out of the tenement districts as soon as they could. It was hard to get out, but there were ways. One was to accumulate money by inheriting it or earning it; the other was through the education of their children. It could take years to cross the boundary from the slums to a higher economic level or social order, but many did it through sheer determination. Eva, for example, had her eye on a job in the library. She doubled her efforts at night school in order to fill the job's requirements to speak English, Russian and Yiddish.

Thrust into a new environment by persecution, the new immigrants met the challenge with native intelligence and a will to succeed that established a truly remarkable equilibrium. If a monument were raised to those days, it should be raised to the sacrifices of the immigrant cultures.

Observation:

In the early nineteen hundreds, Maurice's family was a microcosmic beginning of our political system today. How much did the Russian immigrant import communism that eventually infiltrated American beginning with the unions.

Maurice's stepmother was a microcosm of patience and hard work as his father's philosophy was persistence for the principle of Free Enterprise. Maurice and his older brother capitalized on free enterprise, while their sisters were involved with socialism meetings and the proliferation of unions.

Several letters form a Russian friend to the older sister indicated that those early times the socialist movement in Russia was trying to use the Christian Religion as an argument to start disagreements that would later implore "secular" ideas. Signs of "Jesus Lives" were overwritten written with "Communism Lives." In one hundred years, the U.S. has become a macrocosm of these early families.

Ronald Kelsch

So much empty land, rocks and sagebrush

the Colony

*We would go to Utah and build a new place,
a new independent life with favorable conditions.
The sun would shine 365 days a year and
we would be far away from the tenement district
of Philadelphia.*

8.

The Colony

During the long winter nights we would sit around the kitchen stove to warm ourselves. There would be supper, and our family would be together after the day's work, and we could look forward to Sundays when we didn't have to work at all. In those days the Christian Sabbath was observed by the whole United States. Everything shut down. It was the one thing people of all races, religions and classes shared. But something was stirring in the air at home these days. Julie and Sam had begun talking about a new colony being formed out in the state of Utah. "Why," I wondered, "would anybody ever want to move again?"

Julie and Sam couldn't help feeling they would never live decently or earn a real living if they remained where they were, and they talked about freedom, security and socialism and about going back to the soil to live as our ancestors did in ancient Israel. Various other colonies had failed but they were sure that this one, based on pure socialism, would be different, and they glowed with enthusiasm. I listened avidly to the descriptions of the agricultural life we could have if we followed this course that had so long been denied the Jews.

I began to dream about the land. At the same time, some of the last desires of childhood were getting mixed with the fantasies of adolescence. For example, I was filled with a hopeless longing for the pair of skates displayed in Minsky's window. One of the kids in our tenement house sold me one skate. I was overjoyed, but my father took it away from me saying "One skate would be hard on the leather of one shoe, so one sole would be worn out before the other." Nevertheless, I still dreamed of skating down the street in front of the new girl's house. She would be sitting on the step, her dark eyes watching me go past as I whistled a tune or maybe played one on my second-hand harmonica, all the time skating magnificently straight ahead as though I didn't see her.

One day, Sam and Julie brought home some brochures of different Jewish colonies in the West, with pictures of thriving orchards, berry patches and alfalfa growing taller than I was. A week later Sam brought a copy of the Jewish Exponent. It contained a glowing article by Benjamin Brown dealing with Clarion, the new colony in Utah. Reading it made me think of Dubossar. How nice it would be to live in a small village again! I still have a copy of that paper:

> "The hills West of the colony are thickly covered with pine and cedar trees, affording ample free fuel and material for fences and outbuildings. During certain seasons of the year the nearby rivers simply teem with fish. The Wasatch mountains across the East are covered with heavy timber and there are abundant deposits of coal in its canyons, as well as a limitless supply of gypsum and cement material along its foothills. The sun shines in this valley for at least 325 days a year, the climate invigorating, and few days in the year prevent outdoor work. The blue skies overhead by day and the teeming, starry night and moonlight fill men's hearts both with joy and faith. It seems that no sin can thrive here for it is so open and free that God's eye is not obscured anywhere."

This seemed like a paradise to Julie and Sam. It not only offered them participation in the socialist way of life; it was also an escape from the unrewarding life of the

Philadelphia tenement district. Some of our friends had already left Philadelphia for colonies to the West. These settlers hoped to set an example for other Jewish immigrants to follow. For centuries our people had been limited to being merchants and petty traders who took no interest in the lands in which they lived, and they wanted to prove otherwise.

Father encouraged them by saying "What a great opportunity here in the land of freedom, to give a living demonstration of what can be done when there is no one to stop you!"

Clarion soon became a dream colony which was going to put an end to the awful working conditions and the long commuting on streetcars. There would be privacy, sunlight and clean fresh living in the wide open spaces. I too got excited about the West. "What an adventure," I thought. "Here's the chance to use what I learned at the farm school—currying horses, milking cows, and working the soil!" I could already see myself as a "hero of the land."

Soon, many Jews had already left for Clarion. They would understand each other. A few letters were coming back to Philadelphia from Clarion filled with undercurrents of dissatisfaction, but Julie and Sam shut their eyes to them. Nothing was going to discourage them now. It had taken them three years to get the three hundred dollars required to join the Clarion association, and they planned to leave in the Spring, quite aware that the association was operating on borrowed money and the contributions of wealthy Jews who had subscribed for bonds.

I cannot remember how it was decided that I go along too, but my having attended farm school must have had something to do with it. The fond memory of Mother packing my clothes is with me still. She shined my shoes vigorously and washed and mended my clothes, but she looked unsure about my going. I watched her put a prayer book among my clothes and wished it could have been skates. Did they skate in the new colony? No, no! Of course they wouldn't! I would be a cowboy!

As we were preparing to go, Mother fussed over me as though she wanted to change her mind. We were to make the long journey across the country by rail. Mother and Father would see us off, taking Eda along. The six of us went clown to the station on the streetcar. The others could not get off work to come along.

The station area was crowded with horses and buggies; wagonloads of baggage and freight; passengers with their families and friends seeing them off or meeting them; baggage handlers and loaded porters busily weaving in and out of the throng. New immigrants mixed with Native Americans to make a colorful and noisy scene. The train was far newer than those we had used in Europe, and the entire spirit of the trainmen, ticket sellers and crowds reflected a kind of joyous anticipation of adventure.

Mother and Father hugged us all and kissed us - especially me—as Jews do. I picked little Eda up and held her close. "Be good, Edale," I told her, "and don't grow up too fast before we meet again!"

We climbed aboard. I sat in the last seat of the coach while Julie and Sam sat across the aisle. I pushed my cap back and pressed my face against the train window to watch the rest of the family standing in the crowd on the platform waving goodbye. The chugging engine pulled the train slowly forward and I looked back until the figures on the platform disappeared from view. Tears came to my eyes and I turned my head from the window and looked straight ahead.

Unable to afford a sleeping berth, we sat in our seats for three nights and four days. Mother had packed sufficient food for the better part of the journey. When night came, people adjusted their seats to a more comfortable, inclined position, and I did likewise. I tried to sleep. All day there had been sudden moments of yearning for the rest of the family. I kept thinking of my mother and father, of Joe and Philip, Eva and Eda and my friends in Philadelphia. I even felt nostalgia for Dubossar and the happier times there. This longing dampened my enthusiasm for our new home and in the darkness of the unfamiliar night my spirit of adventure weakened and I wished we could all go back. How I wished for sleep to block out the loneliness coming on!

Daylight lifted my spirits. We awoke to the sight of rich farmlands whizzing by and I stared at the magnificent barns and hefty livestock standing in heavy pasture. There was much to interest a fourteen-year-old boy. As we penetrated deeper into the West the architecture of the passing towns changed. There were a greater variety of buildings and they were newer than the ones in Philadelphia.

The people on this trip were more vigorous, freer and more good-natured than the frightened and impoverished lot of refugees with whom we had traveled from Russia. They were heading for St. Louis, Chicago, Kansas City and points West. Some were very jovial and struck up acquaintance with others, but others were quiet, obviously tired from sitting up the whole night. Small children were bewildered by the changing environment, but despite the uneasiness of the change, an air of cheerful expectancy prevailed as the train crossed the vast and bounteous lands of America. I kept looking for a cowboy.

There were many types of English spoken on the train, but with our limited grasp of the language we were only able to catch occasional phrases. However, those who had made the trip before were anxious to point out the landmarks to their fellow passengers. The children particularly were excited by crossing the mighty Mississippi and Missouri rivers and the grownups were awed by the power of the water and the barges were spotted with enthusiastic interest.

The cars were hot and the passengers finally opened the windows, but the air was soon filled with soot from the engine. There was a crowded washroom and we did our best to keep clean, but we got blacker as the days went by.

After two days and nights the Great Plains gave way to the Rocky Mountains, then to the mountain valleys of Utah, and on the morning of the fourth day the sun, just coming over the eastern mountains, greeted us as the train pulled into the Salt Lake City station. "It will be a city full of gentiles," I kept repeating to myself.

In those days the Mormon Capital had a population of about 75,000 people—a mere village compared to Philadelphia. The city was handsomely laid out in blocks with wide, straight streets, far less crowded than the narrow streets of Philadelphia. We must have arrived in the middle of the week because things did not seem very busy. Yellow street cars with overhead trolleys moved along their tracks up and down the center of the streets. I wanted to ride on one of them, but Sam and Julie wanted to save the fare even though I argued that it "would save time to ride."

No one on the streets looked Jewish, nor did I hear any Russian or Yiddish spoken—only English, some with foreign accents. Little did I know then that this city would one day be the site of my future home and business, nor could I guess that the beautiful idea of starting a new colony where people would live for others' interest, would so quickly fade.

Our train for Clarion did not leave for several hours, and much had to be done before it left. Sam and Julie had received letters from members in the colony warning them to take on as many supplies as possible in Salt Lake City.

In Gunnison, the town nearest our settlement, it was going to be impossible to get the kind of food we were used to, like pastrami. Julie spoke poor English, but it was still better than Sam's - he still preferred communicating in Yiddish. By now, I could read the newspaper and the street signs and the signs on all the store fronts. I played the big interpreter and asked the whereabouts of the synagogue in broken English. The Rabbi put us in touch with several local Jews who could give us advice and they gladly guided Julie to the kosher butcher and grocers while Sam and I shopped for other items. The Salt Lake Jewish community knew all about the Clarion project and wanted to help us all they could and of course, they were the only people we could talk to freely.

The trip to the Gunnison Valley where Clarion was located was memorable. As we left Salt Lake Valley, the mountains seemed to close in on the valley floor. The few orchards we passed were too far off for me to see what fruits they bore. A long stretch of emptiness was dotted with three or four towns, more grey sagebrush and hills and mountains that looked as though nature had clumped sterile dirt out onto the earth in fluid shapes.

I stared out of the windows to see what was going by. After several hours of riding, the train came to a complete stop, far from any sign of habitation. The conductor got out of his cab and after a while we heard voices. It appeared that he had spotted several cows standing on the tracks in time to bring the train to a halt.

The whistle blew again, and the conductor came through to announce "Gunnison." People on the train seemed to know—no doubt from our garb and our language that we were going to Clarion. The conductor seemed to know the place well. He told us that Gunnison was a farm town with a population of 236 Mormons and that Clarion was three miles further West. He helped us get off the train.

My hopes that there would be someone to meet us were clashed, and we slept on the benches of Gunnison's station that night. When daylight came I slipped off my bench and looked around. The early morning sun tipped the surrounding mountains with golden light and they looked as though they were molded against the intense blue of the sky. Having known flat land all my life, I found the mountains fascinating.

The stationmaster showed us the way to Clarion, pointing to some little clusters of houses that lay along the three miles west of Gunnison. In the distance, a wagon and horses approached along the road. I kept watching until it was possible to distinguish the driver and I could see whether he had brought anyone along with him and if there was enough room for us and our baggage in the wagon.

We had expected an exuberant greeting, but the driver was quiet and somber. Although he was from Clarion and spoke Yiddish, he had very little to say. Wordlessly, he helped us pile our things into the wagon and assisted Julie up onto the seat. Sam climbed up beside her and I rode in the back. Julie and Sam began inquiring enthusiastically about things in Clarion, but after a while their talk became subdued and the joy went out of their voices and all of a sudden Julie seemed to be lost.

Not being able to see their faces, I wondered what was going through their minds, and as we neared Clarion I stared at the desolate landscape and listened to their desolate voices and I knew that this was not what they had expected. I thought of all the rich country we had passed through on our journey— the miles of fertile fields, the blooming orchards, the growing things, the green hills. Why did we have to come so far to such an unpromising land?

A committee of two men and four women greeted us when we arrived in Clarion. There were a few houses, but some people were still living in tents. There was a house for us and I hoped that this would cheer Julie up. I watched the faces of my sister and her husband as they looked at the empty rooms, then I slipped outside so they could console each other in private. There was nothing I could say to them that would make things better. Even the water barrel was empty, and it was not until later that a neighbor came by to give us drinking water, which would have to be replenished the next day at Gunnison, three miles away.

That evening Sam and Julie were invited to visit a house across the fields to meet our fellow pioneers. After they heard an explanation of the colony's plans for the future, they felt better. There were fifty families in Clarion who had drawn lots for forty-acre parcels of land. Each forty acre parcel had a small house in one corner and four houses were placed where four plots joined, thus giving those four families immediate neighbors.

We were advised that we would be helped with machinery and the experience of our fellow members. Water seemed to be the most talked about issue. The purchase agreement for the Clarion farmers had assured them of an adequate supply from the nearby state-built canal, so it was difficult to understand the water shortage.

The president of the Colony, Ben Brown, was twenty-three years of age and it was he who had conceived of Clarion and enlisted the cooperation of the Jewish Agricultural Society in New York and raised money from wealthy Jews to give the colony its start. All the members were young people in their twenties or early thirties. They tried to be warm and cooperative. We were introduced to the working arrangements of the Clarion enterprise. There were numerous committees: a committee for working the land, one for making purchases, one for the horses and one that laid out the land and roads and made plans for the houses. The office was run by the president, the secretary and the treasurer. All work was considered equal. The pay was equal, as well: fifteen dollars per week.

At first, everybody seemed to keep his own disappointment a secret. We learned that many were bewildered and disillusioned. In the beginning they had all dreamed of making a great Jewish settlement, although I have since read *"Benjamin Brown observed pessimism from the very start and that people were already divided and not given to accepting leadership."*

That night in the house we didn't know where to begin. Those who greeted us had made a fire, and that was a welcoming note, but I could not tell whether the people of Clarion were glad to see Julie and Sam because they wanted more people to share the colony, or because they needed help desperately. We made our beds on the floor for the night, but our disappointment was so deep that none of us could sleep. Lying in the dark I could imagine Julie withering away here. Obviously, the neighbors had so many troubles of their own they would not be of much help. My own confidence began to wane. Perhaps the knowledge and experience I had learned in farm school would be useless here. I had dreamed of Clarion being just like the National Farm School, with barns and cows and horses, with troughs for watering and feeding them, and with all the equipment to make the work efficient. Somehow, I thought that the crops would all have been planted by now and well on their way, but here it was—so much empty land, rocks and sagebrush.

"How will Sam take to the plough?" I wondered as I drifted off to sleep. "He has had no experience whatsoever."

When morning came, Sam was anxious to roll up his sleeves and get to work. He wanted to give it a try. "We're all in this together," was his attitude, and he was ready to add his best efforts to the community.

The virgin soil was hard to plough and even more difficult to sow. The colonists did not know about dynamiting to make the soil porous, which was something we had learned in school, and I began to wonder if they even knew how to plant a seed or make a furrow, or if they knew enough to give living things the right amount of water. Being a young kid, I would have been happy being just a cowboy, but there was a desperate need to produce food. Our lives depended on it, and when we realized we must face the winter here, the thought of anything failing to grow put us in a terrible state of fear.

However, despite the problems facing us, we pitched in and were able to get some crops planted before the end of spring. This encouraged everyone and a note of hope began to permeate the community. Gardens were a must. Part of the money Sam and Julie brought with them was for potatoes, cabbage and carrots, and the first thing she did, was to put in a garden that soon came up very nicely.

There was also plenty to do to make the house livable; caring for the animals; fencing the stock and weeding. There were meetings to share experience and spread encouragement. I went to a minion (the ten men required for a service) when they could get one together; but Julie and Sam, being socialists, had already drifted away from the faith and did not attend. In Europe, socialist and communist ideals were easy to accept because they seemed the only alternatives to the terrible oppression of the Czar, and when the sweatshops of America blasted their dreams of freedom, the younger immigrants showed their disappointment by joining organizations they felt would put an end to their miserable conditions. Benjamin Brown described one of the early days of the project in exuberant good humor:[1]

> It is here, on such a barren tract of land that I and Hurvitz welcomed our pioneers! Twelve men, they numbered, and I fetched them from this forsaken station, Gunnison.... The pioneers took their places in the wagon, and but they didn't forget to take along their umbrellas [it was so sunny], which they opened up, and traveling so, they stretched out a Ukrainian song (Ach, Doba, Doba). When we passed by a Mormon village children and grown-ups came out to admire the pioneers with umbrellas, dressed in city clothes, that were singing elegantly but so strangely. The Mormon farmers ridiculed them a bit as "Pioneers with Umbrellas"!

> ...At first the days were really very interesting. The umbrella pioneers have brought this virgin wild area into cultivation. We used to greet each sunrise with song and labor, and every sunset used to bring us restfulness and spiritual happiness, the happiness which comes as a result of productive work...We were enthralled by the newness of this machine (tractor). And here I must record my mistake in that I influenced our purchasing committee to buy such a machine... we did not have the tools or knowledge to keep such a thing operating. Nevertheless we did seed about 1500 acres of wheat, oats, and alfalfa ....

There were times and places, such as when we met at the machine shop or the office or hay farms, when there was some activity evident; but added to the fact that it was improbable that the site would ever become profitable or even livable, was the tragic fact that not one of them was prepared in any way for the life they had undertaken. No less unfortunate was the overabundance of leaders and the dearth of followers. The diversity of opinion and the highly individual nature of the persons involved made a truly cooperative enterprise virtually impossible. It became increasingly clear that the project was doomed.

It was sad to watch Julie and Sam realize that things were going to be just as hard here as before. Father had not wanted them to marry before they were self-supporting, but Julie had answered by asking "Have you forgotten your own youth, Papa?" and Mother backed her up. Their whole fortune consisted of five dollars when they married three years before, but they saved hard (and probably borrowed some money as well) to get enough to settle them in Clarion, and I began imagining that they were beginning to wish they had stayed back there in the sweatshops.

Most of the things essential to our diet were not available to us—kosher items and familiar foods like cream cheese, lox and sour cream, It must have been terrible for the very religious ones to have to feel bad about everything they ate. For religious reasons it was even difficult for us to butcher an animal. Our traditions were very dear to us because they were all we had left of our own, and to give them up was difficult for the more religious among us who suffered great pangs of conscience because of it.

There were other problems that beset us, the most urgent of which was the shortage of water. Our wheat was just not growing as well as the Mormon neighbor's wheat, and when it finally occurred to our people to investigate, they found that the diversion gates for the Jewish lands never had been installed on the end of the canal. The older farm communities higher on the canal had all the water they wanted, while the newcomers below went without. The Jews were simply being taken advantage of.

I started wondering "Why weren't all these things looked into in the beginning?" When the engineer laid out the colony into forty-acre farms there were some allocations of good land and some allocations of land so rocky they needed heavy clearing. Anyway, it was doubtful if a family could make it on forty acres of any of this land, with or without rocks.

The colony had purchased expensive machinery of which they were very proud, but not even the best machinery in the world could take the place of experienced farmers. The only reason the colony survived at all was that wealthy Jews from the East and from Utah wanted to see the operation succeed and put a lot of money into it.

The people themselves wanted desperately to have it succeed. They kept reminding themselves of the beautiful sunsets and the blessings of owning their own land. The majority of them became quite healthy looking, but many dreams retain their brightness only in the minds of those who create them, only to fade away when faced with the light of reality.

The cooperative idea was popular, especially among the socialists, but I don't think anyone understands what it is like unless he practices it in reality. It is easy to think of a society in which all are partners and no one is a hireling and there is no competition; but to live in such a colony is quite a different matter.

Julie worked many more hours than she had done in the sweatshops. She washed clothing on a scrub-board and her work never seemed to end. Sam worked long, hard hours and his hands were always blistered, and as if that was not enough, there was the difficulty of finding enough firewood to keep us going when winter came.

In theory, life in a commune should be interesting and equality should prevail, but even a youngster like me could see that all was not well with the organization. There were too many differences. Some agreed for a minion, but a minion no longer had any meaning for some, and the more extreme socialists objected to any religious practice enjoyed by the "old school." They tried to have celebrations but there was no Rabbi to lead them or be a symbol of unity, and those who stuck to religion became isolated individuals who found additional grief in not being able to keep kosher.

People met together only once a week for discussion and study. Each one had a little circle within the community, and although some of them insisted on a literal togetherness, others insisted on privacy. The result was uncontrollable clashing. Mounting dissatisfaction was eating away at the heart of the community. Today, I wonder if human beings will ever be able to develop community souls without competing with each other. Perhaps had they all been socialists it might have worked, but competitiveness is so natural an instinct that it puzzles me how even in Russia people are kept satisfied. Are they completely dominated? Do they have a better understanding of one another, more willingness to subjugate their individuality to the common discipline or is it simply forced upon them?

The Clarion members blamed their leaders, but nothing is more revealing of the frustrations, disappointments, failures and heartbreak of what might have been in another time and place, a noble undertaking, than the writing of its young leader, Benjamin Brown:[2]

> ... even before the first families arrived there was visible the spirit of destruction, and with the coming of the women the disharmony strengthened. "You said, he said" politics developed, and in addition to that the inexperience with irrigation resulted in our not making the best use of the water, so that most of the seeded land went to waste ... [The author writes of his inability to raise more funds and the wrangling which has reached the ears of the backers in New York. The colony got into debt and the creditors came to take away the machinery and even some of the houses.]
>
> ... The spring of 1914 found our colonists in a very serious condition. They plainly didn't have any seeds to plant their fields. Under such circumstances one can easily imagine why some colonists left. The miracle is that others

remained. The stubbornness of those is indescribable. It became a kind of sacredness. I am forced to confess that dedication of the 49 families that remained had influenced me to find new means of carrying on with the work...[new efforts to raise money by reorganization were not success-ful] when it came time to pay the $3,000 we owed the local bank there was a revolt. It nearly came to blood letting...the bank threatened foreclosure. In our despondency we orga-nized our own police in order to cash in from those [mem-bers] who refused to pay. One can imagine the uproar...the end was that the non-Jewish sheriff had to come to bring law and order... Toward the end of the summer the Salt Lake philanthropists contributed a sum of money, purchased tickets on the railroad for those who wanted to go.... About 17 families remained and asked me to take up [our land problems of a legal nature] with the State, which [had as its final outcome] the land and the homes and everything was again owned by the State... Twenty years after it happened I still regret my inexperience then of undertaking a colo-nization project due to ideals... "We dare not forget that such an ideal demands in the practical realization, not only knowledge, experience, a definite market, etc., but also a positive source for financing, otherwise the ideal flies out of the chimney. For self-justification one seeks to blame the next one; friends of old standing become enemies and all this gives the old-time philanthropists reason to pro-claim that Jewish colonization is a failure.

My own summing up is that we of Clarion were just people—average human beings who did not realize that each in his own way gave too little cooperation toward success. In addition, people had to switch worlds: from peace to pogroms in Russia, then to the sweatshops of America, then from the overpopulated slums to the wilderness. All of a sudden there was a small island of Jews floating in a large sea of gentiles, surrounded by a larger sea of empty space. They had ideals, but were too young and burdened by poverty and frustrations to succeed. In time Ben Brown, one of the rare ones capable of living his idealism to any degree, became highly successful in agriculture on his own. Though in his early twenties he could not control people in Clarion, his ability was obvious, and he went on to achieve a unique place in the development of Utah's agricultural industry. He and I were the only ones to remain in Utah after Clarion failed. One might say he was the "ideal" Jewish farmer. The last remarks on the subject in his correspondence said,

> During these ten years I had undergone various emotional episodes. I have to confess that I had lost interest at first in all problems relating to Jews.... I threw myself whole-heartedly in my farm work and found tranquility and happiness in the beautiful landscape of my field. The smooth skin of my animals calmed my enraged spirit. My fine horses took the place of human friendship. My sugar beets, potatoes, wheat and hay always won prizes in the farm exhibits. I became director of the Piute Reservoir and Irrigation Project... and I grew in the eyes of the non-Jews as a practical idealist. Between the years of 1921-1922 I have organized the Utah State Cooperative Poultry Association. And in 1923 my plan for cooperation was accepted by the Utah State Farm Bureau for all the varied departments of Agriculture. Soon after, our neighboring State of Idaho also accepted our form of organization and later a few other states followed, especially in the poultry industry, so that by 1925 our cooperative became one of the largest in the country ...

A banquet was held in Brown's honor by the Governor and he was named by a committee of state and local dignitaries as an "outstanding citizen, outstanding Jew," but he wrote:

> ... after ten years of being torn away from Jews and Jewish life, despite my experiences with the Clarion Colony and notwithstanding the fact that I started my career after the failure of the colony, barefoot, bedraggled and outcast; still, the above-mentioned banquet had an adverse effect on me. In the sweet words of that evening I had the feeling that I was dying a sweet death. As you would douse one in a barrel of sweet water. I felt that I must tear myself away from my non-Jewish atmosphere and return to my people. Later that very year such an opportunity presented itself. At that time I was president and general manager of the State Poultry and Dairy Cooperatives. Millions of dollars worth of our produce were sent to commissioners in the East...their business methods were unsatisfactory . . . the Board gladly accepted the resolution that I should become

their representative in the East... As it happened with all estranged Jews, I became [in New York] an ardent Zionist.

Comparing the Mormon settlers with Clarion shows that the difference in motivation and background spelled success for one and failure for the other. Most of the Mormon immigrants were already experienced farmers when they converted to the Church and came to Utah. They could at least make the most of what resources they had, and their strong religious belief and unquestioning obedience to the new Christian gospel gave them the incentive to survive with their ideals and social structure intact despite the hardships.

As a Zionist, Ben Brown worked to make it possible for Jews to settle in Palestine. Those who farmed on the lands of their ancestors suffered more hardship by far than groups like Clarion, but they succeeded, and finally achieved independence for the country we now know as Israel.

The Clarion Jews were cultured people whose basic development stemmed from a time and place in which open expression was taboo; and despite certain disillusionments they had tasted enough of the freedom of America to know that they could express themselves without fear of reprisal. They were young and fiery, refusing to stifle their individualism. The result was an uncontrolled flood of pent-up feelings playing havoc with the plan for cooperative living.

Now that I have been in business and seen the value of organization, I know a project should be thoroughly studied in advance and the people chosen with great care. For instance, the good Clarion land should have been taken for the crops, the secondary land for grazing, and manpower and machinery put to good use by joint effort for the communal good. When they suddenly found themselves in debt for the machinery they had no way of making the machines pay.

The donors wanted it to succeed, but they did not know about the dissension. Being subsidized kept the settlers from starvation, but it also kept them from facing the basic

142 | *Life More Sweet than Bitter*

issues of physical survival. With all their good will, those who contributed money toward this effort bear some responsibility for sponsoring a project without assessing the qualifications of the participants.

Recently I visited the site of Clarion. There are two Jewish gravestones there which have been protected by the Centerfield Legion Post. On Clarion lands today is a rather dramatic confirmation of both Ben Brown's and my conclusions: Farmers of Japanese background have a paying agricultural enterprise there. Here are highly disciplined, experienced people who chose a free country in which to live, but whose first thought after that is to making a living. They do not sway from that goal.

Man's primary duty is to keep himself alive, and the first step toward success beyond himself is providing for those in his care. From there he can give what his capabilities offer to the wider community. We have abundance in this country, conveniences and luxuries beyond the wildest dreams of most other nations. Even our poorest citizens are wealthy by comparison with the masses of Bangladesh, India, Pakistan, Biafra, and parts of South America. By accepting certain self-discipline as people, and wisely husbanding our resources, Americans have unlimited potential for organization, development and provision for our own land and for helping those unfortunates across the seas, as well.

Sam and Julie had convinced Mother and Father to come out to Salt Lake City with Eda to be near us, so I was overjoyed one day when the postman handed me down a letter off his wagon that said my parents and sister were now in Utah and waiting to hear from me. It has become increasingly clear, even to me as a boy, that the Clarion project was doomed. Now I had the excuse to leave gracefully to the city of Salt Lake.

1   Correspondence of Benjamin Brown, translated from the Yiddish by Mrs. Benjamin Brown.

2   Translated from Yiddish, correspondence of Benjamin Brown, by Mrs. Benjamin Brown

Observation:

When Maurice visited Clarian later in life, it was through my father, who had purchased an old house with property seven miles north of Gunnison from my Mothers Aunt. My Grandmother was born there in poverty a walking pace below. She was 22 in 1914 and new of Clarion. Although we worked for Maurice the place became a summer vacation home and we learned all to well the political problems with irrigation water—essential for watering grounds and feeding livestock.

The Mormon saints practice a more successful method often referred to as a coop. Here each possessed their own land and competed against others. What was held in common was the separate entity that provided the feed, and processed and sold the product produced. Each independent farmer would then share in the business of obtaining feed and selling the product. The share was not equal, but according to the purchases from, and sales to the distributing business. It is like all owned the business of distribution where administrators were elected from the body of members.

At the age of 17 for my senior year, I raise egg laying chickens a few miles north east of the ghost town of Clarion. After graduating the chickens were sold and I went back to Salt Lake to College and work for Maurice. When I retired 37 years later from California and moved back, I received a likely sum for my share in the coop. The coop did not know where I was, but when I returned, the whole county seemed to know I was back from the time I was only 17.

Ronald Kelsch

We had to think of a source of income

M *among the ormons*

*I had come among a group of gentiles
who had no prejudice toward the Jews.
The isolation of my restricted culture broke
like a spring thaw into the warm sunshine.*

9.

Among the Mormons

"You are so tall, Maurice!" Mother cried, alternately hugging me and pushing me away so she could see my full growth. "And you look so solemn! What has pioneering done to you?"

I had found the little house over on the west side of Salt Lake City rented by Eda, Mother and Father, and Mother had opened the door. It was wonderful to be reunited, and tears of joy as well as worry flowed freely. It was true the good, practical farm experience had matured me while the hard work with nothing but impending failure staring us in the face gave all the Clarion people an air of sadness. Father took the news about the colony hard. He had great faith in the Jews going back to the land after the cruel dispersion from their homeland so many centuries ago. In his idealism, he could not grasp why the younger Jews from Russia were so unwilling to be patient and to compromise.

Now that we were together in Salt Lake, we had to think about a source of income. With Father still unable to speak much English there was no question about their needing me. I put Clarion behind me.

Some of the Jews we met here in Utah told Father we could make a good living dealing in junk and referred him to Rosenblatt's, the Jewish junk yard. Whatever my father decided was alright with me. We obtained a pushcart and went collecting and reselling junk. Going from house to house gathering old rags, gunny sacks, bottles and pieces of scrap iron was profitable, but we hated it. We were humiliated and hurt by the suspicion with which many householders regarded us. They watched us slyly through the windows as though we were thieves who would steal from their yards. It upset me to watch my father, a gentleman and scholar in the old country, peddling junk for a living simply because he had never conquered the language. I must have looked old for my age. Father seemed prouder of me and in the months to come our relationship became even closer than before.

People were leaving Clarion now, a few at a time, and they would always stop with us in Salt Lake City for several days before going on. That meant news of Julie and Sam and a chance for my parents to speak Yiddish.

The earlier colonists were downhearted and nearly panicky as to what they should do next. Failure depressed them. Those that had stayed the longest were the most heartbroken. They all hated to leave the beautiful country, and were full of blame for the organizers. Though they had visibly aged, none of these young couples had matured enough to admit that the failure was also due to their shortcomings.

They were now robust. They had tasted sunshine and fresh air. They had worked just as hard as in Philadelphia, but the creative responsibility of farming had stimulated their minds, even though they had not prospered. They hated the thought of going back to the sweatshops. We had meetings about whether they could settle in Salt Lake City; but seeing our family's struggle finally made them go back to Philadelphia.

The new setting in Utah encouraged me to go beyond the traditional life I had always known. There were only a few Jews in Salt Lake City. All were, by comparison to our circumstances, quite wealthy. In the Jewish culture there exists a great deal of upward mobility from one stratum to another, but money, education and family prestige were the social measurements determining these strata. So, it was not surprising that Jews who came from highly enlightened, cultured countries like Germany - as did most of those in Salt Lake at that time, looked down upon Jews from the more benighted and insular areas like Eastern Europe. The boundaries between them could become impenetrable. There existed within the Jewish culture here more discrimination than in the Christian one. It is paradoxical that such a situation could have existed when the Jews themselves had been the victims of so much bigotry throughout history. Under these circumstances it was difficult for me to be accepted among my own people, yet I longed to socialize, especially with others my own age.

Mother tried to help me. She was an understanding and religious person. Little did she realize in her great effort to teach us that "to be religious was good" and that the Jewish religion was the best, she had unconsciously taught us to be wary of others. I feared Christians because the pogroms were still vivid in my mind, believing that gentiles stood ever ready to do us harm, and this made me regard them as anti-Semites or Jew haters. At times, when the memories of our good, Christian friends, the Kolosky family in Dubossar, came back to me, I had to ponder my views. After all, they had saved our lives.

It was not dissatisfaction with the Jewish religion that made me look elsewhere, but the fact that I had no social status anymore. The traditions were a part of me. I believed in God and there was never any question as to what I was supposed to do according to tradition. A good Jewish boy always "does what is right" because he was raised in the Law and the traditions. He knows what they are and what to do, and, when one has been brought up to believe in the sovereignty of One God, it is very difficult to comprehend another, especially a Christian one so foreign to us, who was the God of the Czar and those who had caused the pogroms.

At my impressionable age, the persecutions had created within me a feeling of anxiety and animosity. It was to be years before I could see any symbol of the cross without feeling anguish. The Christians here in America were quite different from those in Russia, and even though they were divided into many different denominations, they were all evidently trying to find a way to live peacefully together. Nevertheless, religion had been the core of Jewish tradition and the Torah was the Word of God. Christians had another God in Jesus Christ. This made the gap between us hard to bridge, even though I had begun to realize that political circumstances, too, had divided us. I started to question the isolation I had been taught. Here in Utah it was obviously not necessary for Jews to cling together for safety or survival. A little verse kept running through my head:

> There is so much bad in the best of us,
> And so much good in the worst of us,
> That it behooves none of us
> To speak ill of the rest of us.

It contained a good philosophy with which to make a transition. My liking for the gentiles puzzled me. Being shy made me especially appreciative of the friendliness of their girls. I was young, needing to expand my life and to become a part of society as a whole. Adapting to new people and changing circumstances was the only logical way to live.

Our gentile neighbors from Gunnison had been friendly, and those in Salt Lake City were trying to be helpful. Our neighbor wanted to teach my mother English, but my parents found more solace in reading the Yiddish books and newspapers that kept them in touch with the Jewish world. With me it was different. I was open to every friendly contact, and my English improved with each one. Perhaps if my parents had been younger they might have taken more interest.

I soon learned that the gentiles could be friendlier than the Jews, and with every friendly contact, my English improved still further. However, I became very sensitive when the other Jewish boys were invited to parties and I was not. The only party to which I was invited where other Jews were present, was when Governor Simon Bamberger, who was also a Jew, gave a ball and invited the entire Jewish community.

It was a gala affair. I was all dressed up in a rented tuxedo and white gloves. I may have been only a dressed-up peddler—the "cat who looked at the king". As a dancer I was "king of the floor." I danced well, and none of the Jewish girls refused to dance with me. I am sure I would have been popular with them had their parents not refused to consider a peddler in their great social ambitions for their daughters. I danced to the end of the evening even though my white gloves were cutting off the circulation in my hands, and I was sorry to see it all end.

Putting on my overalls next morning, I realized how much I hated being called "junkman."

"Having the lowest job on the social scale makes me feel inferior," I confided to Mother when Father was out. "Maybe I ought to try being a doctor or a lawyer. I guess it's the only way to be accepted by my fellow Jews."

But that, too, was only a dream. I had many Jewish friends on a non-social level, but it would be clearly easier for me to rise socially among the gentiles.

About that time, I read an article by Governor Bamberger exhorting his fellow Jews to uplift themselves. He even suggested that Jews could and should be something other than junk peddlers, and I began thinking seriously about my future. "I must move ahead and broaden myself," I determined. Having finally achieved the advantage of speaking English, I could communicate outside the Jewish community, but there were still a lot of other barriers to overcome. This new life in the West, combined with my traditional upbringing, created the combination that changed my destiny and caused me to look ahead rather than back.

Today, I am glad of my choice, for, looking back, I see that life had other plans and another role for me to play other than just being accepted into the Jewish community. Those same circumstances that made me so unhappy then helped develop my inner feelings for other people. Perhaps the misfortunes of youth taught me some valuable lessons, one of which was that, keeping a distance between gentile and Jew for one reason or another, is wrong. Quarrels between families, groups, labor and management, and among churches, all tend to build barriers that slow down production and put limitations on the enjoyment of life and each other.

Utah was primarily agricultural then. One main impression that had remained deep in my mind since I first set foot in Salt Lake City was the wide variety of fresh fruits and green vegetables grown here. It now occurred to me that, if we could somehow manage to get hold of a horse and wagon, we could become produce men instead of junk peddlers. The way was made open. One of the people leaving Clarion (a poor fellow who had been an intellectual with no feel for the land) brought his hors and wagon to Salt Lake City for sale. Since Father did not want to stay in the junk business either, we bought the wagon, the horse complete with blanket and harness, and the next day we started in as produce peddlers.

Peddling got me around the different neighborhoods and showed me how beautiful and relaxing the city could be. Compared to Philadelphia's slums, Salt Lake City was a veritable Garden of Eden with its trees, flowers and green lawns.

When the Jews in Salt Lake City heard what we were doing, the Ladies Auxiliary met and pledged to help Father out by buying all their produce from us. This struck me as humiliating. I was sure we could build up a route on our own.

"That is not charity, Maurice," Father told me. "That is loyalty. We will accept it, of course!"

I swallowed my pride and went along with him. It proved to be a very satisfactory arrangement and I came to realize that we were doing business with some of the very nicest people. Father showed me how we could reciprocate by providing our customers with only the best produce at wholesale prices, and I learned to appreciate the warmth those Jewish housewives showed me. They always helped in every way they could - even loaning me a little money when I needed it to tide me over the seasonal rough spots. It was the first money to be paid back from my next earnings.

I kept hoping that one of the young daughters of these women would come out to say hello, but none of them ever did. Only the daughters of the gentiles came out. It became clear that, to progress socially, I would have to adapt even more.

Education was a worry. True, I could speak English, but the words came out rather mixed up. I decided to spend my little, hard-earned savings on a night class in English taught by Mr. Delbert Draper at the Chamber of Commerce. My creative talent spent itself on a speech about cigarettes. I had heard a woman say that "she would rather sleep with a wet dog than with a man who smokes cigarettes," and I thought it would probably be an interesting speech to make among the Mormons whose "Word of Wisdom" bans cigarettes. The class thought it was hilarious, and they razzed me about it for weeks, to the point where it embarrassed me right out of the literary business.

Mother, as usual, was trying to stretch the family funds as far as they could go, with never a word of complaint.

"Surely," I thought, "she must long sometimes for her former life," but if the thought occurred to her, she never mentioned it.

I always put away for her the nicest things I could find at the market. "She was used to the best in Russia," I told Father. "So she should also have the best we can give her here."

My father never denied me this privilege. I realized how lonely my parents were in this new world out West, and

I tried to ease things for them. The business went well and I thrived on the hard work, but Father was constantly tired and more and more of the peddling route fell to me. "Stay on the wagon, as much as possible, Father," I would tell him, and as soon as we came home Mother would make him lie down, then she'd bring him a little schnapps and have him soak in a bath of Epsom salts to relieve his fatigue.

To me, she always said, "Your father depends on you. Be very considerate of him." She was good medicine for him, always concerned for him, always waiting on him in every way. Seeing how much they loved each other was an inspiration for me and I will always remember it. A love like theirs was not something to be seen every day.

At that time, I was walking about with my hair falling into my eyes, heedless of such details as ragged clothing and the appearance of a needy person I must have presented. Mother would look at me with sympathetic eyes and urge Father to dress me up. Sometimes, if we sold out early, I would leave Father at home and go back to the market for more produce to sell. Mother had to do all the washing on the board as well as all the other household chores, yet she was never too tired to comfort Father or us children. I would tell her of my ambitious plans, and she would call me "Mauresel."

Father had never gotten over the old matchmaking ways. He took me to see a tailor who owned a shop on Fifth South and State Streets, and after a while, I realized he had brought me there to get acquainted with the tailor's daughter. I didn't like her and I hardly said a word.

"What did you think of her?" Father asked when we left.

"What should I have thought?" was my typically Jewish reply.

It was the first time I remember being upset with my Father. I thought he had tried to trick me. I didn't want him to pick a Jewish girl for me just because her father had a good business and could help me out. Nobody was going to "throw me a bone." I had already decided I was going to make a living without anybody's help.

Father was greatly disturbed, both by my attitude and my disinterest in the girl. In my first strike for real independence I risked hurting him more by pulling two pictures of gentile girls out of my wallet. "Father," I said, "I will pick my own girl." The thought of my not marrying a Jewish girl horrified him and his face showed genuine anguish. The thought of having our race dissipated by assimilation was a violation of the promise to survive in order to keep God's commandments alive.

There was no time for reading or shows in those days, and looking back now, I realize that all those sacrifices made it possible for me to be in the position I am in today. We were always encouraged to work hard. In Utah, responsibility was piled on me and I felt I couldn't take any more, yet to do for one's loved ones always gives a person more strength than he thought he had. I am very glad that my life as I grew up was both bitter and sweet.

We sent letters to Joe in Philadelphia telling him to join us. We were doing pretty well at the time, so we suggested he might come out and begin making a living by peddling like we did. Eventually, he came out to see for himself. Philip never came to Salt Lake City, but stayed back East and married.

There were rough times in the peddling business because of the seasons, so during the winter I filled in with other jobs. One, a very hard job in the smelter at Murray, was separating the ore that was "frozen together" in the open cars with chisels and hammers. My partner was a Greek who spoke no English, but we tried to communicate. I gave him an orange at lunch time, for instance. That same day he accidentally hit me with a hammer. He was so sorry he got down on his knees and started praying excitely in Greek, crossing himself as he did so.

"I'm O.K., Stavros," I assured him. "Really, I'm alright! Now I can get out of the cold. It will heal, don't worry!"

He didn't understand me. Actually it was fine with me because I could collect workmen's compensation and leave the job. However, the compensation proved too little to live on, so, with a bandage on my hand, I went out to peddle junk until Spring.

This time I took on a partner, a Mormon named Mr. Naylor who had two horses with rheumatism. That was a cold winter, but we still travelled as far as Spanish Fork. One night we were sleeping in the wagon alongside the road with a fire going. The Sheriff came along riding in a horse and buggy and he was mighty drunk. As he came into our firelight he laid his hand on the rifle lying beside him in the buggy and yelled at us.

"I'm going to shoot you down!"

Much to my surprise, the mild-mannered Naylor yelled back. "I'm going to shoot you down!" he countered, and while I got ready to get out of the way he took the offensive and ran that drunken Sheriff right off our campsite.

Next morning we saw an advertisement in the Provo newspaper about a big sale on lead at the back of a printing shop. We bought the lead and sold it at a substantial profit, but I have to laugh at the picture we must have made with a bandaged arm and two limping horses.

Naylor and I parted one night near our house just as the sun stained the sooty snow with its last crimson glow. Mother and Father opened the door with the news that Julie and Sam were expecting a baby. This started me thinking about Clarion all over again. We could tell from their letters that things were not getting any better, and we learned that, for the past month, they had had very little to eat and had even been tempted to eat pork and beans.

How long could they last? Sam was not a husky person to begin with. Farming was hard for him at best and he had been unfortunate to draw the forty acres with rocks on it when he drew lots for land. However, even if they had drawn a better portion it would have been impossible for them to make a go of it. The Mormon communal "United Order" settlements had failed and it looked as though the same fate was in store for the Jews. The belief shared by both the Mormon leader Brigham Young and the socialists that settlers could work out a society based upon "everyone according to his needs and every man according to his skills" was not turning out to be a practical idea here.

Letters from Clarion now reported only quarrels and fights, discontent and disunity. There was always talk about sinking a proper well, but that was never accomplished while we were there. The diet was always meager. What were they eating now? Who would have believed that socialism could have divided people into enemy camps or created so much poverty, distress and disillusionment?

"Why did they go about things the way they did, I wondered?" I asked myself. "Why couldn't each own his own property? What could be accomplished for one another if nobody had anything?"

The leader, Benjamin Brown, was trying desperately to save the project by travelling to various cities to raise money, but the dissidence and poverty combined to defeat him.

Joe had his own horse and went out peddling. He was finally able to make enough money to send for Sadie from Dubossar. It was arranged through the matchmaker and we all wanted to see what she now looked like. Joe was excited and counted the weeks until she arrived. Joe went down to the railway to meet her. It seemed such a strange arrangement. He took the papers with him, took her straight to the Rabbi's house and married her the same day. There was no real wedding because we were all too poor. It was nothing like the marriage of Mother and Father in Kishinev where there had been such a wonderful feast and ceremony.

Mother fixed the best dinner she could. We all sat down to enjoy it, and we could hardly wait to hear what Sadie could tell us about our relatives and friends in Dubossar. Mother was especially anxious to know about our relatives. The information was sparse and sad. For the most part the Jews who had not fled had been killed. Very few had been able to remain throughout the revolution and the pogroms, and they were so intimidated by the danger and the history sweeping by them that they had practically no information about each other.

Sadie was a sweet person, with no English whatever. She was obviously prepared to make Joe a good wife, but not in any way equipped for the strange new world in which she found herself.

Eva had married Emmanuel Ostrowsky in the spring of 1913. She was still very socialistic in her views and they had not made their vows before either a Rabbi or a government bureau, but before each other and God.

We had a wedding picture of her that Emmanuel had photographed. In it she carried a bunch of daisies in her hand, tied her hair back with a ribbon and wore a white dress.

We received a letter from Julie saying the sweat shops in Philadelphia even seemed better to them now than the disunity and hardships in Clarion. They were going back and would stop in Salt Lake City with us for awhile, at least until the baby was born, as she could not make the long journey right now.

I looked forward to seeing Julie and Sam and planned how Father and I could work hard and help them out a little.

We would be like a family again. The only ones who were not in Salt Lake were Philip who had found a job in Cleveland, and Eva and Emmanuel who had gone there to find work after his photography business had failed.

Eventually he found a job as a cutter for a shirtwaist factory and Eva found a job as a librarian at the Cleveland public library. When we would see the three of them again I did not know.

Observation:

Maurice reflects on Clarion but fallows a traditional view. The view of communism was based on what some brought with them from Russia. The Mormons also practiced similar programs when Brigham Young started the United Order, supposedly after what the Mormon Saints practiced before they were driven west. For this reason many have felt that the early Mormons practiced a form of communism like Clarion. Tradition is completely misleading. The original saints held possession of their own property but consecrated it to be held in common, with common consent the rule of government. Each paid a property tithe for that which they used. Each had a deed, but tradition thinks it was private ownership. It was "with a covenant and a deed which cannot be broken" to pay a tithe on that which one possessed and used for their own enterprise. When Brigham Young changed the tithing from a property tithe to and income tithe, the saints then lost the original method and began to think the original was a form of communism where all put in the same storehouse and took according to need. This United Order also failed.

Maurice was right. Each family must be competitive and possess their own land or enterprise and pay tithes according to Abraham.

Ronald Kelsch

I had both Jewish and gentile customers

On my own

You meet the daily struggles of life with your eye always on the future unless death comes to a loved one - then you stop and reflect on the past.

10.

On My Own

I had never known my Mother to complain, so I was shocked to learn she was in the hospital. I went to see her every day.

"How is Father eating, Mauresel," she wanted to know. "Be sure you see that Eda looks her best when she goes over to help the *rebbitzin* (rabbi's wife). And Mauresel, dress yourself up a little, eh? You're such a handsome boy."

The day before she died I came there and immediately realized something terrible was in the air, because Father was sitting in the hallway, slumped on a bench in a daze. I was surprised, because when I had been there the day before Mother had been in such good humor. This time when I came into the room she looked different.

"I don't want to die," she said. "I am too young to die." I was shocked. I never thought of her as being young or old. It never occurred to me she would ever leave us. It was the first time I had ever heard her ask for anything for herself. We were so used to her giving to us and doing for us. As I grew up

I was so absorbed in my own problems. I felt suddenly guilty. Had we ever done enough for her? She gave so much. She was a wonderful mother to me.

Her life was exemplary. She taught us most of the attitudes by which we could pattern our lives, quoting proverbs like "Never hurt anyone weaker than you." Watching the face of my father I realized that, even though their marriage was made by a matchmaker, they had developed an unusually deep love for each other. I did not know that one day I would be Chairman of the Board of Directors of that Hospital where she died. Our poverty was such that we never dared dream much beyond the next day's survival.

There were just a few people at the funeral, mostly our family and the few people we knew. A neighbor woman, either a Mormon or a Catholic, probably a Mormon, fixed dinner for us after the funeral. I can't remember who it was and I never went to thank her. I was seventeen when Mother died.

Father was inconsolably lonely. Somehow he didn't fit into Salt Lake City. And without Mother the heart had gone out of him. He wanted to go back East and be in a Jewish atmosphere again. He loved America, but he had no heart to be in the West without Mother. With her gone and me grown up he wanted to go where he could talk his own language in a neighborhood where he could understand people, where they would understand him, and where he could participate in the traditional ceremonies and events of Jewish life. He left Eda with me and returned to the East, settling in Cleveland near Philip, Emanuel and Eva.

I got a job working at Auerbach Company's delicatessen and the smell of pickles was always with me.

One night I went to Saltair on the open train. It was a wonderful place then—one of the wonder resorts of the world. The whole place had a holiday air about it and the great Moorish dome dominated a large arena of stands, and rides. The display was an enormous cement platform supported by piles sunk in the Great Salt Lake. Dozens of dressing rooms accommodated the Utah people who swam "for their health" or for relaxation while tourists from all over the world wanted to have the sensation of floating on the salt water. Families or young people in couples or in groups used to come there nightly. The trip out was an experience in itself. The railroad cars had steps the whole length and no doors whatever. Riding out across the Salt Flats west of town, in the good summer air of Utah, was exhilarating. It always put the crowds in a friendly mood. Mothers and children, groups of ladies, political clubs, and tourists flooded the place during the daytime. They picnicked and fed the snowy-winged seagulls. Specialties at the souvenir shop were post cards showing you floating on the water reading a newspaper, and cards with little bags of salt attached. Beautiful crystalized salt in different shapes were popular.

As the sun went down, Salt Lakers in families and in couples, would have their supper on the picnic tables on the first floor of the Moorish "castle." It was vast and open to the wonderful salt sea air. The sunsets were incomparable. Nobody knew what smog was, then. No one was unaware of the superb setting. The color of the setting sun on the sheets of silver water created the impression of quicksilver gliding in beautiful, slippery sheens in and out between the islands and rocks. When darkness came, all the bathers came in reluctantly. The water was warm and comfortable until late. I used to go bathing with a suit covering my chest, and with legs down to the knees. The girls wore fancy suits with high necks, stockings and bloomers.

Sometimes bathers seemed spellbound by the view of purple island mountains and crimson sky floating above the great desert lake.

Then the music upstairs would begin. There was an area for kids with swings and slides to play on, and a nurse in a white uniform would take care of the youngsters while the adults ascended the wonderful broad staircase to the "world's largest dance hall." Dancing was our biggest form of fun then, and for many their biggest form of exercise. I saw an acquaintance of mine dancing with a very beautiful girl with red hair. I couldn't take my eyes off her. Dancing was a friendly affair then, so it was alright for me to ask her to dance. We hit it off right away. We just danced and danced, farther and farther away until we had left her friends entirely. Then we leaned over the railings and looked out into the deep blue night with a million stars flung across the sky, and the clean, fresh air all around us, and we talked. Her name was Inez Williams. She told me she was from a pioneer family and their big holiday was coming up—the 24th of July. This was the day Brigham Young arrived in Salt Lake Valley in 1847, and she had been chosen to ride on one of the leading floats. She was a girl with a lot of sense, but she didn't seem to be more than about fifteen. She asked about me and I told her I was a detective. Then I returned her to the fellow that brought her.

I could hardly wait for the holiday. When it did arrive it was hot and sunny and there was a gala mood about the whole city. It was the biggest event of the year and the preparations for it were lavish. Everybody looked forward to it. It represented the acme of entertainment. In every town in Utah they did something to celebrate the founding of the Mormon "empire" of Deseret, but the biggest celebration was of course in this valley.

An anxious crowd waited all along the main streets hours before the parade began. When the first band struck up "America" every eye was on the approaching floats. They were beautiful—constructed on flat bed cars moving along the street-car tracks. One of the first floats was a beautiful creation called "Rock of Ages," with a great rock and a huge cross on it. On top of this, very dignified and beautiful with her red hair streaming down and looking like an angel was Inez. People applauded this float, it was so beautiful. I couldn't sit still. I followed it down the street, sometimes having to dart in and out of the crowd. It stopped at Liberty Park and I dispersed dreaming of the vision that had floated before me.

I followed the float all the way

That winter I got a job as a doorman at the fashionable Newhouse Hotel, standing by the revolving door in a fancy uniform and a top hat, greeting people and helping them in and out of their cars. A drug store just across the street sold liquor, but it was closed on Sundays, so I figured out how to make money right away. A lot of our guests came in late Saturday and stayed through Sunday with no place to buy liquor. I loaded my locker with bottles on Saturday afternoon and had a good supply for the next day. The scheme was very profitable.

One day Inez, who now worked part time in the office of the Salt Lake Hardware, passed the hotel on her way home from work. Seeing me standing in front of the hotel, she realized that I was no detective. Nevertheless, she walked on the hotel side of the street from then on. My high profit job didn't last long however, because the bell captain realized that I was making more money than he was, and he took it over. My heart was broken, but soon mended with the hope of spring coming and peddling. I would be alone in my venture, yet I would not lose contact with Father. I would write him of my glowing success.

Dear Father: April 1917

Spring is here. New radishes, asparagus, green onions, and spinach are coming on the market. I am starting to peddle in earnest. I am in hopes of making more money now, so I can pay off some of my debts.

Eda is going to West High School and last night she had her first date with a boy. It seemed strange for me to be the one to look him over and decide whether or not he was suited to take her out. They were going to a concert at Liberty Park. She did a lot of sprucing up. I am sure she would have liked to have better clothes, but she is very considerate and never complains. I still owe $40.00 to Mrs. Findling, at the Boston Store for her clothes. This young guy she had the date with seemed very knowledgeable. He talked about things I couldn't understand. I judged that most of what he learned was from high school. After he left I realized that there is something missing in me and he judged me for it. It must be what I do for a living and the way I cannot speak with self-confidence. He dressed pretty good with his checkered vest and shiny shoes. I felt ragged beside him. When things get better I am going to get some new clothes. Things have been hard. I even owe $45.00 to the landlady. She is such a fine lady, I explained to her that I would soon make more money and she is willing to wait. Eda and I have two rooms.

Love, Maurice

Dear Father,   October 1917

Eda has been getting good marks at school. She is beginning to grow up to be quite a lady. You would be very proud of her. I have been trying to understand what she is learning, but am either too tired after peddling all day or too dumb. Eda has been trying to help me but I guess she is ready to give up. Perhaps I am too absorbed in being a good peddler. As you know I tried correspondence courses, but didn't get too far. I enjoy the fellow that dresses well or talks confidently or has a good job or even one that goes to school. I am timid and shy, unless I am on the peddling wagon. Then I seem to become another person. It is hard to explain why. I hope you are doing well in Cleveland. Joe and Sadie talk about leaving Salt Lake and going back there where you are, but I hope they stay here for awhile. Tell the rest of the family that we love them.

Love, Maurice

Dear Father: November 1917

Joe and I have decided to team up and do some peddling. We borrowed a tongue and hooked his white horse and mine together. We have already had two snow storms in Salt Lake, making if difficult for the horses. We have "non-slip" shoes on them, but they still slide all over the place.

We wanted to expand our business and go as far as Tooele and even Eureka so we got together an inventory of oranges, lemons, apples and smoked salmon. It was the smoked salmon that brought us all the trouble. Joe let me buy some bread and milk for lunch and he let me have some salmon to go with it.

That night a lady let us sleep in her barn. Joe made me ask for some coffee. I didn't want to but I am glad he pushed me into it, as the coffee tasted good with the bread and salmon. The next morning we had coffee, salmon, and bread, and for lunch we had salmon. I was tired of this menu so I asked Joe if we could eat one meal in a restaurant. He got mad at me because he didn't want to buy anything until we sold something. We continued to eat milk and salmon, but it became so smelly we had a big fight. He hit me with a milk bottle. I hit him back. I know you don't like to hear that. Joe and I are not being kind to each other, but we will get along better.

Love, Maurice

P.S. I am going over to Joe's house to patch things up. It really was a trying time, the snow was up to the horses' bellies and we came back with a loss, but I have made up my mind that I am going to do everything I could to make up with him.

Like Father, Joe just couldn't make friends in Salt Lake City. There was hardly any time for friends anyway. By the time we fed the horses and ate dinner we had to go to bed, for we had to get up early.

Joe had his stable and I had mine. I think he was jealous of me because my horse looked more shiny and curried than his. My stable was cleaner and I took better care of it. His horse always looked like he had just got up from a manure pile.

Joe soon bought one of the first Ford trucks, with a chain on the outside. When we started it with Joe at the wheel he became so nervous that I asked him to instruct me on how to manipulate it—my first venture of this kind. I started out alright, but when I had to turn a corner I also became nervous and, forgetting the instructions, I hit a man and twirled him clear around. I never found the brakes until we had gone about three blocks. Luckily, there was nothing in the way. The man was not hurt.

Joe and Sadie never seemed able to adjust to life among strangers. The day it was explained to us that the Mormons considered themselves the "chosen people" and we were gentiles made me chuckle, but Joe and Sadie never saw much humor in anything until they were ready to go back east. They seemed to pick up in spirits as soon as they had bought tickets for the train. They decided to go where family members were.

Dear Joe and Sadie: March 1918

It is lonely without you since you left to go back East, but I am glad that you finally decided to settle in Cleveland with Father and Philip. I hope you can be of some comfort to Father and make him understand about me. He seems to think that the best thing for me is to come back East in spite of the fact that I feel better off here.

I know he is lonesome since Mother died and I think you should tell him often how much we loved and appreciated her and how we miss her, too. I think of what she did for Eda and me, when the rest of you were older and only we two were left at home. She really made a lot of sacrifices for all of us through all our years of hardship. It's amazing how she never complained, though she had been used to a beautiful home. Remember her place at Kishiniev when Father married her? And the beautiful house and gardens and the black ebony piano with the gold inlay?

She never seemed to worry about her own security during the pogroms at Kishniev when we were waiting in the cellar, only ours. I hope you are all well.

Love, Maurice

Dear Father: June 1918

Eda is doing very well and I have enjoyed having her here, but she's at an age where she likes to date and there is just not that many eligible Jewish boys around. She says she will never marry a gentile.

I have accumulated enough money for her fare. I need it in my business, but I think I will make the sacrifice and send her back. Summer is coming and I have confidence that I will make it up.

Love, Maurice

Dear Father: July 1919

The roof fell on me this morning. My horse Mod died. The
night before the veterinarian told me that if she could stand
it through the night, she would be all right. I spent all night
in the stable trying to keep her on her feet. What the veterinarian had meant was, if she could hold up through the
night she would make it, but early the next morning she
slipped down from my chest. I could see she was gone.

I can't stop thinking about her. How she used to pull the
wagon with its heavy load of produce. I have made friends
while building up this route and Mod was a part of it. I am
so sad: the stable is empty and the harness is on the floor
and the wagon stands outside with no horse to pull it.

I don't know what I am going to do about another horse.
I can't seem to pull myself together enough to get one to
replace her. I might start looking for a truck. This might
be better anyway because my business is expanding beyond
my ability to service it with a horse and wagon. I could then
peddle both winter and summer and get around faster.

Love, Maurice

Dear Father: July 1919

Today is Thursday. I am writing you again so soon because
I need someone to talk to and someone that will understand. I have enough produce to last me through Saturday
but I cannot bring myself to rent another horse and go out
today. I know that I will not be able to go out tomorrow
either. There will be quite a bit of waste but I hope to go out
Saturday and resume my business.

I just can't believe that Mod is gone.

Maurice

Dear Father: June 1919

I am in debt for my truck but I think that I am going to
make enough money to pay for it. I have started a little business on the side that is compatible with my route. I have
purchased a tremendous amount of jars and jugs and my
landlady fills them with fruit. You should have seen things
at first. Both my place and hers were filled with bottles.

I bought some lumber and last Sunday I put up some shelves. I hope that things will begin to look more orderly here now. Remember when we used to worry when we got stuck at the end of the day with left-over produce? Now I just unload every bit of fruit that I have left. This takes care of all the soft fruit and I have no trouble selling the bottled fruit to my customers. You should see me when I am ready to start everyday--loaded to the top of the truck with hardly any room for me to ride. By two o'clock in the afternoon my load is reduced considerably and when school is out about six boys and I go out peddling the rest. Sometimes I even have to go back to the produce house for more.

I have worked out a great system. Each one of the boys gets a sample tray made out of a crate with a handle across. They go from door to door showing what we have. Then the ladies come out to the truck and buy. I really do better in the afternoon than with my regular route in the morning. I am saving some money.

Love, Maurice

Dear Father: July 1919

I am doing pretty good now and am going to try to get some things for myself. I don't think it is good for a person to neglect himself no matter how busy he is. When the summer is over I will take some time out and go shopping. I wish some of the department stores would open on Sunday, but that is the Sabbath of the gentiles.

I bought two books but so far I haven't looked at them. I suppose one must start early to create an interest in learning. I vowed to myself that I shall never borrow money again, it is so hard to get out of debt. I am breathing more easily now and have only one payment left on my truck. Thank goodness! Of course if I go into a bigger business I will have to borrow money or wait until I can accumulate some. My landlady, Mrs. Proval, has offered me a loan of three hundred dollars and it is very tempting to quit peddling and get myself a fruit stand. Perhaps with what I will have at the end of the summer and her money I can make it.

Love, Maurice

Dear Father,   November 1919

I finally got my fruit stand opened. You remember Mr. Fox and his store on Second South and State Street. I leased the front from him. Joe will remember the place I am talking about too.

I am sure learning a lot about running this business. Most of my stand is on the sidewalk and actually is as much an open air market as an inside one. The stacks of all kinds of fresh fruits are very appealing to the people walking along the street. Lemons are selling well lately. There must be a lot of colds going around. Yesterday one of the restaurants bought all the garlic I had on hand.

Fresh fruits sell like hot cakes. I cannot buy enough. I sell twice or three times as much as on the wagon and make more. A fruit stand is certainly different than peddling. I have to be at the market to do my buying at five in the morning. That means I have to get up by four at the latest. I do not close up the stand until seven at night. This makes a long day, but I am enthused about my business.

It is November but it looks as though we might have a very light winter. I keep my fruits and vegetables from freezing with a few quilts and blankets. It is very difficult to bring in the things at night and then put them out again in the morning. I never get through until 8:30 or 9:00. With all the hard work I am still happy because it is successful.

Love, Maurice

P.S. Remember the girl I told you about, Inez Williams? She is now working for Mr. Fox who runs the meat department in back. I see her quite often and I take her out sometimes when I am through work.

Dear Father,   January 1920

The fruit stand is very successful, but the long hours get to you after awhile. I met this Jewish fellow that wanted to make a fighter out of me and I thought I may be interested in fighting. He kept telling me over and over again that I could make money in the fighting business and it sounded good. He even offered to take care of the stand for me during the time I needed to go to the gym to work out in my training program. He talked me into letting him move in with me and let me pay all the expenses. It was terrible, because he made me take real cold showers all the time and kept the windows open every night. I would be frozen stiff in the mornings. Inez thought I was nutty.

He had me and another fellow get together and stage a fight at the Pantages Theatre for one of those tryout nights. The prize was to be ten dollars. It turned out to be quite a show. We were supposed to fight without hurting each other. We practiced until we thought we had such a good show that we were sure to win the ten dollars. Everything went well until the night of the fight we forgot about the original plan and really lit into each other. I don't know what triggered it off. Maybe it was our pent-up hostilities, or maybe we just wanted to put on the real thing for an enthusiastic audience, for if they started booing us, it would be the clue for the stagehands to put out their long poles with hooks on the ends and pull us off the stage as failures.

As it was, the audience applauded loudly and we were a tremendous success. Besides that, we won the prize, but the next morning I ached so much I could hardly get down to the market. I guess I will get over it. You should have seen our would-be trainer. He took all the credit. Before the fight he called us cowards, afterward he thought we were great. It's hard to believe you could make a man so happy that way.

My fighting experience was interesting for awhile but sidetracked me from my business. I decided fighting was not for me. I have met some of the would-be fighters and they look pretty rough, like real bums. I am going to get rid of my trainer. It is too much for me to pay the expenses for both of us. I will say goodbye to that episode of my life and get back to my business.

How is Eda? Tell her I love her as much as ever_

Love, Maurice.

P.S. I bought Inez a present for $5.00.

Dear Father,   April 1920

I know you want me to come back to Cleveland so I will be with the rest of the family and I greatly appreciate your interest in my welfare, but the country here is new and fresh now, and I would like to try my luck for awhile.

The Mormon Church is very strong here and the Jewish one is very weak, but I am learning to live among others—especially the gentiles.

I am still very competitive in my business dealings with others and have earned for myself the nickname of "tiger." The opportunities seem to be good here and I want to stay at least until I have had time to analyze the situation.

Don't worry about me. It isn't like when I was a little boy and you worried about me so much because I came home so tired every night. Now I am full of energy each day. I know that life has been very hard for you and I hope it is easier now, in the knowledge that the sacrifices you have made for your children have allowed them many cultural advantages that they would not have had otherwise. I know all your children appreciate what you have done for us. I think we have inherited some of your good judgment.

Love, Maurice

Dear Father,   May 1920

The other day I met a man who liked my fruit stand and has offered to buy me out. If I sell I will clear about $1700. I feel very lonely for all of you, so I may accept his offer and come back there for awhile, but I am going to come back to Utah.

Inez is very much against my leaving because she thinks if I ever leave for the East she will lose me. She thinks she is my only tie here and it will be broken if I go. She doesn't need to worry, for I will not seek another girl. I want to come back because "This is the place." I am quite sure I will see you soon. Please don't try to talk me out of coming back to Utah, and have the noodle soup ready for me.

Love, Maurice.

Shortly after, I sold the fruit stand and boarded the train for Cleveland to see Father and the rest of the family. Things had not changed across America much since I had come as a youngster, except that so many more cars and trucks were in use. Tractors could be seen working a lot of the fields of the bigger farms, as well as a lot of new implements like reapers and threshers. Just before my arrival in Cleveland Father had opened up a milk store. It is sad that a philosopher type like him had to be held down to making a living. Like all Jewish scholars he loved the Talmud and much preferred reading it to business. He spent so much time reading and philosophizing while in his small store that he ran his business quite loosely. I criticized him for this, calling attention to his two clerks who looked ragged. He looked up from his book, shrugged his shoulders and said, "This fellow takes a little and that fellow takes a little. So long as they leave me a little, I don't care."

My family considered me rich and successful. My father wanted me to help my brothers. I gave some of the money from the sale of the fruit stand to them and some to father. With the rest I took off on an adventuresome trip to Florida with another young fellow I met in Cleveland. We saw all the sights and had a good time until we were broke.

Back in Cleveland I had to look for a job. Due to my previous experience in the hospital I got a job at Hog Island where many of the soldiers from World War I were stationed. It was quite an experience. There was much disease there. I had to swab the throats of the servicemen sick with colds and sore throats, and was kept so busy there was little time to think about my life.

But I must have been born with merchandising blood in my veins, because even in my busy moments I would ponder this and could really see no other life for myself. Utah became very attractive in my mind again. Besides, I just could not get Inez off my mind. So I took my earnings from Hog Island and boarded the train for Utah. Entering Salt Lake Valley from the East again was indeed "coming home." There was no doubt that my real career would get its start here among the Mormons. As soon as the train pulled in I grabbed my bag and I went straight to Inez's home, only to learn that she was not there. The opera "Hermione" was being presented at the Salt Lake Theater, starring Emma Lucy Gates. Inez had been chosen from her dramatic class at school for one of the roles. She would be busy all day.

I counted the money in my pocket. I had four dollars and eighty-five cents to buy a box of candy and some red roses to present to her after the evening performance. It was worth it. I hung around until the theater was out and met her at the stage door just like in the movies. She was surprised and happy. That night I slept on a bench in Pioneer Park.

I started peddling again, this time, doubling my efforts to find good buys. Father had never scolded me when I made a bad buy, and had appreciated my hustling around for everything to make money. Now my whole business depended upon good purchasing ability. I wanted to assure my customers of getting what they wanted, like pickling cucumbers for one, or certain berries for another. Summers were always, happy, busy days and I enjoyed seeing the same people twice a week. In some ways it was like a social outing.

The window in a certain shop on Broadway was displaying a certain green suit. How I wanted it! That suit was as green as grass, and I could see myself dancing in it at Saltair. I began paying a little on it each week. The day I got it out I asked Inez to go with me to Saltair and to dance in the pavilion where we had met. We rode out in the open-air train on a Monday night when the fare was reduced from thirty-five cents to ten. Somehow or other the mosquitoes were attracted to my green suit. Inez didn't have an easy time herself that night. Her mother had bought her a pair of shoes on a sale that were pinching her feet. She danced anyway, because I wanted to dance all night.

A week later she called up asking me to take her to the circus. Having spent practically everything on the suit and the evening at Saltair, I told her I could not go because I was fixing my false teeth. I heard her gasp with horror so I took the few pennies left and took her to the circus, just to prove that I had my own teeth.

When it got colder I heard that the Newhouse Hotel needed someone to operate its dance hall. I took over the job, hired an orchestra and sold tickets. When business was good

I made between eighteen and twenty-two dollars a week. Inez would come to the dance, but I was so busy running around taking care of things and fixing the punch that I had no time to dance with her. I always had my pockets full of oranges and lemons, which I would slice thin with a little knife and float the slices on top of the punch. The dancing business slowed down, so I decided to look for something that was related to dancing. I then became a "professor" of dancing at the old Odion Dance Hall on North Temple.

After Christmas I had to find another job, so I took one for February, March and April with a Mr. Nathan who peddled rummage-type goods by horse and wagon in Wyoming. We loaded up and traveled from ranch to ranch, unloading some of the goods at every house. Surprisingly we sold out nearly everything. Mr. Nathan was a good merchant and people knew him to be a fair man. He taught me many lessons in merchandising. When we came home I approached Yates and Gladstone, a firm that I knew well, to let me go over the same route I had covered with Mr. Nathan and sell produce. They agreed and my first venture was a carload of oranges and lemons, some smoked salmon that we wrapped in paper, apples, onions, parsnips, carrots and turnips. We shipped by rail to Carter, Wyoming, and used a wagon to load it over to the storage space I had rented in Lyman some miles away. It was no trouble to sell my first six cars, but I had a catastrophe when two carloads of oranges, apples and onions froze. It was during the birthday of Washington and Lincoln and it was very cold. Since the railroad didn't take responsibility for frozen produce, I was stuck with them. We thawed out the oranges, but they tasted very bitter. Luckily I was able to exchange my inventory for hides and pelts, and came out with only a small loss. The incident scared Yates and Gladstone, and I was out of a job. However, knowing it was not my fault, they trusted me from then on and we were to become very good friends.

Meantime I wrote to Philip in Cleveland asking him how he was and subtly hinting that I was going to marry a gentile girl. I didn't want to break the news to father directly. He immediately wrote back letting me know that Father was very upset. Then I wrote a letter to father:

Dear Father,   June 1921

I just received a letter from Philip and he tells me you are very worried about my marrying a *shiksa*. I hope to change your mind. You yourself have never narrowed your life down to only the Jewish culture. Ever since we came to America you have defended life in the United States as the most beautiful life in the world. You have continually admired Teddy Roosevelt for the many things he stands for and have even argued with many Jews that America is truly a land of milk and honey. Then why do you stick so hard to the old Jewish ways and become upset when I want to marry an American who happens to be a gentile? Intermarriage is very common. I thought you were a free thinker.

I understand we are seven million or more Jews in the world, and so far I have seen very little of their acceptance of the gentiles. Isn't it about time we begin to break some of our barriers? Nearly everywhere I go among the Jews I hear stories about anti-Semitism, but among these gentiles I hear very little of this type of thing. This is one of the reasons I want to stay here.

Since being among other religions I have become very friendly toward them and they seem to feel the same way about me. Actually these gentiles seem to have high regard for me and accept me into their social circles. This means a lot to me.

Inez is a fine person and I am sure that married to her I will be able to develop a better life than with the Jewish girl you introduced me to in the tailor shop, even though her father was willing to make things easy for us financially. I think I have enough self-confidence to make it on my own. The Jews think they are the only good people, but I don't find it so. Inez is a Mormon and she comes from pioneer stock of a people who were also persecuted, but they are very good people.

Love, Maurice

Father still could not believe I was doing the right thing. He reminded me that Mother would be very hurt. He also implied that mixed marriages didn't work and that if Jews intermarried the race would soon disappear. So I sat down and wrote him again, trying to appeal to his fine intellect:

> Dear Father,   October 1921
>
> Past experience has left a mark on you, but the United States is a far cry from Russia. Here I own my own truck even though I owe money on it and am able to make a substantial living. So my future is not what it seems. One day I hope you'll take a trip out here and see that everything is fine and that a mixed marriage really works.
>
> This is a new day, and it might be the only way to assimilate into the great melting pot of the United States. Do we always have to have these differences to separate us from other people of other religions and people with whom we do business daily and live neighbors to all the time? When you talk about a bad marriage, include the Jewish marriages.
>
> Our religion teaches us we are the Chosen People out of the billions of people on the earth, and all other religions are lesser than ours. This is hard for me to understand, since I have given it a lot of thought. My bride-to-be and I have discussed our marriage and have decided that we are only aware of one thing: to get married and live happily from then on, including hardship and whatever life has to offer. Her parents share your misgivings. I was the one that proposed marriage, but we have both discussed the objections both you and her parents have.
>
> I am sure Inez loves me, for she wants to marry me in spite of everything. She helps me in every way with my grammar, my learning, and my appearance. I cannot promise her that I will set the world on fire, but I hope someday to become someone she will be proud of.
>
> Love, Maurice.

Inez and I were married on the twenty-eighth of January. A customer of mine who had a car drove us north to Farmington, a pretty little town near Salt Lake where we were married by the justice of the peace. We came directly to her parents and told them about it. The sadness they tried to hide made me feel very bad. We tried to tell them about our love, but

Inez

they had a faraway look. I felt like hiding my head in the sand. Our honeymoon was spent in a hotel room at Second South and State Streets. I had borrowed fifty dollars from Inez to get married on. In time her parents began to accept me. Inez tried

Maurice

very hard to convert me to her religion and she made up her
mind to change my foreign ways. I didn't mind too much about
the latter, because my English was bad and my manners were
all wrong.

Dear Father,

I must confess that I am becoming less active in our synagogue, somehow losing interest. I surely don't feel the same about intermarriage. I guess I am melting into the melting pot of the United States. It is obvious to me that there are good people everywhere, both gentile and Jew. Sometimes I feel that religion separates people. I hope this doesn't make you think I am favoring the Mormon religion. I can see many advantages of intermarriage and not too many disadvantages. I hope you will understand and appreciate how I feel.

Love, Maurice.

We got our first little house at very cheap rent. We lived on the first floor and in the basement lived an old man who seemed to hate the world and could not stand the least noise we made. From the beginning we planned to lay aside savings and live on very little. Except for a little meat and bread, we would eat what was left on the truck after the day's peddling. In time I became very tired of turnips, parsnips and carrots.

Inez often told me how inadequate she felt in trying to cook for me. When we went to visit my friends they knocked themselves out for us, fixing the best Jewish food that only someone with a Jewish background could do. Later she developed a taste for Jewish cooking and came to like it very much.

Religion presented the greatest problem. Once when Inez was pregnant with our first child she induced me to go and hear a prominent Mormon speak at her ward. He was explaining the Bible and how we should be immersed instead of sprinkled. He seemed to enjoy his subject and spoke much longer than he should. Even my wife, who was trained to sit through a top Mormon sermon, became nervous.

Analyzing religion became a habit with me. I was always trying to figure out the difference between people's beliefs. Where was the disagreement? Why did God allow people to be divided so?

On the other hand, Inez and her parents were completely bewildered by customs and ideologies so completely different from theirs. It also took time for them to adjust to me, but eventually they made the best of it.

My father more than anyone, had been against the marriage. He had warned me that before long Inez would be calling me a "goddamn Jew," but of course she never did.

Christmas was the strangest of all customs to adjust to. I don't think I had ever heard of that holiday before I came to Salt Lake City. A girl I had known then gave me a tie for Christmas. I was very touched to think that she would spend part of the small salary she earned working in a bakery on a present for someone else. After thinking it over I began to feel untrue to my religion for accepting it, and finally felt so guilty I told my mother. She had only laughed and said, "So long as you don't marry a *shiksa*."

But I did marry a *shiksa*. We were drawn together and I was blinded to any problems that might separate us. We came before God, each with a different background, different training and, in a way, obligated to different gods. Her God and my God clashed, but our love for each other was nobody's fault. We were to fill the greatest purpose in life: having children. Life itself taught me that we had to come to some agreement, but how? I was forced to do much thinking. Either we had to merge our beliefs or discard them. I wanted to accept her family, her way and her friends in addition to my own. It came to me that my children and their children must not have barriers that would keep them from accepting each other as they are. All at once it seemed to me that a God had to be more universal than just one who righteously judges ten million people, leaving the rest of humanity to be judged by Jesus whom the Jews believed to be neither a righteous judge nor God.

Not only did we face a great shifting of religious beliefs and traditions, but our marriage automatically blended two different cultures. I was used to kosher food. My mother had cooked very differently, and the landlady where I had boarded before I was married cooked the same way. It seemed so good to be invited to a Passover dinner or a kosher pastrami lunch. I just couldn't seem to get over the Jewish cooking and the salads they made. I loved eggplant. It was called *potlashona* in Russian, and chopped with oil and green peppers--delicious. Then there was *momaliga*, a cornmeal loaf, that was cut with a thread, and there were always the herring and boiled potatoes. Our Jewish potato pancakes were called *lotkas*. Even now, I can taste those good dishes as though it were yesterday, but when we have to go without what we are used to, it is not the bitterest thing in the world. There are wonderful things to replace them: good wife, children, grandchildren and the satisfaction of helping people. Gradually I began to put such thoughts aside and became blinded to everything but hard work.

After peddling for two years and working extra hard, I made enough money to buy a lot for five hundred dollars. It was up on Kensington Avenue above Thirteenth East, on the "East Bench," one of the levels of the great prehistoric Lake Bonneville. While our house was being built, we used to push our baby Marjorie in her baby buggy, all the way from Washington Street up the Ninth South Hill to the site on Kensington Avenue to see how the house was coming along. There were many lovely homes being built in that area for the "rich" who made as high as three hundred dollars a month. If you made two hundred dollars you could still swing this "upper class" lifestyle comfortably. Since we had come to Salt Lake City we had lived on the "West Side." Inez also had been brought up there, but it was very important to her that we build on the "East Side." She had already saved up enough to buy a piano and a phonograph.

I was trying to do some reading, but by now was so distracted by everything I had to do it was impossible to concentrate on anything outside the business. In fact, the house had not been done long before we were faced with another trying decision:

The peddling business just did not make enough money to carry us through the winter. I tried supplementing our income in various ways. For instance, one winter I made a couple of thousand boxes out of orange crates I had bought for five cents a piece. I took them apart, changed their shapes to apple boxes and sold them for twenty-two cents. This kind of thing just was not enough to support a family on however and it ate up all my time. Marjory was now three years old and Inez was pregnant with Keith.

Observation:

The reason the Mormons were not anti-Semantic was due to the concepts Joseph Smith received in the Book of Mormon. The book expressed the American aborigines were descendants of scattered Jews from Jerusalem about 600 years before Christ. They brought the teachings of Isaiah. It allowed the Mormons to understand that God was going to use the gentile Mormons to gather the Jews in America. Joseph was specifically told to purchase lands in Missouri "between Jew and gentile." The reference to Jew was to the Indians further west. East was the gentile Christians, and the city between was the New Jerusalem

Maurice got along with Mormon's, hired them in his business ventures, and stood by them. My father, mother, and myself were only three of the Mormons he employed from the early days of Grand Central Stores.

I new Marjory, their first child after she was married. Keith, the second child was only fifteen years older than I. First I worked for Maurice from age 16 and when I returned from my LDS mission to Boston, I worked for Keith. My father had the longest running record of employment.

Ronald Kelsch

My family grew along with the business

Califomia interlude

*A business so limited by the seasons
could flourish and grow in a climate where
there was little difference in winter or summer.*

11.

California Interlude

Unable to face another winter in Salt Lake using up the little money from the summer's business, I decided to try my luck in California where the good winter weather would let me make enough to send for my family.

I left my wife in Salt Lake in the house we had built at 1425 Kensington Avenue. The only money she had to live on was the collectable bills. In California I could take advantage of the good weather during the winter and hope to make enough to send for them.

Driving my second-hand half-ton Ford truck I headed south through Utah Valley and on through Southern Utah, passing numerous Mormon towns and thrifty farms. The roads then were rugged and places to get a car repaired were practically nonexistent, but it was common in those days for travellers to help each other. Salt Lake to Los Angeles took me six days; but at a lemonade stand in St. George I met two men who were determined to make it in forty-eight hours! They were in some sort of record-setting contest and they were strapped into the car for the utmost speed across the desert.

In Southern Utah the grades became steep. The foot brake on my truck gave way, then the hand brake. I took my life in my hands coming out of St. George with no brakes on those terrifically steep hills.

Las Vegas was merely a stop in the desert, on the edge of an alkali basin which could not be crossed if it rained. My car joined hundreds of others on both sides waiting for it to dry out before they could go on their ways. I continued on through Needles, which was nothing more than a rough layover point out in the heat of the desert. I had brought bedding and slept in the truck. A cold autumn was coming, and the nights were beautiful. I lived on pomegranates fresh from St. George for two days, so my mouth and hands were blood red.

Finally I pulled into the suburbs of Los Angeles. On the outskirts on Lankershim Blvd., fourteen miles from the main produce market at Seventh and Central. I rented a fruit stand with a back room for forty dollars a month. With a couple of bales of hay to sleep on and a little tin stove I set up housekeeping.

The man I rented the stand from also owned a walnut grove and an apple orchard. He let me gather the walnuts which, sold from the stand, paid the rent. I put up a good-humored sign saying, "nuts wanted" which attracted a lot of customers. A man would come in and say "I brought you some nuts," pointing to his wife and kids. They'd all laugh.

I took in a partner named Hebe Burmingham. He very soon decided there wasn't enough business for both of us so he left, but not without this parting advice: "Maurice, you should quit trying to own a business and work for somebody else. You'll never be a good merchant."

This shook my confidence somewhat, but then I realized we had different outlooks on business. He believed in starting with a high price and coming down; I was already volume-oriented and believed in giving the customer a good buy to start with. The first thing I did when he left was to take the little money I had and remodeled the fruit stand. I put up four strands of electric lights so that people going down the boulevard could see me a long way off. This immediately boosted my sales. It advertised me in other ways, too. I was held up four times.

I hired an elderly man to watch the stand while I hustled different real estate places that were subdividing orange grove properties. They gave me all the oranges that fell from the trees to sell on the stand. I myself lived on oranges, hamburgers, and hot dogs.

There were very few people living out on Lankershim Blvd., but one source of customers was the busloads of people being brought out to see real estate. We laughed at them getting gipped on that bare land, but they always bought fruit. The farmer across the street sold his land when California real estate was booming. Who would have dreamed he could get rich on that isolated land, or that the population of California would multiply so fast?

The Universal Picture Studios were nearby. Out of loneliness for my family I would occasionally go over to watch them making a movie. They asked me to be in a film being produced by Carl Lemele. My role was to drive my truck across the street and wave my hand. The hero was supposed to be in deep thought and was reading a letter as he walked in front of my truck. I had to put on my brakes to miss him and also just barely miss hitting a taxi. So that it would look authentic, I loaded the truck with fresh produce each day as if it were for my regular route, and I was paid both for my work in the film and the produce. When it came to the theaters I sat through the film four times in order to see myself "act."

When I delivered fruit to the Universal Studios restaurant, the cook would spend a little time "pitching" cards with me. One day he wagered all his furniture and lost. His wife of course objected vehemently, and despite his insistence on being an "honest man" who paid his debts, I couldn't take their furniture.

I tried to take advantage of the crowd coming out there, and business improved, but it took all I made for expenses.

My next project was to buy a press for making apple cider and fresh grape juice for my customers. One day a man came into my stand with a gallon of whiskey and wanted to leave it there. Prohibition was in force then and many arrests were being made. Not wanting it on the premises, I gave him a very emphatic "no," but he pestered me until I gave him permission to hide it in the orchard behind one of the trees until he returned the next day. I never saw him again.

There was a lot of building in California at that time and a great deal of sand and gravel being hauled out to the building sites. One of the truck drivers came into the stand one morning and told me he was thirsty and would like a drink. I knew what kind of drink he meant and refused. He pressed me though and finally the temptation of an idea was too great for me: I went to the orchard and brought back a little whiskey, and poured it into some apple cider. That made my income two dollars and a quarter on the three glasses instead of fifteen cents—quite a profit. He came back often and brought other people with him. I felt funny about doing this sort of thing, but I was desperate to get my wife and child to California. By the time the whole gallon was used up I had enough for their fare.

Inez wrote me she had found some renters for our house and was on her way with little Marjorie. When they arrived at the railroad station Inez broke down and cried, we were so glad to see each other. She was horrified though, to see what kind of living conditions we had. The house had indoor plumbing but was made of nothing but clapboard and you could even see through some of the cracks.

I went to my landlord and asked him to build us a house behind the stand that we could lease. He had gained confidence in me and agreed to do so. When the house was built I still had to sleep in the stand, because it had only three sides on it and the front was open to any passerby.

Occasionally we had some pilfering trouble on that account. Once two fellows came in by car and took ten dollars. I jumped on their running board with a wrench in my hand and threatened to break their windows. They started so as to throw me off, but I held on to the cracked windshield. They decided to give me back the ten.

I went down to the big Los Angeles market to purchase the produce, unload the first part at Universal Studios, the second part at my stand, and then go peddling among my many customers that lived in Beverly Hills and North Hollywood. Sometimes the hills were so steep that the ladies had to let down baskets for me to fill and pull them up again by ropes. My time was now divided among my customers, my stand and my fresh juice business. Inez minded the stand while I was out selling. I fixed everything up before leaving so it would be easier. But she had little Marjorie to tend.

The juice business had the problem of attracting the bees and flies every time I went to press some juice. My wife didn't know until later that I did a little bootlegging to accumulate the money for her fare from Salt Lake or she would have said, "I would rather starve than use that kind of money." I was finally forced to tell her because one day while she was keeping a watchful eye on the stand a customer came in and asked for a drink and she found out about my former customers.

There were other complications. Somebody told Francis X. Bushman and Rudolph Valentino that I sold wine. They got their stories mixed with my grape juice business and the other incident. It gave me an idea to sell wine to movie stars.

Francis X. Bushman learned to drink wine while he was making "Ben Hur" in Italy. Valentino was already a drinker. I sold wine to other actors as well. Once Bushman was embarrassed when the actor's newspaper claimed he was in with a "certain bootlegger." He had borrowed five gallons from me, but bringing it in and out gave people the idea we were partners.

Noah Berry wanted his son to become a businessman and he gave him some orchards of Satzuma plums. He made me give his son the price that he wanted, and he paid me the difference. Now I opened a second stand and sold one stand, to Ben Turpin, who had the same name as the "cross-eyed" actor. He put up his name and a big X, which made the actor furious when he came out of the studios across the street.

Inez was lonely, and about to have our second child. So my mother-in-law came to be with her. When she first arrived I wanted to impress her with our success so I took her for a ride in my truck. About four miles out the wheel fell off. When I had put it back on she didn't want to get back in and said she'd rather walk. Inez was of pioneer stock and could withstand many hardships. This was fortunate because I could not afford to have the first baby, Marjory, delivered at a hospital, and when it came time for the second child, Keith, to be born I still could not afford a hospital bill. I had been working desperately to get enough money to pay the doctors and the landlord for the house he had just built for us. I could never convert any of my inventories to cash for anything, and Inez refused to let me borrow money. Anyway, there was no one to borrow from. Both our daughter Pat and our son Keith were born in California in the little house behind the stand. I will never forget how humiliating it was not to take her to the hospital. The doctor was kind of rough with me and I felt like a two-cent piece.

Everybody liked my small daughter and the little fellow, Keith, was the apple of my eye. He was a very good baby, no bother, and I liked to be able to glance out and see him sitting in his high chair under the trees in the fresh air.

We had so much to do to make a living we hardly had any time for ourselves. For outings I used to take the kids and family - with one kid on the floor and two on the seat, over to see a friend in Burbank. We would eat dinner and talk awhile. Driving back I had all I could do to keep my eyes open. Another form of outing was to go twice a week to a stand for barbecued beef on a roll. Today if I see it on a menu I shut my eyes.

I hated to leave this business in California, but Inez became increasingly homesick for Salt Lake City. And she wanted to go home. By now I was thirty years old and had sufficient confidence to believe that I could make a living there for my family. So we packed up the kids and left California.

Observation:

It was often the case that many Utahans' would go to California and try their luck. Because of this there were eventually more Mormons in Southern California than in Utah.

I myself tried it and was successful at age thirty-nine. In looking for work, I was accosted by a commercial production for a man on the street. It was a Good Year commercial that ran during the Super Bowl. The residuals made it possible to get into a home. My first job was advertising for a Daily Newspaper using a recommendation from Keith for creating commercials for his Keith Warshaw and Company in Salt Lake.

The parallel is very interesting to me as I left most of my family behind until I got established. Maurice died while I was there and eventually retired early and returned to Clarion country after my Father died to run the Bed & Breakfast.

Ronald Kelsch

We kept adding on to the original store

S a upermarket isborn

One cannot say that the success of any man is due to one single factor, but rather to a combination of things. The right time, the right place, the need for something at that particular time, the ability to see that need and the driving ambition to fulfill it..

12.

A Super Market is Born

When we arrived back in Salt Lake, we ran into my short time fruit stand partner from Los Angeles, Hebe Burmingham. When I told about the success in California and that I was thinking about going into business for myself in Salt Lake, he took me aside and repeated his advice to me: "Go get a job someplace. You are a good worker Maurice, but you're no manager." "Why would he say that?" I began to ask myself. "Am I too aggressive? Am I over enthusiastic? Am I any good at all?" We needed money immediately. I did not mind working day and night, but I just could not make enough on wages under somebody else.

We moved back into our home on Kensington Avenue, but we had no income at all. Not only were we shabby and needed clothes, but I worried about food for the children. The tenants had abused the house while we were gone. There were five of us now: Inez and myself, Marjory, Keith and the new baby, Pat. I rented a stand on Thirteenth East and Fifth South and started a good business, but had no lease. When the landlord saw how well I was doing he evicted me and took over himself.

There was a great decision to make: Whether to go into business for myself again or take a job.

For advice I went to my old friends in the wholesale produce business, Yates and Gladstone, whom I respected very much. I told them my quandary: Hebe Burmingham's judgment as opposed to my own strong affinity for independence. They hit the ceiling. "You are a business man," they said. "Don't let anyone ever tell you that you are not. Look for a location and set up the kind of fruit stand you know how to open." I returned with a light step, my confidence restored. They had inspired me with enough courage to go out and begin again.

I did not have to look for a location, having picked out a spot a long time ago, just in case I ever had the chance to open my own business. It was on Ninth South and Main Streets, which I felt would be the future center of things.

Ninth South and Main was to become the center of my world, even though it marked the place where the city sidewalk ended. There was more traffic on State Street from people coming to the city, but Main Street carried a lot more of the local traffic.

State Street was filled with businesses, but Main Street had plenty of room for expansion. The next day I rented the lot for forty dollars a month, and that night I counted the rest of my money out on the kitchen table: sixty-two dollars and thirty cents—the only cash we had in the world. As I recall, that seemed more challenging than frightening. It was hard to ask Inez to make more sacrifices. Every time I asked her to be more economical she would get that look of "How much more can I do?" Nevertheless, she agreed that night that we would buy nothing until we were really in business. It was urgent to build a stand and make enough money to pay the next month's rent. Spring was coming. That was in my favor.

I started building the next day. A lumber yard on Seventh South and State Street gave me credit on condition that I would sign over the completed fruit stand and display stands if I could not make it pay. Determined to keep my word, I constructed it so it could be moved off the ground and turned over to them if I should default.

I believed my building was at the best spot on earth. Looking five blocks up the main street you could see the beginning of the business section of town, which continued up past the Brigham Young monument standing at the head of Main Street at South Temple. On the north hill overlooking the city stood Utah's fine State Capitol Building. And if you looked at a right angle a few blocks from my site, you would see the big tower of the City and County Building with its huge clock that chimed out every fifteen minutes.

Toward the east, the city sloped up to the brown foothills of the Wasatch Mountains, at the base of which one of the levels of the great prehistoric Lake Bonneville formed the "East Bench" where we lived. Main Street ran north and south and really divided the city into two different sections. Those living on the East Side came from the "right side of the tracks," and those from the West Side were from the wrong side. I remember once, when Mother, Father and Eda and I were living on Salt Lake's West Side, I came home from work one day and found our furniture on the front lawn. We couldn't meet the rent. It had been just the opposite in Philadelphia: the old East Side was where the immigrants lived. I remember how important it was to Inez to live on the East Side.

East side, west side, it made no difference to me. I would now be in the center and people from both sides would be my customers. No matter where they lived they had to buy food, and people ate pretty much the same everywhere. Hoping the store would one day be as busy as a big station, I planned to name my store "Grand Central Market."

For the next few weeks, every time the clock chimed in the City and County Building I would chime to myself to remind me to really hustle. I hired a part-time carpenter, promising to pay him after the store was opened, then worrying constantly that he wouldn't show up. Whenever he came there were a hundred questions to ask him about building and what to do to get by the inspectors.

We had lots of problems. I tried being an amateur carpenter and walked around with both thumbs bandaged half the time, and when they were not bandaged they were chapped. At night my wife sympathized and encouraged me with my hard work, for she knew how much I wanted to be in business for myself.

The electrical wiring worried me the most. The electrical materials had to be obtained on the same conditions as those with the carpenter. I will always be grateful to the owners of the surrounding business places who cheered me on. They came to watch and offered to help. After I had struggled with an old saw for awhile, thinking it was dull because the lumber was wet, someone brought me a good one. One man brought me some tar paper and helped me put it up. Everybody watched what I was doing. The produce people were interested and enthused. My stand would be a good outlet for them.

The problems were offset by great hopes. I walked around in a daze dreaming of how I would display my fruits and vegetables. I was never building a fruit stand, I was building a castle—planning out every little stand and corner. I was overjoyed when it was nearing completion. Each night I would come and tell Inez and the kids about it, reassuring my wife that we would soon be able to buy groceries.

Worrying whether Inez would think me a failure made me try harder to prove myself. I wanted to lay the world at her feet.

It took us three weeks of hunger and worry to complete three sides and the roof. The floor was gravel. The open side which I used for displays faced the street. I built false bases so that when the fruit was arranged on them it looked like huge stacks of fresh produce. Looking at pictures of my first stand now makes me wonder how I could have been so proud.

Good luck brought me a cash register for twenty-two dollars, bought on the same terms as I had bargained with the others. I went to sleep each night worrying about how much I owed and who I was going to get credit from next, but determined to justify everybody's faith in me—especially my wife's.

Opening day was set for Tuesday and I wanted everyone to know where I was. I rented the lot next door and bargained with the florist on the comer to advertise some of his items if he would help me erect a sign. It was sixty feet long with a platform running in front of it so I could walk along to paint the letters, and so tall I had to reach to get at the top. The letters were seven feet high and visible for blocks around. I put up four times as many electric lights as usual so my place could be seen at night. The signs were painted with Mrs. Stuart's Blueing on butcher paper and hung all around my stand. From the beginning of my dreams I planned on doing a volume business.

Twenty boys were hired for opening day. Just as I had finished putting out all my inventory and the stands were looking beautiful, it began to rain. I wanted to cry. It seemed as though I was starting out with bad luck. I never saw so much rain. The roof was leaking in many places, the gunny sacks I was to use for a bed that night became soaked, the tissue paper on the oranges turned pink and Mrs. Stuart's Blueing began to run on the signs. I sent a boy onto the roof with some tar paper to see if he could fix the leaks, but when he climbed out onto the roof, the strong wind caught the tar paper like a sail and blew him off. I thought he was dead, but thank goodness he fell in a mud puddle and was unhurt. At nine o'clock we opened.

The boys waited on the customers and I stayed at the National cash register I had been sold on credit for twenty-two dollars. (The salesman of National later became president of his company.) All the produce on the stands was on three days' credit. We would have to sell enough to pay for it on Friday. That "Grand Opening" was more exciting to me than any since. My stand was my castle and my customers were the visiting royalty whom I treated like kings and queens. I had stayed awake nights dreaming how I could build up a great business with good customer relations and I was determined to be the most courteous merchant in the whole Valley.

At midnight I lay down on my damp gunny sacks, rejoicing in my successful day and planning what I was going to do next. Everything on the stand was sure to sell and the supplies could be replenished. Sunday would be a bonus day, with plenty of customers, and my creditors would not have to be met again until Monday morning.

As soon as it was clear that the stand would flourish and people were going to give me credit, I started figuring every way possible to increase business. A truck load of oranges could be brought over from California, sorted and sized and still sold for less than anywhere else. Piles of bright oranges on the sidewalk attracted customers to buy them by the buckets. I painted new specials on my big signboard every other day. Weather damage was kept patched up, and the signs and lights brought people in droves. My old customers from my peddling route came to buy. I felt so complimented to have them come that I found myself watching out for choice fruits and vegetables for them with "Let's see what I have in the back room for you."

During the week I tried to wait on every customer possible and carry their produce to the car or baby buggy, or fill up the little coaster wagons they brought with them.

It was not just a continual story of success, of course. Not being the greatest carpenter or engineer in the world I had not figured how much weight my roof would hold. So when a hundred stalks of bananas were hung from the ceiling, down came the roof and squashed all my inventory. In the middle of this chaos a boy I had hired by the name of Ruth Laughlin came to me with a customer's check for a million dollars! I was in no mood for pranks and lost my temper so I threw him out. (It turned out he was demented and known to every business in Salt Lake for preposterous checks.) The mess was disheartening, but I fixed the store and the next day made a good buy at the market and things again looked sunny and bright.

It is hard to describe the difficulties of running a stand open to the wind and sun. Neither heat nor cold was good for keeping produce at its best. There were no refrigerators or advanced ways of storage. I did the best I could with my sprinkling can to keep the fruits and vegetables from drying out, but the heat nevertheless took its toll.

There was so much work even with the help of the hired boys it was still necessary to work late every night, then to be down at the market by dawn, buy my produce and get the displays set up before the customers arrived; but I could now tell my wife she could go ahead and buy things. Five months later still sleeping in the back room with no front on the store, I could never lock up and go home.

Difficult or not, these were very happy days. The only thing that really bothered me was the exhaustion and never having any time with my family. How I longed to go home at night. I soon got my wish. Winter was coming and there were two choices: either close the stand in or close it up. I decided to close in the front, and put a pot-bellied stove in the center of the stand with the pipe going up through the ceiling which would keep the fruit from freezing and help keep the place a little warm. Though it was still cold for both me and my customers I could dress warmly and wear gloves most of the time. Best of all I could lock up and go home for a few hours sleep.

I tried to keep up with my wife and fast-growing children. The hobby all the family shared when the children were young was music. With Inez playing the piano and leading with her lovely soprano voice, I would harmonize and the children all joined in. In later years they were to remind me that I was better at making money than making music. I took the family to a circus occasionally, or to the State Fair or the Coon Chicken Inn which was so popular then out on Highland Drive. But for the most part we kept our living to a minimum so that we could take a loss on the produce if we had to in order to build up the business.

I put almost every nickel I made back into the business. I hated to deny Inez and the children so much, yet to expand would still require cutting our living expenses. I had let Inez buy some furniture from Axelrad's and we were paying ninety dollars a month for it. It was hard to pay this and still keep my inventory up, and I kept thinking that if I didn't have to pay that money out for furniture it would ease my situation considerably. I talked her into letting the furniture go back. Axelrad's were very upset, but they let us return it. All we had left was a table and two chairs for the kitchen, the piano and phonograph, and the baby buggy that Keith had to sleep in. All the rest of us slept on the floor.

Business got better and better. It was the first time in Salt Lake City that customers were allowed to pick out their own fruits and vegetables. Other merchants thought I was crazy, but I was sure I knew what I was doing. Then one day a Mr. Leaver came by and wanted me to sell Kellogg's Corn Flakes (he later became chairman of the board of Kellogg's Company). I made a big display of the boxes and immediately sold more corn flakes than anyone had dreamed. He awarded me a big clock with the Kellogg name on it, to the envy of all the other merchants. I decided it was now time for me to go into the grocery business.

Again I consulted my friends Yates and Gladstone, but this time they discouraged me, saying, "The grocery business is a dangerous business to be in."

Respecting them very much, I hated to go against their advice. My ambition was greater than my fear, however, and the next week I started to build on the adjoining lot to house the grocery and meat departments. Knowing little about these, I leased them out for others to run. The whole business continued to grow. Many customers still walked from their homes, but now those with cars were stopping along the streets, as we had not planned for parking. Neon signs were just coming in and were very expensive, but I decided to be the first one in Salt

Lake to put one up. It had required high payments, but it drew many customers who, upon arrival, found nice, fresh produce, meat, and groceries. When the butcher and grocer were asked to help with the costs of the advertising which benefited them as well, they refused. My sign was so expensive that I consulted an attorney (Hugh B. Brown, later in the L.D.S. First Presidency; we are still friends). His advice to me was: "You can't break the lease, but there is nothing to stop you from adding a grocery and meat department on the north side of your store, as their lease involved only that portion on the south side." I advised them about what I was going to do and it still didn't convince them to pay anything. I soon built an addition on the north side and opened up my own meat and grocery departments. We did so much business that in a few weeks they moved out and we continued to expand.

Inez was now able to start replacing the furniture in our house.

I started buying all my groceries from Western States Wholesale Grocers. This became a problem because L. S. Skaggs, head of Safeway, happened to be the president. Hoping to eliminate me as a competitor, Western States cut off my credit. I owed them fifty thousand dollars at the time, but I figured a way out. AI Smith of Utah Grocers extended me credit and I manipulated a few deals to pay off Western States. One was to buy four thousand cases of canned milk from Morning Milk Company on credit and sell it on special to get enough to pay on the old bill. I then had thirty days to find enough money to pay Morning Milk.

Automobiles had become widely sold, and looking ahead I could see that expansion would require parking area.

One policy I developed very early in my business was "night straightness"—leaving everything in the stores clean and organized to do business the next day. This was a policy which added to our efficiency gave our store a reputation for neatness.

Many of the boys who worked for me in the early days have become very successful in their own businesses. I wonder if something rubbed off from me. For the most part they were all wonderful young people and some are still with me.

Observation:

If Keith was about 3-5 years of age, it would be between 1924-1929. My father would be about 9-11 years of age.

I reflected on those few boys that stayed with Grand Central stores all those years. I could not have been my uncle Jack because he left the company many years before this book was written, but could be one of the boys. I was unable to ask my father, because he passed 5 years after Maurice at the age of 68 due to cancer. At about 9-11 my father was a young boy from the west side and also a hard worker.

When I was about seventeen, Maurice had three stores. The first was just across the street of the original stand and my father several times referred to the original stand across the street where at that time a Dutch Boy paint store had replaced the original.

I can only think of one other that could have worked his whole life for Maurice. It is hard to imagine any others because I later worked in the central office where all the long timers were now buyers. They would have to be about 57-62 when the book was written. Only two long timers fit that description.

Ronald Kelsch

Price was the key

the great depression

*One does not let the failure of any system
be a deterrent to progress - rather it becomes
a challenge to success.*

13.

The Great Depression

Struggling so hard to start my business blinded me to the gathering dark clouds of the Great Depression. Now they were closing in. At first, even the newspaper headlines couldn't make me believe that the national economy was collapsing. It seemed that overnight people were walking the streets looking for work. I still didn't take much time to think about it, but grew uneasy when someone would come into the store and ask for a bit of cardboard to put in his shoes to cover the worn-through parts of the soles they couldn't afford to have repaired. Gradually, I noticed that people had less and less money to spend, and finally, the time came when I rarely saw a dollar bill anymore. Most of the intake was now in small change. The way people purchased in single items reminded me of the immigrant days.

"FOR SALE" signs began to appear on the front lawns of many of the lovely homes that I had once peddled to. People were leaving the high rent districts because they could no longer afford to live there, and many of the mansions were being turned into housekeeping rooms. Numbers of people became dependent on the Salvation Army for their meals. The rich and middle-class that was experiencing poverty for the first time were bewildered. It was to my advantage that I didn't have to be conditioned to poverty. For me, there was only one way to go—up. I also knew that the first thing a person bought when they did get money was food.

Even though I had enlarged things considerably, my main drawing card was produce—nice, fresh produce. If one price painted on my big signboard did not bring them in, I would lower it. To increase my business even more, I added a lunch counter where a customer could get a sandwich and a cup of coffee. This caused an unexpected turn of events. There were a lot of hoboes riding the rails during the Depression and I suppose I was still performing mitzvas (good deeds), so when one turned up I would give him a cup of coffee and a roll. The railroad tracks were just behind my store, so the word spread and I was soon dispensing so many rolls with coffee that it was getting to be more than I could afford in such a small business. Furthermore, my customers were beginning to object. Saying "no" to a hungry man was almost impossible for me, but in the end I put a stop to it.

One thing I could not understand was the high suicide rate during the Depression. Our family had lost everything once, including our country, yet we still regarded life as too sweet, too great a gift to throw away. As times got worse my business got better. I still did all the buying, putting up the displays, doing the bookkeeping and janitorial work. My biggest worry was keeping up the health of both my two-ton truck and myself, which had to be loaded so heavily that I feared a broken axle.

It was to my great advantage that there were good buys to be made in Utah. Many of the large farms in the nation had folded because the farmers could not get enough for their produce to pay the workers for harvesting it, but there were still a lot of small farms down through Orem and Provo, and up through Farmington and Bountiful, that were producing many kinds of fruits and vegetables. There were luscious raspberries, strawberries, and all kinds of currants, blueberries, apples, pears, peaches, grapes and prunes. Besides these, they grew all kinds of green produce and root vegetables.

About the only substantial outlet these farmers had was the Growers' Market, where they took it every day. I would go down to the wholesale market every morning and buy all kinds of produce at a low price and sell it at a slightly higher one. If the market was overloaded, I learned to wait until the regular customers were supplied. Then, when the farmers were anxious to dispose of their products and get home, I could often strike a bargain by taking a whole load.

Many times, by taking the whole lot, I could get five hundred or maybe even a thousand cases of berries at fifty cents a case, and I would sell them at sixty-nine cents. I did everything to make the business pay, determined to support my family and prove that my creditors could trust me because I had to depend on them to advance the money for my market buying. It was not a time when one could go to the bank and borrow money. I also had to stock my store with groceries and meats. The whole operation had to be based on mutual trust.

There were no welfare or food stamps in those days. People just had to shop where things were cheapest, and I kept thinking I must find a way to get the best merchandise at the cheapest price so I could pass the benefit on to the public. No matter how little the income, people still had to eat. I never took credit accounts, but tried to supply my customers with as many foods in season as I could, thereby saving them money, and this helped me to build up a good, steady volume of customers. Individually, they did not have much to spend, but their spending mounted up. Practically every family put up all the seasonal fruit they could get. They would also store away foods like bushels of potatoes, apples and cabbage.

Looking back now, it seems I worked twenty-four hours a day. Sometimes my wife wanted to go to a show for a little recreation and I would go along because it gave me a chance to get some sleep. While she watched the movie, I would dream about the morning when there would be fresh decisions to make on what to buy and how much to sell it for—how to make a profit while still taking the customers' needs into consideration.

In the strange paradoxes of the Great Depression, surpluses began to pile up, not from overproduction, but because the system of distribution had broken down. Crops lay rotting in the fields because the big farmers couldn't get enough money to pay off the pickers, let alone to meet their mortgage payments. Manufactured goods piled up in warehouses for the same reason. Everything slowed to a standstill. There was deadliness about the Depression that seemed to stifle the very energy of the people. President Roosevelt was by now trying to get money flowing again by initiating various projects such as hiring the unemployed in the Works Progress Administration. The W.P.A. took on projects for the public good, such as roads, soil conservation and re-forestation. A distribution system serving as an outlet for mass production of goods at prices the public could afford was badly needed, and a new star was beginning to shine on the horizon: the "Supermarket" was going to come into its own, and I was going to hitch my wagon to that stars.

I did not get into the Supermarket business by way of the small, independent store or via the chain store system. I guess you could say my operation was unique, for, like Topsy, "It just growed." The supermarket was not actually a creation of the Great Depression. A sprinkling of ideas in this direction had already taken root in the minds of a few merchants scattered throughout the country. It was the conditions created by the depression that caused the supermarket to mushroom and grow. The small neighborhood store and the more efficient chains had preceded it; but these were having a hard time now and would be somewhat eclipsed by the fast-moving system of the larger outlets. I remember that when the chain stores first became popular they threatened to push out the little independents with their more efficient system of merchandising. The independents fought back, claiming that the chains might gain in efficiency, but would lose by mechanizing people instead of maintaining the warm, personal relationship of the small, friendly, independent store. Remembering the old days in Dubossar, where my father's customers were our dearest friends, I could understand the value of this. On the other hand, I remembered the disadvantages of a small store—the slow process of selling over the counter and the storage and sanitation problems. The old butcher shops rarely closed their doors in winter, even in zero weather, I guess to keep the meat fresh longer.

In the new era of "cash and carry," I had to eliminate many forms of service that I had formerly offered the public. I also lost some of the nice features I had enjoyed in my peddling days, like being invited in for a cup of coffee by one of our customers, or having my old customers come clear across town to patronize my fruit stand when I first started up.

In this day of the most modern equipment and fixtures it is hard to realize that in the beginning the emphasis was only on "bigness"—enough space to make piles and stacks of merchandise. Any old building that was big enough would do. I just kept adding to my place because I soon found out that, if the customer had to make a choice between shopping in the cruder buildings with little or no personal service, or paying higher prices for these extra services, the lower price would always win out. Besides, it was clear that displays attracted the customers more than just a few, tidy items on a shelf, and, in some mysterious way, made them feel as though they were truly getting a bargain—something that could not be achieved without merchandising.

Variety was another advantage we had over the small stores (and even the chains) especially in our produce department. They carried only a few of what we called "hard items" such as potatoes, apples, a few cabbages and things that could be kept in boxes and set in the aisles. My produce department was like a green and luscious growing garden, displayed with great care for freshness and beauty. We also kept attractive fresh produce out on the sidewalk. The combination of such variety in addition to the low prices pleased the public, and business grew so rapidly that I just kept adding on to the building until it was many times its original size.

One great Supermarket did not spring up like a shining light for others to follow. I think it was rather a simultaneous thing with different merchants in different parts of the country responding to the needs of the people of the nation. The Great Depression was a different situation than our recession of the 'seventies', in which there were actual shortages. In the Depression years, there were actual surpluses and there was an urgent need to find an efficient means to move large quantities of merchandise to the people. How the great merchandising markets were formed to distribute these surpluses and make it a permanent way of life is one of the romantic stories of America. I am glad I was part of it.

The essential features of the Supermarket were huge displays of merchandise moderately priced and easily accessible; the displays were large enough for the customers to serve themselves, not one at a time as in the old days at Dubossar, but many at a time. A display man was needed to put them up, then keep them replenished, but less help was required throughout the store. Although the public had little difficulty adjusting to the new system, we promoted it wholeheartedly, and they came to accept it as soon as they realized how much they saved on their overall food bill. Price-appeal became the theme of the Supermarket.

Now we had to be sure of always moving the large inventory. Newspaper advertising was the ideal medium for that. I didn't mind using my showmanship, either, and I put out "hot ads" to bring in as many people as I could. I found that people would travel from as far away as Provo and all the surrounding towns to buy the 'specials' advertised. For my week-end specials, I would use "leaders" consisting of the items my customers would need for week-end dinners—usually meat or fowl that would fluctuate between twenty-five and thirty cents a pound.

Butter was regularly at a quarter, and in my ad I would often run it for seventeen cents. Other leaders would include ground beef at ten cents a pound, onions ten pounds for fourteen cents, bananas five cents, and eggs from fifteen cents to a quarter a dozen. These prices were designed to bring the customers into the store where they would buy their whole supply of groceries at other low prices. Pot roast by the pound was eighteen cents, pork roast twenty cents, lamb seventeen cents and ham twenty-nine.

A staple such as flour was five pounds for twenty-seven cents, Heinz soups were nine cents a can, peas ten cents, rolled oats ten pounds for forty-three cents, peanut butter seventeen cents, and marshmallows ten cents a pound bag. Apples were seven pounds for a quarter, sweet potatoes three pounds for a dime, oranges thirteen cents a dozen, and lemons fifteen cents. Apple cider was ten cents a quart, thirty-five cents a gallon and a dollar sixty-five for a five-gallon barrel. Ice cream sold for twenty-five cents a quart. With prices like these, the shoppers in my place never seemed to stop buying. One man who owned a restaurant in Delta came every week and loaded up his truck. I had underestimated the magic power of saving a few pennies, but to each customer, a few pennies saved each week was magic indeed. Sometimes, a family spent as much as five dollars to lay in a supply of groceries. They would pick up their non-food items such as soap, at a nickel a bar, and toilet tissue at six rolls for a quarter.

Governor Blood used to call me up on the phone and modestly ask, "Would you please put four rolls of toilet tissue in a paper bag so I can pick it up?" Then he'd come by in his big automobile. Naturally people were curious what he bought, so, even though I tried to keep his secret, my place soon gained added luster as the store where the Governor bought his toilet paper.

One cannot burn the candle at both ends without burning it out. I became so tired it was obvious that the only way to manage was with better organization and planning so I could get more sleep, all of which were necessary to any future expansion, anyway. I needed a square meal every day instead of hot dogs and hamburgers. My wife and I talked it over and we made a plan to eat better meals and hire more people to take some of the burden off my shoulders. She understood. More stores required turning some of the responsibility over to others anyway. I had been a one-manager operation with only the boys to help me. From these boys I would develop new managers. I put on my one and only suit and stopped rushing to wait on my customers. This was relaxing, and it felt good to be out of my overalls—a first real lesson in management.

The first consideration in expanding was the leasing of a building. To get into a building and equip it with fixtures and supply the inventory would cost sixty thousand dollars. A good manager would cost forty dollars a week and clerks sixteen dollars apiece. I needed a cashier and a fruit and produce man in each store. Altogether, the running expenses would be around two hundred dollars for help. I believed so much in advertising that I was willing to spend fifty dollars a month on that. With careful projection I would be able to swing it. If I could get the credit, I would go ahead.

The Depression was really not a hindrance to my expansion plans. Many companies who were stuck with large inventories were willing to give me credit to move the merchandise.

My first expansion was Number Two at Third South and Fourth East on the south side of the square cut out of the corner of the block. Today, it seems incredible to me that I could have accumulated enough money by 1932 to even think about building another store, but I had surmounted so many problems between 1928 and 1932 that I felt I could tackle the world. I leased the building there with the idea of converting it into a large establishment for retailing foods and household items. Many said it would not work, but by my own test I thought it was a sound idea.

This Number Two covered 6,600 square feet plus backroom space enough to handle volume business on the same block as a hamburger store and a Snelgrove's Ice Cream Parlor. My entire layout of fixtures was cheaply constructed, giving a rough-looking appearance. I built cheap, rough tables and loaded them with merchandise. A hundred and fifty baskets were piled by the front door so that a customer could pick up a basket, go around and pick out the merchandise he wanted, and carry it to the checkout. The checkout stand was not like the sleek, modern ones we see today, but a rough, counter-type idea with a place to put the groceries while checking. The meat, delicatessen and produce were checked out of each department, but all were under one roof and one management.

In preparation for opening day, we hung dozens of banners from the ceiling, put up blaring signs everywhere, inside and out, and planned a big, splashy ad in the newspaper. When people read the ad featuring their favorite brands at such low prices, they flocked to opening day in such crowds that it exceeded my hopes. That first ad was really hot: Quaker Oats at three cents; Lifebuoy (extremely popular then) was four cents a bar; Maxwell House Coffee, "Good to the Last Drop," was twenty-two cents a pound. We had record sales on opening day, which continued right through the week, totaling the unbelievable sum of close to five thousand dollars. (Today one of our openings brings in four hundred thousand dollars.) More than half of this business came from the grocery department, but we were making history in food distribution, and right in the middle of the Depression, too. It also marked the beginning of a new type of retailing that was to revolutionize the whole industry. I found that signs saying "Help yourself and save the difference" had a strong psychological appeal to customers who had to stretch every penny as far as it would go. It also enabled me to understand my competitors.

More men were hired to work in the store. There was so much unemployment that they were glad to get any kind of a job. Super marketing required a totally different kind of personnel than was needed when I hired the boys to wait on customers. With self-service and a checkout stand, fewer people were required to run a much larger business than the smaller one. It was a matter now of having men to put up the displays and a checker to check out the customers. Our bookkeeping was still simple but our bookkeeper still had to balance up whatever was in the till each night against what had to be paid out each day. Employees were paid on Monday. They received their wages in cash in little envelopes. This still gave me the advantage of weekend business to meet the payroll. It was no longer a one-man operation but I still continued to do all the buying, planning and checking on things every day.

My critics and the skeptics waited for my luck to peter out, but they were proved wrong. Business only got better. Each week, the crowds grew bigger and many drove from Ogden and Provo to buy. This method of catering to the masses while handling costs and sales under one roof eliminated costly service and created this tremendous volume which started a chain-reaction of mass-production, mass distribution, and more and more volume purchasing. Hence, we were increasingly able to purchase and retail food at such bargains that we could advertise prices lower than the chains like Piggly Wiggly, O. P. Skaggs and Safeway. The joy of it all was that people could eat so well for so little. Slowly, the skeptics started coming to buy, but the critics and competitors remained aloof and hostile. Their comment was "Give him enough rope and he will hang himself." We seemed to defy all these predictions and within six months opened up Number Three at the corner of Twenty-first South and Lincoln Street in Sugarhouse.

As we grew, so the management problems grew. I didn't like the way my head produce man was behaving toward others. He was authoritarian and worked the men under him in a cruel manner. Talking to him a few times about it was of no avail. Being of a different nature myself, I am uncertain why I ever allowed him to work those people so late and so hard. I asked him to please change his attitude toward the help. When he didn't answer me I assumed my point had gotten across, but whenever I checked on him I would find that he had made the men work even longer hours than before. They tolerated his abuse rather than lose their jobs.

A good friend hauling produce from California for me invited me on a fishing trip. Before I left, I appealed to my manager not to overwork the staff, but when I came back, I was angered to find that he had worked one man eighteen hours a day. I fired him on the spot. Deciding not to be away from the business any longer, I turned down my friend's invitation to go to California with him to bring back a load of produce. I took him out to the airport. Five minutes after the plane took off it crashed.

We also had the problem of pilferage. Heretofore, it was only some of the clerks who pilfered and even then if it hadn't been for some of my honest boys we would not have made it. Later, Roy Simmons, who became president of Zion's Bank, and Izzy Wagner, the millionaire, jokingly said, "We really saved you, Maurice. If we had taken just five dollars out of the till each day, we would have broken you." But as the business grew pilferage became a real problem because now the customers had a better chance of pilfering. No matter how many we caught, we couldn't seem to stop it. We were always worrying about losing our gross. One girl was caught and taken upstairs. She took out a gun, and I said, "Put that toy away!" she shot at the floor and that floor shook. A man jumped on her back and she ran down the stairs with him still on her back. Near the bottom of the stairs, one of our men held out his arms to stop them and she shot him through his shirt, barely missing the flesh. She had shot her husband the week before.

Through all our struggles we came out very well though. From everywhere I heard stories of successful Supermarkets through M. M. Zimmerman's magazine, and I came to realize that we too were in the Supermarket business.

I met Mr. Zimmerman who was a leader in the Supermarket field. He gave me some good advice because he had such a vision of the future. He told me that this sort of market was advancing so fast that I would be wise to watch. I went to see how other markets were doing things whenever I was able to get away, to copy any ideas that seemed successful. Since "copying was cheap" I did incorporate many ideas into my plans, but seeing different markets also stimulated my own thinking, and besides imitating others, I did some innovating of my own. I also continued to think about not only customer relations but about our dealings with the people who served us in our business. I wrote a letter to Phil:

Dear Phillip,

Remember our merchandising days? I now have three stores and am doing a big business in groceries, produce, and meat. We have added a bookkeeper to our staff and a manager that does all the buying for the groceries. I still do all the produce buying, and am gaining a reputation for having the best produce in town. I suppose the reason is that it's true. Not only do I buy a variety of fruits and vegetables, but I buy it in large amounts so the customers have a feeling of plenty.

I can be as hardheaded as some of the cabbages I buy, however. If one of the salesmen doesn't give me a price that I want to pay, I just don't buy from him anymore. Price is my middle name.

The other day though, something happened that I did a great deal of thinking about. Bill and Art, my grocery buyer and bookkeeper, came into the office laughing. When I asked them what the joke was they told me a prank they pulled that they thought was hilarious. But it didn't strike me so funny. We have chairs where the salesmen wait and sometimes they are kept waiting a long time. Bill and Art had sawed a couple of inches from the chairs' front legs, making it uncomfortable for them to sit down while waiting their turn.

This really bothered me. I locked myself into my little office for about two hours. I mulled the situation over in my mind and decided that it was very wrong to treat anyone with so little respect.

That afternoon I called a meeting of all my employees. I really laid down the law about being rude to salesmen or anyone with whom they came in contact. I told them we could not expect to have good business relations with others if they built up enmity towards us. I wanted a complete change.

You would have thought that no one had heard the word "courtesy" before. They seemed surprised I insisted on it.

This turnabout brought almost instant results. Already the people that sell to us are different people; acting differently towards us, and even giving us better buys. I am glad now that I was so shaken by the episode that I did something about it. I intend to make it a crusade.

It is ridiculous to hurt people and it is an especially poor way to treat potential customers. I do not like the idea of being rude to salesmen because they seem to be more or less at our mercy. It is going to be hard, for many people have a tendency to slip back to their old way of insulting bread and milk salesmen and telling them to get the hell out of here, but this is one policy I intend to keep up from now on. I'm hoping to be able to expand my business and build new stores in the next few years. I think back often on those days that started our marketing career when we went out selling our merchandise from those baskets.

Try to come out here this year and see the stores I now have.

Love,

Maurice

Observation:

If Maurice started his expansion in 1932 my father was now sixteen years of age. A few years after Maurice opened the third store I would have been born, because I remember the third store in detail as a young child about 1942-45. During the summer or on Saturdays, my father would take me very early to that store and he would set up the produce. He was fast and meticulous. I often wondered where he leaned such a trade because his skill was a sign painter at home— something he learned from an art school in Salt Lake. After he finished, I would follow him up the stairs into a dark storage room with special lamps over a long banner table. It was here that all the store front signs were made. This store was closest to our home. His sign shop was later moved to store #1 across the street from the first stand. Maurice had rented a wrestling ring after the depression. He kept the wide stairs going up to the balcony's, which was later a toy and hardware store. The drug and groceries were on the lower level. The sign shop was up the back stairs where the general offices were. I distinctly remember someone named Art. He was shorter than my father and in good humor all the time as depicted by Maurice. According to Maurice he was the buyer of the produce and would order signs for the front of the stores.

Maurice mentioned a buyer for the grocery or can and packaged foods. This was my uncle Jack although Maurice did not reference him by name.

Often on Saturdays I would explore the back rooms and take a tour to see the new displays and signs that my father would build.

I was not hired until I was about 15. This was when the sign shop was moved again to the other side of the back stairs. My uncle Jack took some of the old sign space for his office. This is when I was trained to paint signs, but mostly to fill in and paint displays. I mentioned this in the preface.

Ronald Kelsch

9th South and State store just east of the 9th south and Main food mentioned in this chapter. Note the garden center to the right and the sign designed by Clarence Kelsch longest time employee and friend.

Transition

*To be able to incorporate the old and have
the courage to try the new - to be aware of
one's surroundings and alert to his opportunities,
makes way for progress.*

14.

Transitions

Meantime our children had been growing up. Marjory was a teenager - pretty and full of fun; Keith was a good-looking, all-round American boy, and up-coming athlete, and Pat was a brunette with a great zest for living. They were wonderful children who always brought us a lot of happiness.

It was soon clear that we needed to move from that little, two-bedroom house on Kensington Avenue to something bigger. "We bought a two-story house on Yale Avenue near Thirteenth East, just a few doors east of the Garden Park L.D.S. Ward. (By now Inez had taken all three children to be baptized into the Mormon Church, which made their Grandfather and Grandmother Williams very happy.)

Buying that house was a bold venture, but it was very comfortable, and especially nice for the youngsters. Our backyard sloped down into the lower part of Red Butte canyon, which extends into the residential district. There was a cabin down there in the woods, and a stream which all the family could enjoy in the summer and where we liked to entertain our friends.

We came to love our neighbors there. Next door to us lived the Sterling Sill family. I used to tell Sterling that my property was worth more than his because mine was next to a Mormon, while his was next to a Jew. Our new home seemed to open a new way of life for us.

In 1935 we bought the New England Bakeries that had belonged to Mr. and Mrs. Chapman. We had become acquainted with them because one of their fifteen outlets was next to our store on Ninth South and Main Street. After Mr. Chapman died Mrs. Chapman sold them to us and they became another merchandising venture.

No longer were there neat rows of cookies behind glass cases, but following our pattern of business, we piled bakery goods all over the counters and made displays for the people to choose from.

But there were other problems--our competition caused us problems with the Union. They promised the Union that if they could get us to join first they would follow.

At first we refused but the picket lines was playing havoc with the business so we gave in and joined. Our competitors never did.

In spite of all these problems we were on our road to expansion.

I was ready to open another store. The Supermarket was going to be a great innovation in the nation. By this time the customer was well aware of the differences between the Supermarket against the chains and independents. Our type of stores would allow the price-conscious wife to buy the majority of her food needs as well as other household items at competitive prices.

I leased the property at North Temple and State Streets for my fourth store from the Mormon Church, constructing the whole building with the understanding that it would revert to them in twenty years.

In spite of the Depression, I was very optimistic about our country's emerging from it. On opening day in late summer of 1937, we had a parade that went right down Main Street. I had arranged for the wholesalers to fill their trucks with groceries and ride in the parade, led by a brass band. On each side of the trucks there were banners that read "THE DEPRESSION IS OVER," and "FORGET THE DEPRESSION—THINGS ARE LOOKING UP." People were already leaving the W.P.A. and businesses were beginning to hire again. My opening helped to stimulate trade and I wanted to go all out in creating an atmosphere of hope. We built a platform in front of the store and had the band playing and entertainment going during the opening.

I continued to learn from other successful merchants. This is a great world for adventures if you don't overestimate yourself and are willing to learn. It was a very competitive time. We had a price war going all the time with Safeway, Sewell and Piggly Wiggly. I undersold many, of my products to promote business. At first they paid no attention, but the more successful I became the greater concern I was to them. I was a fighter and when they invited a fight I loved it.

They even tried to go through legal channels to stop me. The Fair Trade Commissioner came and said I would be arrested every week until I agreed to stop lowering prices, and I was, until I was brought before a judge who was a customer of mine. He announced to them that he could not see anything wrong in lowering prices for the public, and he threw the case out. I couldn't have stopped lowering the prices. My business was built on low prices. This was among my most trying times. They tried other ways to get at me. One day, an inspector came in and insisted one of our clerks sell him a certain can that had no label, to trap me on a technicality. Next, they tried to get us on our weights. This was hard to watch, because the shrinkage that took place in the time between selling and buying potatoes, for instance, caused many of the problems in weight control. Once an inspector found a lesser weight and thought he surely had a case against me. The potatoes had shrunk.

Another time, one of my butchers thought he would please me by putting tomato juice into the hamburger to make it appear redder. I found out in time and fired him. Had we been caught I do not know what would have happened.

It was a problem to sell things at such low prices and still make my men feel responsible for a certain amount of growth in profit, and in making and maintaining a good reputation. Men who did not cut a good gross would be in trouble as managers.

Advertising seemed to me a must. At first, I did not make enough profit to justify the advertising so I just kept on finding ways to improve and increase business until it did "pay to advertise."

Things seemed to go quite well after that and the country started to emerge from the depression which helped us.

It was the rumblings of war around the world, a war that the United States would enter in 1941, that was to change the patterns of our lives and our business.

By this time I had started to become involved in civic affairs and one of the first trips in this venture was a trip with the Arthur Bohns to the Southeastern part of the Untied States for the Exchange Club, stopping in Chicago on the way back. There, a wire was waiting for us, saying that our son, Keith, had been stricken with paralysis while playing on the East High Football Team. He had excelled in all sports when, overnight a tragedy happened. He went into the game with some infection, and he was thrown all over the field by the other team. The coach tried to take him out, but he begged to be allowed to stay in, and play the game out. He often told me afterwards that he could hardly stand the pain. The nervous system at the base of his spine had burned out and he was left a paraplegic. The pain of seeing my strong athletic son stricken was more than I could bear. Inez and I had a hard a time adjusting to the situation as Keith did.

Keith was bedridden a long time. The use of his legs was never recovered. Penicillin had just been developed, but it was difficult to get because so much was going to the armed forces.

One day, Abe Guss, a young businessman who through polio had also become a paraplegic, came to visit Keith, and told him: "Bed is no place to improve." Keith was challenged. He fired his nurse and got out of bed. It wasn't long before, with certain contraptions, he could drive a car and we bought him one made with special hand controls that made it easy for him to drive manually. The car helped a great deal in making him mobile and restored the "sense of speed" that he had enjoyed before. Abe and Keith became friends and developed a social life once they were able to get around together.

Our daughter Marjory was at the University of Utah. We all felt for her when her fiancé, Don Mackey, went into the Service. Later during the war Don returned home on leave and they were married in a garden ceremony at our home.

My daughter Pat soon married Tom Panos, a Salt Lake man with a Greek background in another wedding performed at home. Tom came into the business and it was wonderful to have him working with the family.

After Keith married Pat, a Catholic, at the Cathedral of the Madeleine, our family was a mini-United Nation. We all have been very frank with each other. The wide variety of ethnic and religious backgrounds reflected in our family has been a source of pride rather than of dissent. Religion is a personal thing. To this day, I am proud and happy to say that my children and grandchildren feel very free to talk with us on any subject at all. We all respect each other's beliefs, from the youngest to the oldest.

After the war when the young men of our family was working beside me in the business I was proud and happy. I was proud of their confidence in my merchandising style and ideas for the future.

With their fresh ideas added to my experience, we were very ambitious. They broadened my outlook on becoming better merchants.

It was a time of reconstruction, of getting our country's economy back on a peacetime basis and it was exciting to be a part of that development.

The first non-food items were introduced with just a rack at a time. My two main men who had helped me build the business threatened to quit if I ventured into the drug business. I was thinking of Keith and his future and nothing was going to stop me from developing a department he could handle. I let them go.

Keith had already begun learning various aspects of the business. The idea of a companion business to our food markets: drugs and toilet goods, household utensils, toys, cosmetics, hardware, had intrigued me for several years. I started planning this in earnest the last year of the war. Keith and Don pitched in and we tried to get that end of the business going, but they didn't have it rosy. Because industry had not yet re-adjusted to peacetime production, there were still many products made of metal which were doled out in allotment to the different retailers. We wanted to give our customers drugs, cosmetics and similar needs for a better price than they had been getting at the current Drug Stores. Yardley's were the only people who would allow us to retail their cosmetics. The others wanted fancier outlets, separate from food stores, but as time went on and we proved ourselves others sold to us.

Keith had an understanding of the medical items and was very valuable in building up the pharmacy business so that it got a good foundation.

Very few stores were handling drug store inventory of such variety. Still to come were new drugs developed during the war by the armed forces and which were now beginning to be made available to the public, such as antibiotics (which had been a Godsend for Keith personally).

Like every other war, this one had reaped a bumper crop of war babies. That was going to help our toy business.

We were glad to see our employees who had served their country come back. Women had done a fine job of taking over while they had been gone. We immediately undertook to employ as many handicapped veterans as possible, and I took an interest in developing a training program so they could get back to normal civilian jobs.

Don and Keith took on a good deal of the non-food part of the company and in 1946 we formed the Grand Central Drug Stores.

Tom and I took over the food stores, and Don and Keith the new Drug Chain. I proposed a four-way partnership, and when they consented, I had the business put into a four-way ownership right then.

All metal had been used for war production and there was still practically nothing made of metal yet to be bought. We sent our clerks out with pocketsful of money to buy whatever they could anywhere that was made of metal: toys, egg-beaters, pans, anything at all that could be picked from here or there, even other retail outlets. Don heard of a sale on tricycles. We ran over there and bought them all, took them out of their boxes and put them together, advertised them for sale and brought in many new customers. Our trouble was being new in the non-food business. Factories sold their products to their old customers first. I still recall our first all-metal ad after the war: toy trucks, aluminum kitchen ware, hairpins, and electrical gadgets.

In New York the wholesalers turned me down on toys, and I finally bought anything available in desperation. Mr. Pensick, a California based wholesaler, also in New York for toy purchases asked me what other toy companies had sold me. I told him, "You wouldn't sell me anything so I bought these," showing him the invoices. He took one look. "That stuff's no good," he said. "Go downstairs and get a secretary to cancel all those orders. I'll sell you some good items."

Now we were really in the toy business. When his shipment arrived we put a full-page ad in the comic section of the newspaper and parents flocked in. Our fixtures for displaying toys were still made of orange crates, ply-board and crepe paper. Price, like everything else, was always the drawing card. We used the same techniques to sell non-food items that I had found so successful in food retailing—volume buying, low prices, large displays, signs and large newspaper ads. Actually, the response to this allowed us to sell more in a week than we formerly sold in six months. It was not advertising per se that did it, but advertising designed with mass merchandising.

We learned to be guided by the customers as to how to display toys. For instance one time, I took the dolls out of their boxes and hung them by their necks on strings above the counters. Needless to say, that didn't go over at all! We learned fast how to display each product for better sales.

We made great efforts to procure for our customers the best quality at low prices. There was real enjoyment in searching out the items people wanted, finding them first and getting them to the public first

As more goods came into production, the old excitement of the competitive market came back.

Of course, my most energetic period had been when I was young and strong, ready to fight at the drop of a hat to win out over my competitors, but I still found this very stimulating. Competition makes people produce. The young people with families coming along worked hard, trying to outdo competition. Competition is natural to man, and if it is channeled into productive lines, the individual himself benefits, as do those depending upon him as well as the community at large. Henry Ford was always a good example of how a competitive spirit brought the American masses a car they could afford. This stimulated many other industries, such as steel, rubber, fabric and plastic.

Don had a good many ideas for merchandising. One of his best moneymakers literally backfired, though. He had a wonderful display of fireworks on the mezzanine floor of our big store on Ninth South and Main Street. He had a selection in plastic bags and they were "selling like hot cakes." Because of Utah's two July holidays—Independence Day and Pioneer Day. We had an unusually big stock on hand.

One afternoon a ten-year-old boy set a whole row of fireworks alight. A blaze started that soon got out of control.

"Get out!" I yelled at Art Bowen, our cashier who was counting the money. "Forget the money!"

We cleared everybody out, making sure there were no children left inside the building as the crowds of customers and employees moved quickly out of the store, just before the whole place went up. For a few minutes it was quite spectacular. Fireworks and Roman candles were shooting off in all directions. There was little the firemen could do. They did their best, but finally were forced to just keep it from spreading to adjoining buildings. The crowds gathered to see one of the biggest fires of the season and I thought "There goes up in flames the best slides of Russia I will ever have."

To stand by and see something you've created—something valuable and personal go like that is a terribly helpless feeling. We were underinsured and we suffered quite a loss. It was especially bad for us because we were just opening up a new non-food store on Ninth South and State, on the adjoining corner and had put out an enormous amount of money. The burned building was to have been remodeled into a large food market with offices upstairs.

Because of the financial strain from the fire, we decided to sell all the grocery stores to Mayfair. The time had come anyway when the non-food stores had done so beautifully and that whole field was such a challenge we could go completely into junior department stores. I hated to part with produce and groceries for sentimental reasons, but we made a handsome profit and new ventures of expansion awaited us.

We opened new Grand Central stores in Idaho and Wyoming, where we tried to establish good relations, and I think we have. The public responded well to every grand opening and made us welcome in their communities. Grand Central stores had long since become known all over the Intermountain West for "good shopping" and shoppers came from everywhere. It is not unusual to see stockmen, Indians, farmers, sportsmen and tourists mixing with the regular shoppers from the urban areas in our aisles. Our growing reputation for wide variety and good value has been sustained by constant administrative attention to quality.

I had promised Mayfair when I sold them our grocery business not to go into competition with them for five years. That time was up. I opened another group of five food stores called Warshaws, which were equipped with the latest of everything and very handsomely designed. We featured fine delicatessen and gourmet foods from around the world and we imported fish in variety from New York.

It was good to have fresh fruits and vegetables in my place again. The produce in the past several years had vastly improved in quality and packaging and beauty. Tom and I did well and these were stores of which any owner would be proud.

But Grand Central's unique merchandising style was becoming more popular. This was the company's overwhelming commitment. If we wanted to expand we could not divide our efforts. Once again a good offer came, this time from Smith Food King, and the other partners and I concurred on selling the Warshaw Stores. This freed a lot of money for the expansion of non-foods.

Public relations have always been important to both the business and the family. We have tried to play our role in a forward looking community and to set a good example as merchants, but we realize that people are people. We have never expected perfection of the public or ourselves. Making an effort to relate to people, in the family and in business, has paid off.

There were times when we had our labor troubles. As the unions increased their demands with changing times and conditions we always came to terms even though people are never at their kindest in a fight. From the time Grand Central started making money our pay was generally better than other comparable firms. Together with the unions, we have an excellent combination of fringe benefits. Grand Central is the only non-food retail company in Utah that is unionized. We always paid more than the minimum wage, and have the highest paid clerks.

With young people in the business, it grew more creative. While for a long time it was no less work for me, at least I had some good company in the struggle. We still had to be very much on top of the job, running to this store or that store, seeing to problems night and day. The fact that my partners were good at business, and that all our managers and buyers were energetic, and had the business as their first interest, now freed my mind for me to spend more time in service organizations.

Observation:

Transitions covered my families entire experience with Maurice from about 1939 to 1979. I remember the war when my father had no automobile because of a waiting period. He walked a block or two and took the bus down twenty-first south to the Store #2 where he set up produce and then spent the rest of the day painting signs. When I was sixteen I started working at the 9th South Store in the sign shop while my father created newspaper ads.

I actually witness the start of the fire as the fireworks were igniting one after another. I ran to get a fire extinguisher out side of the printing press room, but someone had beaten me to it. I remember Maurice telling everyone not to worry about loosing their jobs.

We opened up shop in an old drive in restaurant. Both the advertising and sign shop was located their until I went on a mission for the LDS Church. When I returned a new central warehouse and general offices had been built. I started in the sign shop with the same familiar faces. In time I was moved to advertising and newspaper layout for the out-of-town stores. I had to reduce four pages to one and keep everything in.

Eventually I became the director of all advertising. I was managing all the non food—including production, printing, and signs while my father designed the layouts for the new Warshaws foods.

When Maurice's latest food store effort was sold to Smiths Food King, I left the company and went into advertising production My father remained as the in-house agency for television. At times there were complaints about the advertising and I was asked by Maurice to come in and help adapt new techniques. The one in charge was actually from a 100 store company that was my client until it was sold. Resentment was too strong. I was even asked to help D. Smith assume to regain the quality of the food ads, but that was far too political. In both cases I said, "I could help them." I did however continue producing TV commercials for Grand Central and Keith Warshaw & Company. Keith left shortly after me to do his own thing for the same reason I do not care to mention. It had nothing to do with his father or my relationship with Maurice. Keith Warshaw and company had everything from produce and meat to high fashion. It was like old times to Maurice who visited the downtown store almost daily. Keith even hired many familiar faces from Maurice's last attempt at the food business. It was a great downtown idea, but it failed because of poor financial management by someone too young for the job. I continued to work along with Maurice in the production of documentaries for the March of Dimes.

This was the period that my mother spent all her time with Maurice just to write his history. I spent as much time in Maurice's office as I did with Keith before I left for California. When the book was first publish, it was popular in certain circles, and the LDS church created a musical around the book and performed it at the Promise Valley Playhouse. I remember producing a record in an excellent sound studio I used to create TV commercials.

When Maurice died shortly after my father retired, Grand Central Stores was sold to Fred Myer. As of today Kroger owns the residue of both food and drug from the original Grand Central or the stores were given up to other merchandising. So many business clients that I had over those years, continually made the same mistakes—they do not adapt to changing markets as Maurice proved so essential. First downsizing and then it always ends in a sale for a lack or hard work and adaptation to the needs of local clients. When everything started to decline, I went to Los Angeles and witnessed the very same thing. I later retired to our small family business just seven miles north east of the old deserted Clarion.

Ronald Kelsch

PART TWO

*The previous chapter covered along time. What
follows covers perhaps Maurice true spiritual love that
that overlap his greater successes to the time he died.*

Ɛnriching our lives

chapter
one

15.

Enriching Our Lives

My affiliation with service organizations really started back during the war when the affairs of Europe interested Americans vitally, not only because the future of our fellow democracies was at stake, but because most Americans came from European backgrounds. The roots of our culture come from there. The public responded well to such appeals as British Relief, when the Luftwaffe besieged England.

I had meantime been made president of the Jewish Community Center. We had three types of synagogue in Salt Lake City. In addition, there was a community center attended by members of all three. It was a beautiful mansion on South Temple, and is now the Deseret Business College. At that time, the Jew was more isolated than today. Most clubs restricted their membership to a very small quota of Jews, or denied them membership altogether. The Community Center was the club where Utah Jewry expressed themselves more often socially. I served as president of that Jewish Community Center for six or eight years, and also of the B'Nai B'rith organization of Jewish men for two years.

One time, we had a social affair attended by nearly all the Jews in Utah. Suddenly, someone came in with the news that the United States had been attacked by Japan and that President Roosevelt had just declared war on Germany and the Axis countries.

We all left the party in sadness, scarcely able to believe it. Everyone knew the consequences of war, but everyone agreed that Hitler must be stopped. At that time, the entire Jewish community united in patriotism for America, where we felt so safe. Few realized at that moment that if Nazism won, every Jew, his children and grandchildren, no matter how little Jewish blood they had in their veins, would be hunted down and annihilated.

Americans were frightened by the idea of communism. The Russian Revolution's beginning as a people's honest effort to free themselves from tyranny was obstructed by the fact that Russia's counter-revolution resulted in tyranny under another name. Disciples of free enterprise in particular, feared the spread of communism. When the U.S.S.R. signed a non-aggression pact with Hitler, she lost many American sympathizers. Nevertheless, when Hitler attacked Russia, the Allied cause became linked with Russian survival. By the time America was attacked in 1941, the whole world seemed aflame, for practically all of Asia had fallen victim to the Japanese, and the other members of the Axis, Germany and Italy, had subjugated most of Europe. It was then that the soul of the Russian homeland, her people, appealed to the American heart.

For military reasons, America began to ship vast supplies of arms to the Russians east of the Nazi invasion lines, through Iran. The Russian people burned their farms and towns, practicing the scorched-earth policy for which they were so famous in Napoleonic days. Millions of them died and millions were homeless and without clothing or food. It was a time to forget politics and reach out to those who were now our allies in a mighty death struggle against the devil himself. Allied leaders appealed to Americans to help the Russian people on a personal basis. The job of organizing a Russian Relief organization in Utah was up to Arthur Gaeth and me. As co-chairmen we were to gather clothing to be shipped by boat from Portland in time for them to reach people in the U.S.S.R. before the freezing winter set in.

It was for me a time of soul-searching. Somehow, in the Russian people's hour of need the bitterness of the past fell away. I did not for a moment feel we would ever be able to relax our vigilance against communism or any other form of dictatorship, but I remembered people like the Kolosky family and others who had, in our time of peril, rescued us from certain death. I accepted the job.

It was at that time that I learned to appreciate the talents of the blind. People had contributed clothing generously, but they were so busy doing defense work that there seemed to be no available manpower to help us match the shoes and sort the clothing. The blind took on the job. Our headquarters were at the old fire station on First South and they worked there diligently until everything was shipped.

I had put so much energy into Russian Relief that they asked me to become chairman of the U.S.O. and the contact man for Bushnell Hospital, where many of the worst of the wounded were coming in from the theater of war in Southeast Asia. This so commanded my interest that, in addition to running my business, I had no time for social life. With the exception of not living in poverty any more, my wife was not much better off than before.

There were so many problems connected with the U.S.O. that I wondered how I would handle them all. Before becoming overall chairman of Utah's U.S.O. I was head of the Black U.S.O. (at that time there were two). I remember one incident vividly: A black man named Paul Robeson, the famous singer, came to entertain the men. I was able to make arrangements for him to stay at the Hotel Utah only on condition that he would agree not to eat there. When he arrived and found out that the White and Black U.S.O.'s were separate organizations he refused to perform. I had a hard time changing his mind, but he finally consented. The more he defended his people the more he was accused of being a communist, until he moved to Russia. I knew better.

My first job with the U.S.O. had been only with the black division and I had created a lot of hostility because I put locks and bars on all the storage we had. Too many things, especially food, had disappeared. In time they got used to it, and when I induced Fort Douglas to donate fifty-four beds and mattresses, pillows and bedding to the Black U.S.O. Club house, and filled them with soldiers who needed a place to stay, they calmed down. Meantime, there were beds going to waste, so I began admitting white soldiers to the black club, which was a Catholic project. One of the clergy objected, but it worked out very well and the men got on alright together. If the people of Utah wanted to invite some soldiers to dinner they had to contact me. I screened the invitations. Many people offered help, but wanting the boys to have a good time, I suggested they invite some young women to the dinners so the boys could communicate with others their own age and would not feel at such a loss in strange homes. Occasionally a letter from an irate mother would follow.

The entertainers were very generous during the war. Marion Anderson, one of America's greatest living singers, came to entertain the troops. She was not allowed to stay in the hotels and I had to make arrangements to have her stay at the home of a black family.

In spite of these problems, the public responded to help the soldiers. They did much to make a home away from home for them. Many people supplied money for hotel rooms or to tide a soldier over who was broke. I organized busloads of girls with chaperones to go dancing as well as entertain groups for the bases around Northern Utah.

Bushnell was a hospital for the most badly maimed. Here was my first real awakening to the terrible ravages of war. All kinds of damage to what had been beautiful, healthy people was seen there: mutilated bodies, broken spirits and ravaged minds. Even though I was worried about my business, this experience above all made me come to see that just making money was not enough to make me a good citizen and successful person.

I tried hard to learn how to help the soldiers at Bushnell, not wanting them to have just a crumb here and there, but to have as full a life as possible and to help break the loneliness and homesickness they must have felt. I learned that people who were isolated by illness, especially by crippling wounds, became timid, shy and weighed down by a sense of inferiority. It struck me that no man is master of his destiny, nor does anyone know when misfortune will come, but when it does come any agency or person who can help is God's blessing.

Being head of the Central Hospital Committee in charge of handling personal relations sometimes proved a more heartbreaking job than dealing with the patients themselves. Many letters of inquiry came to me from parents and sweethearts and wives whose great hope was to be united with loved ones. Sometimes they would not accept my answers and came long distances to visit particular boys. This was extremely difficult for me. How do you say to an eager young girl, "Forget him. There is nothing but pain in trying to continue the relationship." Sometimes they would insist on seeing their boyfriends, fiancés, husbands or brothers, and when they persisted there was nothing to do except let them see for themselves. Often three doors had to be unlocked before we arrived where the patient was. They didn't even recognize each other. It was not easy for them to give up the men they expected to love forever.

Bushnell also showed the hatred between nationalities, brought on by war and I began groping for an answer as to why men cannot get along with each other.

There were German and Italian prisoner-of-war patients who wanted a radio very badly, but no one would agree to contribute for that. People even criticized me for buying them one. These prisoners wanted even more to have haircuts, but the barber answered this request by saying he'd cut their throats. Finally I got a barber to realize that these P.O.W.'s were only kids who had been drafted. They had a right to look presentable.

We did what we could to help train the patients to use what was left of their remaining faculties. By now my son, Keith, had mastered so many obstacles that he could function very well. 'Ve brought him in as teacher for the many paraplegics there who were still trying to hold on to life. Working for the Government he brought his fellow paraplegics a lot of encouragement by his example alone. He memorized the books from the Surgeon General's office and read everything he could get to help him teach the men at Bushnell. He helped organize trips and shows for them, as well.

It was heartbreaking to watch the wounded in what we called "The Olympics" trying to participate in sports. Some of the amputees even tried riding horseback. The outpatients were every kind of amputee as well as victims of malaria and other devastating diseases besides the wounds.

Another idea was to give the men some art classes, and give them nude models. When those classes started men who couldn't draw an apple suddenly became artists and they came on crutches, in wheelchairs, on litters, everything. Was I glad when that day was over! We discontinued that class.

The different religions of course were catered to as far as possible. The Salt Lake Jewish community saw to it that kosher food was flown over from Denver for special Jewish holidays, and that they had a nice sitting room for services. Some of the Jewish boys from extreme orthodox families in New York were subsisting mainly on candy bars and koshered beef sandwiches made by Mrs. Eizen for fear of getting non-kosher food. They still mostly refused to take a chance on army food even after we wrote to the Rabbinate back East and got permission in writing for them to eat whatever was provided in an emergency.

Once I was on my way to Bushnell with three chaplains - a Protestant, a Catholic and a Jew with a load of small copies of the New Testament. My car skidded on the icy road and barely missed being crushed by a huge sand and gravel truck. The priest and minister reminded me that the Bibles in the trunk had saved our lives. The rabbi and I referred to the two huge kosher salamis.

I tried in those years to give the wounded men as much personal friendship as possible, but there were so many and they were so ill I was never sure how much contact really got through to them. However, once later in Chicago I was getting out of a cab and four veterans in wheelchairs hailed me and were glad to see me. They asked me to join them at a show the incapacitated men were giving that night.

The rewards to me from my war work were ample. It was a privilege to befriend the young men who passed through the U.S.O. clubs. Their eager faces—often showing great fatigue and loneliness. Their faces reminded me of our defenders—youth set aside to face a time of danger. They knew their duty and, while they grasped at any friendliness offered them and departed their loved ones with sorrow and even fear, they knew their duty and why they had to do it. That was a war most Americans felt they understood.

The patients at Bushnell symbolized what people will give for each other. Each man was there because of an enormous sacrifice. Each was now trying to rejoin the human race, to be whole again in mind if not in body. Those men's valiant struggle had just begun with the war's end, when the public would begin to forget them and they would have to go the long, hard, uphill road virtually alone. They showed me the work cut out for my future: to try to give the handicapped that extra boost which would help them attain their rightful place in our society.

The war's end brought much rejoicing everywhere, which for a time outshone all the sorrow it had caused. The

242 | Life More Sweet than Bitter

countries of Asia and Europe, which had been occupied, plundered or used as battlefields, lay flat on their backs. Very slowly and painfully, the world started to pick itself up and move forward again. Next followed the emergence, one after the other, of newly independent nations wanting their place in the sun. Some had been almost totally ruined by war. Others were almost untouched, but greeted their freedom by plunging into civil war that created huge refugee problems. Many were handicapped by eroded and worn-out lands and illiterate, underfed populations without the skills to meet the Twentieth Century. It is to the everlasting credit of President Truman and the American people that our country embarked upon an unprecedented program of help to former allies and enemies alike to get back on their feet. America had suffered a terrible loss of life, but we had not been invaded; we had food, medicine and machinery to share in abundance. We gave money, supplies or technical aid to countries in need. We set an example which made the next twenty years, as Mrs. Golda Meir put it, "Not only the era of the outstretched palm, but the age of the helping hand." It was in our own best interest to get the world economy moving again. We also gave with a good heart. The most significant movement of our time was the United Nations, where world leaders sought to avoid future conflict by discussion, debate and argument.

The U.N.'s specialized agencies, brought· help to the multitude of refugees, displaced peoples, and starving and homeless left in the aftermath of war by giving technical assistance to restore their countries to productivity.

I became associated with the Utah State Vocational Rehabilitation Organization for the Physically Handicapped.

This marked my serious entrance into the field of health and rehabilitation. I became active in the Utah Society for Crippled Children and Adults. In the next few years I was to join in the work of the National Committee on Jobs for Veterans; the American Cancer Society; the American Heart Association; the National Foundation, March of Dimes; and the Utah State Mental Health Association.

It is important that volunteer groups do not duplicate each other's functions, yet a combination of them working in a spirit of cooperation and coordination can be very effective.

Some of these have allowed me to accept awards for service as representing the many devoted volunteers with whom I work. They are not all recognized in the press and with medals; nor can all of them travel as I have. When American officials or heads of foreign states or institutions gave me a wonderful welcome and extended themselves to let me see their institutions and their countries, I considered this recognition of the organizations I represent. That is why I want to share my experiences in the field of public service.

More than anything else, I enjoy an organization that is producing well, running smoothly whether in business or philanthropy. I believe one should approach volunteer work with the same sense of responsibility as if being paid.

Today's young people are in some ways spoiled, while in others they are an improvement on their elders. They are getting a much bigger kick out of doing for their fellow man than they used to, and we are finding a lot of them in public service. Today on the March of Dimes TV Telethon I am the only old person on the show. Great! Young people can express themselves in a growing, creative organization, and no organization can survive unless they do.

I had in no way lost interest in the new developments in the postwar period, but in the back of my mind was always the picture of the young soldiers going through on their way to war, and the patients at Bushnell Hospital, with their broken bodies and disturbed minds—a terrible waste of human resources. I wondered whether man would change from this mad course, now that another war was behind us.

For some time I had reflected on the strange attitudes of man, who, with this great, beautiful world at his feet, filled with conveniences and luxuries beyond his forefathers' wildest dreams, periodically twists the useful employment of these luxuries and advantages into the pursuit of conflict.

Why do we not see how much more profitable peace is than war? The enormous sums spent on war could provide a high standard of living for the whole world. Does man prefer war to peace?

In the early fruit stand days I would teach somebody not to steal from me by punishing him. After I developed a big company I got used to giving orders and getting results. During the war, however, working with all kinds of people outside my family and business over whom I had no authority showed me how difficult it is to accept the slow pace of negotiation. Persuading volunteers to go your way takes giving a little and sometimes giving quite a lot. I learned that progress by negotiation is possible, and I began to envision the same potential for peace as my father before me, this time through the United Nations.

For the first time in my life circumstances permitted me to really explore my thoughts about peace, and I found that many others in the community shared my earnest belief in man's capacity to improve.

A widely representative group of Utah's outstanding leaders, led by Bishop Moulton, had organized the United Nations Association to gather support for the U.N. as a unifying body where nations could resolve their disputes without war, and for its specialized agencies. This Association stimulated me to a new awareness of the global character of man's problems, and the various approaches to their solutions. The one that claimed my attention immediately was UNICEF: United Nations International Children's Emergency Fund, whose program was to rescue children from malnutrition, disease and homelessness. My first assignment was to handle the "Trick or Treat" campaign, and I poured so much enthusiasm into it that they soon asked me to takeover the program for Utah.

One of my beginning projects was a brunch featuring the child star, Margaret O'Brien, at the Hotel Utah. People paid handsomely, but received a meal exactly like the one most of the world's children hoped to get from UNICEF: mush and a glass of milk. They saw, at a hungry hour, a little of what it takes to help a child, what it was like to go without, and the price of their tickets went for the children's fund. This sort of dramatizing and gimmicks, which we know the American people enjoy and respond to, have always paid off in raising money for the many causes I espoused from then on.

Not long afterwards, I met Mrs. Roosevelt at the United Nations in New York. In our. several conversations she impressed me very much with her sincerity and concern for the future of Americans and the part we must play in helping the world.

Inez and I have traveled to most of the countries on this earth in behalf of numerous organizations such as Care, The International Society for the Welfare of the Disabled, Unicef, Child Welfare, and many others. These were not just tourist trips, for which I paid for. We visited with many persons, concerned as we were with the handicapped, the homeless and dislocated, the sick, the blind and others in need of help. We visited hospitals, day care centers, and workshops. We traveled to remote areas to be on the scene to see the great need as well as the great accomplishments of the many organized groups working for the betterment of mankind.

Observation:

The map shows the many places that Maurice and Inez visited. In one of their trips to Russia, my father and mother accompanied them. The four were close. From my perspective it was a common event for my father to design special advertising in behalf of fundraising for

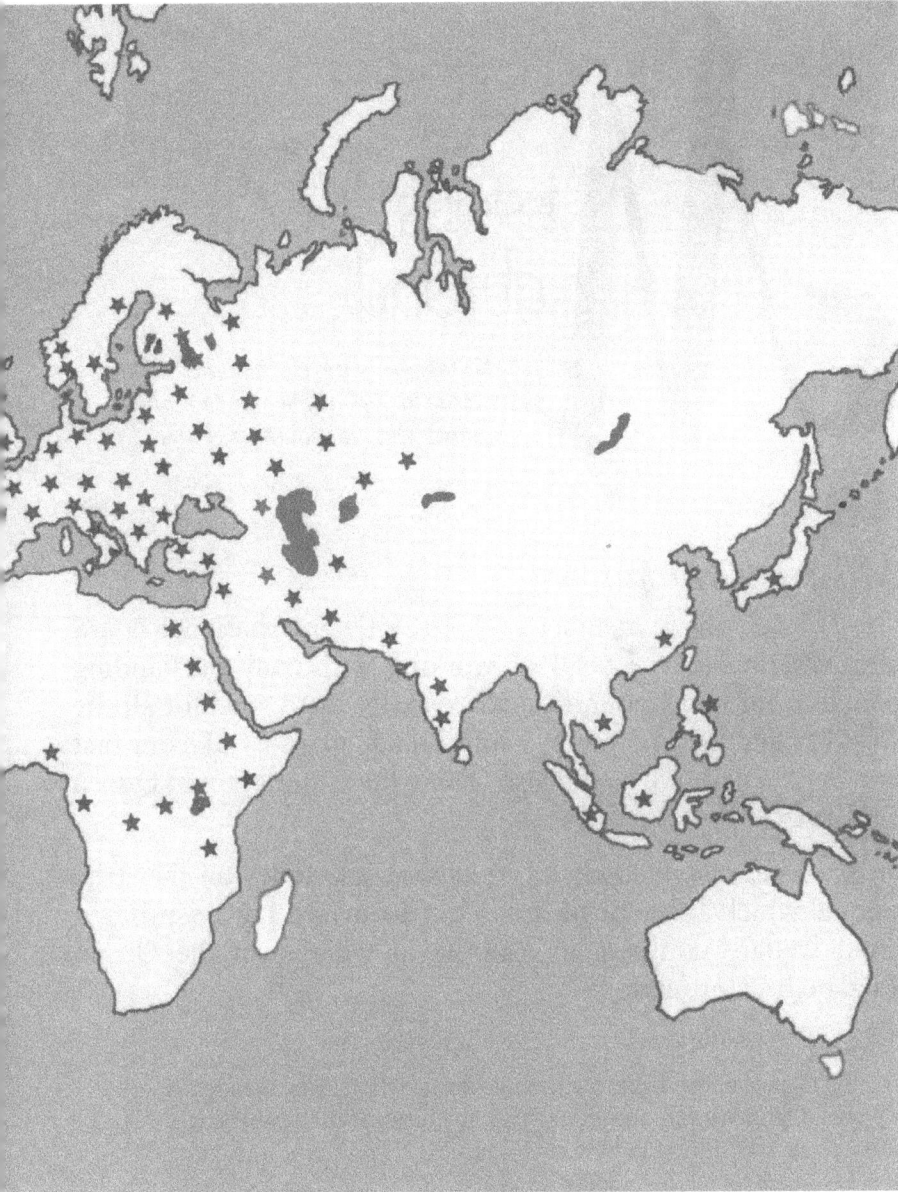

various organizations. One time he designed a full page depicting the history of Grand Central Stores. The headline was, "From push cart to supermarket." It won a national McCall's award. This was the first trip that the four took to New York to receive the reward.

Ronald Kelsch

M issions abroad

Maurice was a traveler from his youth,
Because he suffered, he was concerned.
Maurice was a philanthropist indeed.

16.

Missions Abroad

I became a member of UNICEF's international board and experienced the thrill of working with truly outstanding people from many countries, all devoutly concerned for all the world's children, and my wife and I made plans to take our first journey abroad. We would also take in the Coronation of Queen Elizabeth.

There were some very pleasant interludes on that trip, one of which I described in a letter to my Father regarding a child welfare congress in Yugoslavia while visit the Queen Elizabeth's Coronation:

Dear Father: July, 1953

I just came back from Yugoslavia where we attended a Child Welfare Congress. Tito, the head of the country, was very enthused to have it in Zagreb.

Our congress was held in the army barracks. When we had our banquet, the children were let out of school to see Tito, who was on the way to the army barracks and to our banquet.

One incident that was different was that some of the cookies for the banquet were hauled over in Tito's car, but anyway, the streets were lined with children waving small Yugoslavian flags.

Tito took a liking to Inez and invited us to his beautiful castle. I am happy to be part of the Child Welfare Organization. Am in a hurry right now, but will write you again soon.

Your loving son, Maurice

P.S. It rained all during the Coronation of Queen Elizabeth.

While abroad, I became acquainted with the work of CARE, and my interest in their program has proven to be a lifelong one. The officials of CARE projected with me a tour for each year to see one section of the world which was in need of their help. These were some of the most rewarding times of my life—times in which I would have the privilege of seeing CARE's work first-hand, which has been so successful in helping people help themselves. CARE's first project was sending food packages abroad from individuals to individuals. Soon they were sending tool kits with instructions for leading the poor peasant farmers of Asia, Africa and South America one step from their primitive agriculture. One very effective project was supplying sewing machines and related equipment to young village women in most of the countries of South America. I delivered to the young State of Israel's Hebrew University CARE's gift of $21,000 worth of books, and visited the project for teaching building trades to Arab refugees in Gaza.

One of the great lessons I have wanted to teach my fellow Americans interested in philanthropy is that giving money if you have it is easy. Giving yourself—your personal interest, your skills and experience along with the heart multiplies its value many times over. It brings you into contact with those who need what you have to offer, and you have the matchless rewards of seeing your contributions come to life in the improved health and minds of the receivers.

The more I traveled the less foreign people seemed "different" to me. They came to be just more of my fellow human beings with problems which, under other circumstances, could have been my own.

I became very enthusiastic about the United Nations specialized agencies: UNICEF, FAO (Food and Agriculture Organization), WHO (World Health Organization), ILO (International Labor Organization). In fact, most of the international agencies, helping the less fortunate to do something with themselves, attracted my participation. It is not possible to tell about them all. My travels of the past twenty-five years have spanned a period of extraordinary humanitarian advancement across the globe in a number of areas of human health. Some agencies have made such far-flung contributions we will probably never know the extent of the good they have done. No less important are achievements in America, of course, but I have not related them in detail here because they are already so well known. Unfortunately this is not the case with the overseas work.

The United Nations has let itself begin to favor one country against another—far from its original purpose. When that happens the same old causes of war are just around the corner. The peace we expected from the UN never showed up. We have not yet had a chance to prove that bringing advancement to the underdeveloped nations would actually enhance the possibilities of peace; but this is the hope upon which all the UN specialized agencies and many other international groups based their activities.

I began the first of several very long trips through Central and South America for the CARE Organization to investigate the most pressing needs of the people of those countries, including a survey of relief requirements for the area of earthquake damage in Chile. We also presented for CARE gifts such as sewing machines to village women in Costa Rica and jeeps for the agricultural work in Mexico.

Here were countries untouched by war, but also untouched by progress in many, many areas. In countries where the wealthy had lavish homes, the hillsides are covered with the shanties of the desperately poor, provided with no water or light or sanitation services nor have they any protection from the weather. There, in these dreadful heaps, stood the children of the UNICEF posters with staring, hollow eyes, distended bellies, distorted bodies with honey skulls and skinny little legs. These were the children we were to see everywhere in our future trips around the world.

It is the children in all the countries whose eyes follow you when you leave a country, and you feel those eyes upon you wherever you go, forever. But it is also the children who smile when you return, who show hope where hope has long since gone out of the faces of their elders, and it is the children who make you go back again and again.

I am not the first to ponder the question of why countries. such as those in South America have conditions of suffering as bad as those that were war-torn. I believe it is because they have no precedent set for them. We do not realize our good fortune in getting our country off to a good start through the free enterprise system which kept new persons and groups constantly setting precedents for change.

The Peace Corps should have a book written of its own. Its most successful programs were largely developed in South America. Our American young people in the Peace Corps at its height were the best ambassadors we ever had, and they left permanent change and new hope in many places where they worked. I met them in jungle and desert and city slums. They always took on tougher assignments than most diplomats.

Of course some of those with the greatest needs around the world are young people—young couples with responsibilities for aging parents or for younger brothers and sisters, and for little ones coming along of their own. They don't always look young, but they make up the majority of the farmers and workers helped by the Peace Corps.

At first it was thought by many that Peace Corps people would be too young to command respect in countries where older people always had the authority, but they were able to win over those of all ages and for the most part get the jobs done.

They took on everything from working in hospitals to teaching home economics to village women, to building sewers and roads and helping schools with recreation and teaching trades. Wherever we met them they were enthusiastic and glad to talk. Their living conditions were not the best so they were always happy to come to our hotel rooms and get a warm bath and have a get-together.

CARE had interesting projects throughout Latin America: a truck to bring water to the poor living in slum huts on mountain sides, for example; a derrick to help dig wells.

The Alliance for Progress was active on development projects in South America. In Colombia, for instance American loans were helping on low-cost housing.

We toured many wonderful projects, including UNICEF's malaria eradication project on the Amazon River.

Everywhere I went I showed slides of my markets and enjoyed showing people how we handle our produce. I even tried persuading the farmers to grade and clean their produce. Some of the ambitious ones would study my slides and ask many questions. I enjoyed talking, laughing and joking with them.

I also made two trips to Russia in the early fifties. I wanted to visit the Soviet Union to see at first hand the conditions left by the second "war to end all wars." They were staggering. Years after peace came many cities had still been unable to rise from their ruins. Not only did the troops suffer crippling wounds, but, because they had been invaded, their civilian casualties were horrendous. I found myself in the Soviet Union going through miles of hospital corridors studying methods and sharing experiences with the doctors and therapists of the country which probably had more disabled victims than any other.

As guests of the Organization for the Blind in the Soviet Union, we went all over the country and had the unusual opportunity to photograph its natural beauty, its many types of people, and the institutions for the blind which far exceeded ours.

Russia during the fifties was still secretive about her policies. The war had left her weak, both economically and socially. Soldiers had returned to a civilian life not much more amenable than the military one they had left. One Russian told me that "The Americans went home from war to prosperity, while the Russians came back to poverty and hunger. Many of us were reduced to eating cats and dogs to keep alive."

The average tourist in Russia never felt welcome. The Russians seemed evasive and you knew you were seeing only what they wanted you to see. In the medical field it was different. We were welcome visitors. They were enthusiastic about showing us through hospitals and rehabilitation centers.

Because I went to Russia in behalf of The Organization for the Blind, I did an intensive study in this area and found some very amazing facts. There were 165,000 blind people in the country. According to an old law which was still on the books, which had not been changed during the new regime, they themselves still owned 280 factories and apartment houses. I was amazed at how they functioned. They could produce as many manufactured goods as many of our modern factories.

When their doctors graduated from Medical School the government sent them wherever they wanted them to go. Graduate students were usually sent to practice in remote areas, or small villages. If they proved themselves there for two or three years they would then choose where they wanted to settle down—any place except Moscow.

One night we were all asked to a party and one of the young doctors asked if he could bring his girl along. We thought he would be all spruced up but when he came he had the same suit, shirt and socks he had worn for the last several days. Another young doctor told me he had gone to a Medical Congress and had met another doctor from Canada who actually had four suits.

From my tour of the hospitals, I saw people much the same as in the United States. The same patients, the same problems, sickness, and people in wheelchairs. They had their returned veterans and all patients were given the kind of medical treatment and nursing care that is given in the U.S. It seemed as though we had not left our own country. The Russian patients I met seemed to be at peace.

Of course in other areas it was not the same. They were always talking about their five year plan: that is, they planned everything out. In discussing it with them they would ridicule us because we had a waste economy. According to their propaganda the chief economic task of the U.S.S.R. had one aim in view: that is, a country on the road to peaceful enterprise. They spoke about a new factory daily; they spoke about conquering diseases in the interests of all mankind. They wanted to build six thousand new industrial plants a year and complete a fifty room apartment house every half hour. They were continuously talking about raising the educational, cultural, and technical level of their working people, attaining a high level of labor productivity, and economically surpassing the chief capitalist country which of course, meant us. They spoke a lot about the wealth of Siberia, and how they were going to open up 50,000,000 acres for industrial development.

They were concentrating on education for scientists, engineers, and skilled artisans. They made no bones about wanting to out produce us in the business of education and were always trying to show the difference between our waste economy and their controlled economy.

They taught that our economic system carried the seeds of its own destruction within itself, that lynching occurred almost daily, that minority groups were not well treated, and finally that the United States, with the help of other nations in the Western World was plotting the overthrow of the Soviet Union. They believed that we were building a military machine with the sole purpose of destroying Russia. This was the propaganda they fed daily to the people through any means possible.

In discussing merchandising with them I tried to tell them that our way of doing things, our way of advertising, acted as a stimulator to the merchant, consumer, and manufacturer, that through price range and many other factors there was a control on distribution. I tried to tell them that our way developed judgment and understanding in the consumer. It informed them of what was new and what was quality; it developed their art sense. I wanted to put the idea over that if things were presented in an artistic way people could develop their artistic sense and still choose the good from the bad. I wanted to say that in America people develop their ability to choose materials, ingredients, colors and styles. They could not understand. They did not have any choice.

Moscow was one of the cleanest cities in the world though. Wherever you went you would see people sweeping the streets. They would scrub the city twice a day. Lenin and Stalin were still in their tombs at that time—under glass. There was a continuous line filing past. It was a kind of procession. The lines were about a mile and a half or two miles long, all marching to the tombs.

Before we left I decided to go around to some of their libraries. The big library at Moscow had nineteen million books in it including magazine publications from all over the world. The whole library was patrolled by the police. They were stationed everywhere.

I went to visit the Red Cross. They certainly operated differently than we do. We allow other people to take part in it by giving a donation. They receive their allotment from the government. I tried to tell some how we did it but they didn't seem to know what I was talking about.

As we left I took one last look at their billboards—not used for advertising but for pictures of their leaders. Wherever you went you saw them. I saw a poster of the black man and a Russian shaking hands, very happy with each other. I saw a billboard about the five year plan, with the people looking forward and happy.

When we were out of Russia it felt like a breath of fresh air. As an American I was not used to the atmosphere, its tension and all that was behind the iron curtain.

My father was getting old now, but he still took great pleasure in hearing from me. The following letters summarize for him some of my visits to India and other countries:

Dear Father,

I just came back from India. I was there, representing CARE. Orin Mieker and his wife were there. They are a great pair. Both are writers and they are doing a book on India.

I also met Mrs. Ghandi who is the President of the Congress. She is very much interested in elevating her people from poverty. She and her advisors are now traveling through India teaching family planning.

Looking over this country, one sees nothing but poverty. Ford is manufacturing what they call a 'bullock pump.' It is a piece of machinery that draws the water from the ground when a bullock is attached to it and made to circle all day long. All around these operations you see green fields. Ford must be spending lots of money on these.

India is so poor that in Madras, I was told that 400,000 people are sleeping on the street. It is very surprising that in spite of eating and sleeping in the streets, where there is little or no sanitation, they don't all get sick. The government built latrines all over the cities for these people, which is good. They are a friendly lot and sing together and help each other all they can.

We of CARE have shipped many boatloads of food from American surplus. I cannot say enough for CARE. CARE is doing the greatest job of distributing food and feeding people, in the world.

Our Ambassador's wife is up early every morning, helping feed the many hungry children of India. She has a small truck, and mixes powdered milk each morning for them.

I am trying to be helpful. I travel from village to village. Some of the things I see make me very sad. I am glad to be an American. I wish other Americans could see the things I have seen over here. They take America for granted.

Love,   Maurice

Dear Father,   1958

Iran is a country where there have been great strides since I first knew it. It seemed that people didn't take their illnesses seriously here, and that hospitals reflected an indifference to suffering. They were not well run, and only the most extreme cases were admitted. They were terribly backward in every respect. However, the Shah has been stubborn and his country is moving ahead, especially with the sudden influx of wealth from oil.

The Shah wanted to open supermarkets in Teheran. His American advisors from USOM advised against it because it would upset the servants who do the shopping. That seemed like a shallow bit of reasoning. A better reason came from the two Germans who opened a fifteen cent store-type operation. The first day all the merchandise disappeared under the heavy floor-length veils of the women shoppers. In a Moslem country no foreigner would dare ask a woman to reveal what is under that veil. The Germans suffered a terrible loss.

The Shah insisted on seeing my slides and hearing my talk on super marketing. He gathered his ministers together for the evening.

Love,   Maurice

Dear Father,   1958

I just came back from Pakistan. ·what a poor country! CARE is here also. They have imported a staff to study the best way CARE can help.

The markets are about what we had in Russia. They don't seem to get away from the Old ·world. Most of them do not understand that other countries have advanced much more than they have.

Their life is as interesting as nothing. I feel very sorry for them and I am sure I have influenced them with my two cents.

The Minister of Health invited the CARE staff to his ocean home. I never had such a day. Beggars of all kinds, with every sick problem in the world, dragging camels, other animals and children one after the other, and there were snake charmers, too. We gave away all our money and that only brought more and more beggars. I felt sorry for them. I don't call that a home for relaxation. One had to be made of iron to see all that.

CARE is doing great work and I am glad to be part of it. I love America and appreciate everything about it.

In Pakistan, it is considered a disgrace for a high-caste person to do hospital work, so it is difficult to get really good personnel in government hospitals. For the same reason, there are very few women nurses, but one charming young Parsec woman wanted to become a physical therapist, and with our help, she studied in the United States, graduated, and returned to Pakistan to open a private practice. She came from a wealthy family, and we hope she will set an example for others so they would go into this kind of work.

Love,   Maurice

P.S. I will be leaving for Ceylon soon and will write you again from there.

Dear Father,   1958

Ceylon is an island which would look like paradise if it did not make for itself so many problems. When it got its independence in the late 1940's it had plenty of foreign currency, a trained civil service, a good educational system, plenty of foreign currency and was rich in tea, rubber, coconuts and other things. But they immediately fought amongst themselves and by the time we arrived there a civil war between the Buddhists and the Hindus was over but riots and strikes over political issues were ruining the economy.

I was as usual photographing the market when trouble broke out. Before I knew it four men came running out of a store, blood running down their chests. Someone brought four chairs out for them to sit on. A policeman was fanning them, for the flies were gathering on them. One man went completely out. I asked the policeman to step aside so I could get a picture of them, which he did. Other police were whipping the crowds to disperse them. The CARE mission chief ran up to me and said, "Are you crazy? Let's get out of here." A man was getting into his cart and we jumped in with him.

CARE is distributing milk here in the schools.

Love,   Maurice

Dear Father,   1958

Israel is another country where there are great changes. For one thing the settlements that started out with very poor settlers and sometimes with many handicaps are now prosperous. Undoubtedly they had much more in common than the settlers at Clarion, as these Jews have made a success of communal living in the agricultural areas.

CARE has some excellent programs in Israel. Israel had food rationing until 1954 so CARE food packages were very much in demand by relatives as a dietary supplement until the austerity period eased up.

Now CARE is involved in orphanages, vocational training schools and helping to solve problems in training immigrant children for skills to meet the demands of industry. CARE has also equipped three sewing centers for the Israel Women workers Council. Also we provided hundreds of kerosene stores for schools in Jerusalem and Galilee as health authorities noted an increased   incidence of rheumatic fever among children in these areas where heating is inadequate.

In the category of rehabilitation CARE has contributed one braille workshop, hearing aids for the deaf and didactic toys for mentally retarded.

We visited the very interesting project for Arab refugees in Gaza. This is a Food for Work program designed to help rehabilitate men who had been unemployed for many years in their refugee status, when Gaza was under Egypt's administration. This project includes repairs to hospitals, clearing roads, building maintenance, and planting 2,500,000 trees for dune control and sand stabilization.

At the request of the Israel government to help alleviate the poverty and ill health of the Bedouin people of the Sinai Desert, CARE has contributed manpower and funds to several work projects for clinics and food distribution, as well as several water control projects to provide permanent ponds for the herds.

These Bedouin have been among the poorest people in the world and I am proud of CARE's accomplishments there, together with the government of Israel.

Love,   Maurice

That was the last letter I wrote to my father. We returned to find him ill in the Cleveland hospital. We went to see him and my mind traveled over the years of his life and all that he had stood for. He was not comfortable with the idea of death, but he told me, "I am about to die and nothing can be done about it." A week later he left us.

Asia

Our travels in Asia introduced us to a world dramatically different from our own in climate, customs, costumes and ideas about life. The religion, and history and art of Asia have given Asian peoples a very different outlook. Humanitarian work as we know it was introduced from the West, mainly at first by Medical missionaries, teachers, or colonial government officials. Today organizations like CARE are doing something remarkable in relief work and in cooperating with existing medical organizations in primitive areas. One of the most interesting visits in that part of the world was in Kuala Lumpur in Malaysia. Among the projects we inspected there was a hospital for aborigines, an eight hour drive away on winding roads on which the government had to keep a crew working all day to keep them from being overgrown with foliage.

By the time we arrived at the hospital, we had seen many aborigines in trouble. Some of them had dysentery, abscesses, arthritis, tuberculosis and leprosy.

At that time, war was brewing and the General we met told me that the aborigine would never make a good soldier because he believed that meat is to be killed only for survival, and that they would never understand what fighting was all about.

The hospital was run mainly by doctors from Canada and England, since the British had been in that area for many years. CARE was aiding them with supplies. We arrived to see the families of the patients camped around the hospital grounds. When an aborigine child enters the hospital the whole family make their home there, usually with a lot of children. I handled some of their babies. They are very cute and playful, like any babies. The families cooked their meals over open fires. Their meals consisted of game and herbs.

Some of the visiting doctors became so interested in their work that when their two year assignments were up they sometimes continued on. They felt they could do more good there than anyplace. One of them carried an X-Ray machine on his back while he went in search of T.B. patients. This poor doctor became very thin because he was unable to eat the food in the wilderness, and he would have to come in periodically for a checkup and some nutrition.

It was my particular job for awhile to check on the babies in the ward, and I called them bouncing balls.

The hospital was overcrowded with many patients, mostly lepers. We took many pictures of them so the United States people could see the conditions and help.

While we were in Kuala Lumpur we stayed at the rest home. It was very inconvenient and the toilet was on top of a hill. Our bath tub was a barrel cut in half and the waste water ran onto the floor. Inez wouldn't go to sleep the first night because the head boy would not give us clean sheets until next Thursday, and this was Friday. The netting that kept the mosquitoes off us at night was very dirty too, but we decided to sleep in the sheets and put up with the netting anyway.

When we ate at the nurses' home the food was pretty good, but the little 12x12 restaurants we went to were so unsanitary that it took time for us to get used to eating there, but the doctors and nurses ate there and we finally got used to eating there too. It was surprising that the Hospital staff could accept the conditions they had to work under, but they were dedicated people who worked with lepers and other contagious diseases without worrying about becoming infected.

Vietnam

From there, we went to Vietnam, where we found the most beautiful men and women in the world. They were also the kindest and sweetest people one could wish to meet.

Vietnam was one of the most agonizing periods in our history. We not only lost men in a war whose meaning our people could not grasp, but through television we were for the first time able to experience its horrors in our homes. Moreover, by travelling and being enlightened by Americans participating in humanitarian projects there, Americans can relate to the people of Vietnam, both North and South in a new and very human way.

Recalling a trip as far back as 1959 may not seem relevant now. Nevertheless, my memories of how it was, tell me the tragedy may never have come about had our approach been constructive instead of destructive. It was a preview of what might have been—Southeast Asia with vast expenditures on technology and equipment. We failed to build up the area and perpetrated our longest and most futile conflict.

We went in to "make the Vietnamese behave." No one can doubt, after what we have seen there, that developing their agriculture, their medical and educational facilities and their industry—in short to strengthen the country for a peacetime economy. We could have avoided most of the anti-Americanism rife throughout the area that resides now. We would not have lost our men and boys, nor have the peculiar drug problem that is unfortunately going to be with us for a long time to come. Public indignation has been raised about waste in foreign aid. At its worst, can it compare with the ghastly waste of war?

In February 1959, my wife and I were met at Saigon's Tan Son Nhut airport by the staff of the CARE office and of the Disabled Rehabilitation Center, and by a group of disabled veterans, carrying a large, colorful banner that proclaimed "Welcome, Mr. Maurice Warshaw!"

The climate was hot and sticky but the ride from the airport gave us a chance to enjoy the panoramic view of the peaceful rural life outside the capital. Pleasant, clean people in brightly colored, cool cotton garments were carrying baskets of fruit along the roads, hung from bamboo poles over their shoulders. Farmers, men and women wearing conical rattan hats were tending the rice paddies and children rode on the water buffalo at work. Once in the city, we rested awhile in the Majestic Hotel, then went to visit the Rehabilitation Center for the Disabled. There were many patients there who were victims of Japanese occupation and the war of independence from the French, but war seemed to be a thing of the past. Everyone, doctors, staff and patients alike, were charming and overwhelmed me with their welcome, despite their afflictions.

That evening, there was a reception in our honor held on the lawn of the CARE staff house. The night was delightful with cool breezes and the air was heavily scented with the perfume of oriental flowers. The Vietnamese ladies lent a great deal of charm to the occasion with their dainty manners and pretty costumes. Saturday we visited the school for the blind, and we derived a great deal of pleasure out of presenting the school with many kinds of musical instruments, including a piano donated through CARE by American businessmen. We then proceeded to Hoi Due Anh orphanage. The children were all dressed in beautiful uniforms, but they had very few supplies to help their studies. Much to their exquisite delight, we distributed one hundred school kits which included paper, pencils, and erasers.

"Boys Town," the Don Bosco orphanage, was next. With quiet pride, the boys showed us a workshop equipped almost entirely by CARE with lathes, saws, circular saws and other tools. They had made all the classroom furniture themselves. The orphanage was a clean, well run organization with a competent director.

As in any country I visit, my greatest delight is visiting the markets. An Asian market is filled with color and interest. Everything there is related to the climate. Baskets are used for everything because they stand up to the damp climate. Inez was entranced by their wide variety of shapes and wondered at their uses. There were beautiful handicrafts of rattan and bamboo and very unique lacquer ware. Conical Vietnamese hats were a popular item.

We enjoyed a wonderful Vietnamese dinner in Saigon at the home of one of the doctors. The many courses were served one or two at a time by graceful servants moving silently on bare feet. First came cha-gio (a little sandwich made with meat), then nem (ham squares) and cha lua (goose liver paste). Next came chao tom (shrimps fried in batter) and bahn trang (rice pastries). The food was all arranged on delicate crockery and our hostess was dressed in the elegantly simple costume of the urban Vietnamese ladies: a light-colored long, fitted chemise, slit up the sides, over silk trousers. Curving her slender, pliable fingers back in a classic dancer's gestures, she signaled for us to be brought bahn uot (a thick, rubbery and very tasty dish), then baby pigeon, fresh cucumbers and greens in spices. More rice came with ga tim (a thick, soupy combination of chicken, peanuts, mushrooms and berries). The highly flavored nuoc mam sauce into which we dunked the various foods is a mainstay of the Vietnamese diet. It is a concoction of raw fish and salt pressed until liquefied. The dessert was lychee nuts and tea. Very early in the meal I had given up chopsticks and was provided with a fork with which to finish off this delicious repast.

On a beautiful Sunday morning we drove about eighty-five kilometers north of Saigon to the jungle village of Hung Phuoc (Lucky Hamlet). This was one of the most interesting experiences of my life. Jungle clearing presents problems difficult for the Westerner to comprehend. The 'tree hog' was being used to clear the land, and was another gift from CARE. This machine cuts away jungle undergrowth, vines, tree stumps— almost anything that stands in the way. I spent five days there with a crew. It was a real jungle, full of Southeast Asian wild life like monkeys, elephants and snakes, and as we cleared the land the animals penetrated further and further north into the jungle.

The land clearing project was making room to build houses for the immigrants coming into Vietnam from China and surrounding countries, and when we first came into the forest there was only a makeshift dirt road that was constantly and very quickly being covered over by the fast-growing jungle foliage. Five days later this growth actually scratched the station wagon when we tried to get through it. One time the driver got out of the car to move a fallen tree, but he jumped right in again when he discovered that there was an active beehive in it, and resorted to moving the tree with the front bumper.

Our living quarters were tents of netting. We had medicine to take regularly against malaria carried by mosquitoes. We cooked outside. The watering hole was quite a way away from the camp and was obviously a popular gathering-place for the monkeys in the area. They were being decimated by hunters and I thought that monkey-shooting should be made illegal, but there were no laws enforcing this.

One time, some soldiers came through our camp looking for rebels, and we could easily have been taken for rebels had not the CARE man with us known one of the soldiers. A day later we saw dead monkeys lying all over the forest. The soldiers had shot them to pass away the time. That was my first confrontation with the coming troubles.

There were quite a few voluntary agencies in Vietnam, such as CARE, Catholic Relief Services, Foster Parents' Plan, Mennonite Central Committee, and the Asia Foundation. There were many missionaries among the immigrants that had flooded into Saigon and the American Women's Association and the International Women's Association were active there too. All these efforts combined with the Vietnamese people's own desires to pull their country forward. Little did I dream that the many children we helped through CARE, who had been so happy and appreciative, would soon die, or become homeless and made to suffer hunger, disease and wounds which would affect their whole lives.

In the country one could see life as it really was for most of the natives in Vietnam. Farming was the main occupation of the people. Fishing was important but was not as fully developed as it should have been. Most rural Vietnamese lived in shelters made of bamboo with thatched roofs made of dried palmetto branches. Bananas, oranges, papayas, pineapples and *pampelmousse* (a variety of thick-skinned grapefruit) grew all over the countryside. It was a beautiful country, tropical with great rivers like the Meckong which could be developed for power, irrigation, and navigation. There were many interesting tribes and even aborigines in the hills.

It was relatively easy to get transportation in the Capital at that time. The taxis and cycles (pedaled by manpower) were all over the place. The taxis all had meters and the minimum fare was six piastres. We took the cycles for about five piastres. They went almost anywhere and were far safer than the taxis that travelled too fast for city traffic and were dangerous besides.

There were a number of restaurants serving both Chinese food and Vietnamese food, particularly in Cholon, a sister city to Saigon, three kilometers away.

One of the most enjoyable moments of the trip was a walk up and down Tu Do, or Catinat Street, looking in all the shop windows. There were many little Indian merchants who seemed to handle almost everything. Tailors, craftsmen, sidewalk cafes, milk bars and night clubs catered to a population which seemed to include people from almost every nationality in the world besides the Vietnamese. We departed from this lovely city on a bright and beautiful morning after breakfast at the CARE staff house. I said goodbye to everyone, promising to return, and return I did.

Our plane had to turn back before we flew over much of the ocean because something went wrong with it. We returned to the Majestic Hotel but were unable to get a room because the place was all filled up. We tried the only other hotel in the city and were given the worst room I'd ever seen. I called up the mission chief who had a friend who was a General and lived in the hotel. The General moved to the Mission Home and we got his room.

It is heartbreaking to think back on a peaceful Saigon with its lovely people, their cleanliness and their artistry. War seems such a waste. Why weren't negotiations chosen instead of war? With the riches and ingenuity of our country we are always in a position to negotiate. Vietnam is the best possible illustration of how war can weaken us and be utterly profitless to all concerned.

Dubossar Again

Memories were stirred up for me as my wife and I embarked on our third trip to Russia in 1963 in behalf of the International Society for the Welfare of the Disabled. This time we were going to visit Dubossar for the first time since I left there so many years before. On the other two trips my travels had been confined mostly to large cities but now I had letters of introduction to the staff of all the hospitals and medical facilities in the Soviet Republic to take me wherever I wished to visit. No matter where I went it was open to me. Leningrad, Odessa, Kiev, Sochi, Yalta, Rostow, Muldovia, Kohen, even to remote Dubossar.

The terrible pogroms that caused us to leave seemed far away now, but like my father before me, those years had developed in me, a philosophical nature that eventually led me into the humanitarian work I was now engaged in. Not in a religious sense necessarily, but into a social consciousness of other human beings.

By nature I am a *questioner* rather than a *believer*, more the *observer* than a *proselyte*. This had given me the opportunity to observe people everywhere and I found them basically the same in whatever country I had visited.

Even the cries of "Christ-sellers" was only a distant echo in my memory now, but under any circumstance I was glad to visit the place of my birth even in a country that was in such sharp political focus at the time by all major countries of the world. I wondered about a Dubossar behind the Iron Curtain, and how much it must have changed under a system of government that had changed so much since our family had been forced to flee our home there so long ago.

I knew I had changed. The bitterness was gone now and I was grateful for the experiences of those years in between that taught me that underneath all the outer hostility and competitive aggressiveness there is an inner quality, common in every individual, that identifies with each other. It is only the dogmas throughout history that has separated us. But paradoxically, people whose religious principles teach love, mercy and justice do not necessarily develop better attitudes toward each other.

Our train ride from Bucharest, Roumanian, to Kishinev had some interesting facets to it. It was an old relic of a train and we were surrounded by curious crowds from the moment we boarded it at Bucharest. Mostly women in route to their homes in Kishinev, showed a great interest in things of feminine American. An English-speaking Muscovite woman in our car made it possible for us to communicate. They told us that Americans are seldom seen in Moldavia, which lies in Southwest Russia, bordered by Rumania on the west and the Black Sea on the South. Judging from some of their questions, such as "Do all people in America really have all their meals completely prepared in the factory?" and, "Do all Americans, marry, divorce and remarry many times?", it appeared to me that the people of Moldavia, of which Kishinev is the capital, saw very few Americans.

After an hour or two of questions and answers, I presented some lipstick and nylons to our translator and to her girl friend. The supply of American lipsticks, costume jewelry and nylons made excellent "get acquainted" articles, and soon we were enjoying the kind of relationship that makes travel for us a real pleasure.

One of the women who received our gift gave my wife a beautiful set of beads to express her appreciation, and she invited us to her home in Kishinev for dinner. We accepted, of course. She was a charming person, a 28-year-old widow named Anna Molotov.

Customs inspectors boarded our train at the Russian border during the night and snapped on the lights in our compartment about four in the morning and told us to prepare for inspection. I had been sleeping in my clothes because we were sharing our compartment with two Russian women and there was no dividing curtain.

The inspectors hit us in three separate waves, much to the delight of the crowd that gathered around our compartment. The first inspector was typical of the two who were to follow although his duties were different. His uniform was frayed and his blue cap ragged, but he stamped our passports sternly with an officiously attitude. The second inspector was a crowd-pleaser. His job was to inspect our luggage, and never before or since has our luggage been eyed so critically, as if he were expecting a roll of highly dangerous micro-film to drop out. The audience enjoyed the show immensely, and for that matter, so did I. If the Russian people desired to see the possessions of Americans, why shouldn't they see ours?

The third inspector's manner was the most threatening. It was his duty, he said in English, to accept our declaration of the jewelry, cameras and so forth, and to confiscate any items we might have above the permissible amount. Excess jewelry would not be tolerated. I made our declaration. It's strange how the mere threat of a penalty in Russia sounds so much more serious than it does in other countries.

"I'm glad that's over," I said, once the last inspector was safely out of earshot.

"I'm afraid I have something to tell you," my wife said nervously. "I didn't declare all my jewelry."

She had it in a stocking tied about her waist because when we toured South America recently she had left most of her jewelry in our home safe and burglars had broken in. Although the police caught them in time it scared her. In the last minute packing rush she had impulsively taken the items she valued most and placed them in her valise, thinking they would be as safe there as anywhere, since we had never encountered any threat to our personal property during previous travels. Unfortunately she had not given much thought to customs regulations. She whispered all this as we sat side by side in the compartment of a train whistling through the early morning toward Kishinev, our first stop in Russia.

For a moment I considered summoning the customs inspector and amending our declaration. But then, I thought, who is going to believe such an oversight? So I decided to leave things as they were and avoid any situation that could possibly lead to a search of either our persons or our luggage.

I was still pondering my decision when an incident occurred that decided the issue. I had a small amount of Roumanian money left and had decided to give it to the Muscovite woman who had interpreted for us the day before.

"Oh, no," she told me quickly. "I couldn't take it. I didn't declare it to the customs officials."

"Couldn't you amend your declaration?" I asked. "It isn't much, and you could tell them you merely overlooked it."

"No," she said quietly, "I couldn't do that."

Her manner convinced me to keep silent. Our train reached Kishinev about eight-thirty that morning.

It was from here that we had escaped from the cellar. All the memories flooded back and for a short moment we were in the wagon traveling toward the border. I remembered the old fears but most of all I remembered the Koloskys. My parents had corresponded with them a long time after we left. I remembered the letters they had written to them, not only keeping them up to date about what was happening to our family but thanking them over and over again for helping us escape.

I especially remembered how Father had gathered labels from candy containers and sent them to Mr. Kolosky. We wanted to show him how they sold candy in America. He told him about the chocolates that were put in little cups and arranged in attractive boxes and tied up in beautiful ribbons. He wrote to them about ice cream and how people bought it as much as they did candy. He even sent him a recipe for ice cream and for some of the different candies they made in America. Once he had sent him some salted peanuts to show what they ate instead of sunflower seeds. He thought he might. be able to grow and market them in Russia.

I remembered all these things and wondered if I would be able to find the old neighborhood of both my Mother and the Koloskys. But things had changed so much that even the shrubbery looked different and where my last memories were of destruction I saw only a peaceful city which had grown to a quarter of a million people.

I had made prior arrangements for an interpreter-guide from Intourist, the Soviet State tourist bureau, to meet us at the station. We left the train in the company of Anna Molotov at whose home we were planning to dine three days later. She was still with us when we met the interpreter, who introduced himself to us as "Yavon," and since she needed an interpreter at our dinner together, she also invited him.

Yavon first drove us to the hotel to get a room and then took us for a tour of the city. At one busy corner we noticed something like a Coca-Cola machine, with people queued up for drinks. The machine was automatic, with only one small water spigot and one glass. The spigot was turned up so that each person would up-end the glass and wash it before filling it to drink from. Yavon drew our attention to many small libraries and bookstores. Inside one library many people were browsing through racks of daily newspapers, some of which dealt with religion. One was titled "Who is God?" Another was, "The New Religion," which was, of course, communism. All the publications were put out by the government, but recently there has been public criticism against government censorship. More than three-fourths of Kishinev was destroyed during the war, but there had been a great deal of reconstruction. However, the new apartment houses still looked drab. Some had television antennas on the roof, and we were told that there are many privately owned radios.

Yavon wanted to be with his family that evening, so I asked him to telephone a certain Dr. Malinsky for me before he left us. Dr. Malinsky took us from the hotel to a hospital where he gathered his night staff for introductions. It was a small but busy hospital with two shifts on a twenty-four hour schedule.

Two of the doctors who could speak English acted as interpreters and our visit became a very pleasant one. We exchanged information on vocational rehabilitation, and they impressed me with the quality of their work.

They became quite sociable and served us a light supper complete with the traditional vodka. They were interested in our laymen's polio, cancer and heart organizations, in our public and private hospitals, medical schools and research centers. Everything in Russia is run by the government, and one doctor boasted that everyone in the U.S.S.R. is entitled to free dentistry, free medicine, and free hospital care. I could have argued that point and told them I had seen too many of their people with bad teeth and in need of hearing aids and eyeglasses.

The women doctors were very much interested in what my wife was wearing and watched her intently. It was obvious that the Russian people were becoming more and more insistent that the quality of consumer goods be improved.

It was difficult for them to understand why small countries like Holland, Belgium and Sweden could be so far ahead of them in everyday comforts, and I could almost speculate that a silent revolution was beginning—a pending change that even a normally observant tourist could spot.

On our second morning in Kishinev, I arose at five-thirty and set out for the bazaar. Since marketing has been my life, observing marketing methods in another country is as enjoyable for me as reading a good book is for someone else. In the market I can "read" the people, the economy, the agriculture, the food processing, the distribution, and, to a certain extent, the government of a country.

Of course, the market was the place I most wanted to use my camera, and naturally I did not anticipate any objection. The bazaar covered an area of about six city blocks and seemed to be the business hub of the area. There were lines of waiting people that stretched from every place of business, ending in another line that formed at the streetcar stop. It was July and all of the marketing was being done in the open air. Even at that hour, the bazaar was crowded with women enjoying the coolness of the early morning, eager to get their choice of the produce and other items available. Fruit seemed to be scarce, but cabbage, potatoes, cauliflower and cucumbers were plentiful and inexpensive.

I began snapping pictures, for the scene was fascinating. Steaming glasses of tea were being served to shoppers from a samovar mounted on a pushcart. The Russian people drink great quantities of tea, and the samovar is the traditional way of serving it. There was no evidence of salesmanship as we know it. There were many clerks waiting on customers, but none of them seemed in the least concerned about making sales. Because everything is government-controlled, one does not hear the usual bickering that is so common in the European marketplaces. There is a conspicuous absence of free competition.

At a stall full of fish, tea and other foodstuffs, the old woman in charge had fallen asleep, and I wondered if she would be penalized for stealing a few moments of well-earned rest while her fish and tea remained unsold. At another stall, wine and packaged meat were being sold, surely an odd combination. The meat was not butchered into chops, steaks, or roasts. Nearly all the cuts had bones in them and were packaged in pieces weighing about a pound and a half. The packaging consisted of flimsy waxed paper with the price (very high) marked on it.

The stores were small, with an old-fashioned barrel of olives, oil and pickled watermelon, open bins of grain, cornmeal, tea and coffee, while preserved foods were kept in glass containers. The Russian people shop for fresh food every day because refrigeration is a rarity in stores as well as homes. With long lines outside, the stores resembled depots.

The clothing of the women shoppers was as quaint as the decor of the shops—a mixture of the old and the new with stiff, heavy skirts, heavy shoes or thongs and large babushkas that made them look frumpish. The leaders of the U.S.S.R. believe that women should be natural-looking, without paint or powder or fancy hairstyles, but the ladies I talked to about this would have liked to look and feel feminine again.

Altogether, the marketplace in Kishinev was a photographer's paradise. I took many pictures of the stalls with their scrawny fruit. Both shoppers and sellers were affable and receptive to my photography, except for a man and his partner who were loading a stall with fresh meat from a wagon. When I clicked a picture of them the man stopped working and ran over to me shouting angrily and trying to grab my camera. A small crowd gathered quickly. The man soon desisted, and I walked away quickly, thinking he had stopped because of public embarrassment. But I was mistaken. Within five minutes two men began to follow me. As soon as I snapped another picture they approached. No one spoke, so in order to break the silence I asked them where I could catch a taxi.

"Come with us," one of them replied, "and we'll show you where you can get a taxi." They fell into step on either side of me, and I didn't need to be told they were policemen, even though they were not in uniform. I gathered from their apparent sense of purpose that we were not going to catch a taxi. It was impossible for me to protest, so the three of us merely walked along through Kishinev's broad streets.

Soon we entered a drab, windowless, two-story building - a police station, evidently. The men directed me across a dimly-lit hallway to a wooden bench against a wall and told me to sit down and wait. There were about fifteen Russians sitting on an identical bench opposite me. There were both men and women, all poorly dressed and all looking despondent. I wondered why they were here.

After a quarter of an hour I was summoned. I arose and left the Russians still sitting on their bench. The two men in civilian clothes and a third man directed me to enter a small room down the hall. Inside there were only two chairs and a table. I was directed to sit in one of the chairs. The third policeman took the other.

He began speaking in Russian, and I indicated that I did not understand him. The three men talked among themselves for a minute and then abruptly left. I sat waiting for forty-five interminable minutes, worrying all the while about the concealed jewelry. I knew that a search of our hotel room could have serious consequences.

Finally one of the arresting officers reappeared and once again told me he would show me where to catch a taxi. He led me back in the direction of the bazaar and left me abruptly, without a word. I stood there dumbly, wondering what next? Am I supposed to leave? So I said to myself, "Nuts. I'm not waiting for a taxi, I'll take a streetcar back to the hotel. It would take forever to find a cab."

Although it was before 10:00 when I returned, Yavon was already waiting with the car and driver. I asked him why he had not warned me about taking pictures, complaining about my treatment by the police.

"But you can take pictures," Yavon said, and then, shaking his head slowly, remarked half to himself, "Sometimes you don't know what they are talking about." Then he brushed the incident off with a laugh, saying, "Anyway, when you are with me, feel free to take pictures of anything you want, unless I tell you not to."

Relieved, I went up to the room to get a few things but did not see any reason to bother my wife by telling her about the incident. I took the film of the bazaar with me, but curious as to whether the police were actually interested in my photography, I arranged three magazines on top of my film valise and made a sketch of the arrangement in my notebook.

The maids had already cleaned the room, so if the arrangement was disturbed upon our return, it would indicate someone else's snooping. Then we set out for Dubossar.

During the ride out of the city, I once again tried to imagine what our people had sacrificed in the terrible pogroms to preserve a religion that taught them tolerance and brotherly love. While there was appreciation for the ideals of my parents and those before them, my feelings for religion had long since altered to an attitude of skepticism because so many of the heartbreaks in history came about by some of the most deeply religious peoples warring against others in the name of God.

At last we were on our way to Dubossar. It was a twenty-four mile journey to the northeast across the winding Dniester River. The scenery was magnificent, with the fields all in bloom. The beautiful reds, pinks and oranges of the poppies gave a cheerful aspect to the whole landscape.

"How will the people and the little village have changed?" I wondered as we neared my native place. Undoubtedly everything would be different.

Excitement and curiosity mounted in me, for this was where my mother and father, my brothers and sisters and I were born. Here is where we were children. Here was the scene of much love, of my father's singing and story telling. My mind moved on to the good business my father had built up, and then I recalled the discouragements and the hardships and the sorrow of parting with our relatives and friends, leaving everything behind.

My family and I were forced to flee, so I could not regard this trip as a nostalgic return. Bodies lying about with their throats cut remain in a man's memory, often crowding out the pleasant memories. The consequences of the pogrom in Dubossar were etched into my mind, even though I was a child when it occurred. Often during later years I relived the terrible shock of that violent day when Bola's family was murdered.

When we arrived at the Dniester River, I saw how much things had changed. As a child I used to cross the river on a huge ferry barge, but now two steel bridges spanned it. Nearby stood a power plant which Yavon assured me was the largest in Russia. He also told me that it was perfectly permissible to take pictures both of the bridges and of the power plant.

As we drove into Dubossar everything looked strange. The only familiar landmark was the river. Yavon said that the population was now 53,000, much larger than in our time. Even now, however, there was only one paved street, and the small stores had an uninviting look, with badly painted fronts and dull looking signs. Most of the windows were dirty, a condition that could not hide the fact that there were very few displays inside.

We stopped for lunch at a restaurant which Yavon recommended. He assured us that it was the very best in Dubossar, and I had no reason to doubt his word. Nevertheless, it was not something an American would call good. My wife declined ordering, saying that she had no appetite, but I ordered a meal with the usual borscht made of potatoes and cabbage. Finding it unpalatable, I ordered a glass of beer, which was served warm in a dirty glass. Somehow, I managed to drink it.

The rest of the patrons were poorly dressed, and I wondered how they regarded the food. I noticed one man shoving some rolls into his pocket. Yavon and the driver braced themselves with vodka throughout the meal. The driver kept an eye on the doorway. He did not want a policeman to come in and see him drinking, but he did not seem to think that he should mind. Although I minded very much, I said nothing.

Since we planned on a two-day visit, we next went to a hotel to arrange for rooms. Perhaps because of the low quality of the restaurant, the thought of sleeping in a hotel in Dubossar brought to mind another childhood memory—the uncontrollable infestation of bedbugs and lice. As we were registering, another guest informed us that they were still a very real problem.

Our room was furnished with a Chinese rug and heavy furniture. The walls had not been painted for a long rime, and although the largest electric plant in the world was within ten miles of us, there was only one electric light globe in the room. Later we learned that our driver and Yavon had slept in the hall, which surprised me. Such arrangements did not sound to me like what communism was supposed to offer.

As soon as we were settled, we decided to start our tour, and I soon saw that things had not changed as much as the bridges and the power plant had suggested.

There was an occasional automobile, an occasional tractor, an occasional television antenna, but it was odd to see so many old things and so few new. There were many more horse-drawn wagons than trucks. The town had grown considerably, but the streets were still unpaved and the houses were drab affairs.

As we were walking about, I was able to talk to several Jewish people. Among my childhood memories was the rabbi who had instructed us and made it his business to punish us severely for wrongs, both real and fancied. Sometimes the punishment was just for laughing out loud and sometimes if he thought we had not learned our lesson well. I had a sudden desire to see how the Torah was being taught now. I knew Russia had abolished all parochial schools, but I was interested in seeing if any Hebrew traditions were being taught to the younger generation. So I walked to the old synagogue.

As I approached my heart quickened. Would it look the same or would it have lost the splendor of my memories? As it came into view it looked familiar, but faded and isolated. I had the feeling that it had been a long time since the joyous spirit of Passover and Rosh Hashanah had been there.

Inside there were about thirty-five Jews praying. I asked for the rabbi. When he came over to speak to me he was cordial but evasive. I could see that he wondered what our purpose was.

A few of the congregation gathered around. To allay their suspicions, I immediately told them that I was born in Dubossar. They relaxed and drew closer, so I asked, "Have you ever known or heard of any Ramples or Warshawskys in this area?"

A few vaguely recalled a Rample family, but they seemed to have little interest in recalling things from the past. Perhaps the events that had transpired since the Revolution had made the old way of life unreal to them. At least they showed little interest in my relative's whereabouts.

I then asked them, "Have you heard of the Koloskys in Kishinev?" After some thought, one old man answered. He seemed to recall that there was a grandson in the food business there now. Perhaps some of their disinterest rubbed off on me, because I found myself becoming less intent on finding out anything. It all seemed so long ago.

I looked around at the synagogue of my childhood. The long benches facing the eastern wall were still there, with the reading desk in front of them. The table where they had read the Scrolls was there and in the center of the wall stood the Ark. I wondered if the same richly covered Torah was still behind its closed doors. I saw the Star of David on the eastern wall and for a moment it was as if I could still hear the shofar and the singing and my father's voice above the rest. But no one opened the Ark that day or carried the Scrolls with their little tinkling bells to the table to be read.

I wanted to find our old home. I knew the direction to go, but I was not sure any more just where the street was. Yavon helped me to identify the old landmarks. Finally, I recognized the street and began to walk quickly. I could almost see the lace curtains at the windows, but when we reached the spot where I was sure our house had been, the only evidence I found was the remains of the old foundation, almost buried beneath the weeds. The well had been covered over with some weathered planks and there were gnarled and twisted trees where once had grown our beautiful orchard. I felt downhearted as we returned to the hotel.

That evening we ate at another restaurant, which appeared cleaner and more orderly than the one where we had eaten lunch. As was our custom, we ordered compote, which in Russia is a glass of light, watery syrup with a small amount of rather mediocre fruit. We were also served a tasty soup made of carp, but were warned not to speak while eating for fear of the bones that might get caught in our throats. We ended the meal with potatoes and herring, making it the strongest fish dinner we had ever eaten.

After supper we went to a drama called "The Bedbug." It seemed hilarious, but then we could not understand much of it.

The next morning we went out to learn more about the conditions that existed in Dubossar. I was shocked to see that there was more anti-Semitism here in Moldavia than in other parts of Russia. From my conversations with the people in the synagogue and with the Jews I managed to speak with on the streets, I gathered that their situation there is unfortunate. Moldavia has always been anti-Semitic and still seems disinclined to outgrow it. It also surprised me that I could still immediately recognize a Jew on the street or in a store merely by certain mannerisms.

I learned from my conversations that the Jew is always the last person to be given a job and must perform the most undesirable tasks. The police and the people are always on the alert for an excuse to harass Jews, and many expressed fear that they might be seen speaking with me.

One man, who ran a vodka and soft drink counter, told me that his apartment was very crowded but he was repeatedly denied larger quarters. Even though the authorities had promised him a more spacious apartment, their promises had been continually broken.

At one restaurant we were served by a Jewish waiter. I inquired about his life as we ordered our meal. He talked freely at first, but later when he brought our plates he was silent.

Two young Jewish men in Dubossar did strike a positive note, however. They told me that Russia was their home, it was where they would have to raise their families and spend their working lives, and that they must do the best with it they could. They believed that by working and studying hard they could make a reasonably good life. These young men were confident that anti-Semitism would disappear within another generation. They claimed that even now there was a lessening of anti-Semitic incidents.

Yavon had some relatives in Dubossar, and at first he was reluctant to permit us to visit with them. But I talked him into bringing us into their home to get acquainted. The relatives were of the "old school," the real Russian type, with their home quite barren except for necessary furniture. But the crucifixes on the walls set them apart from other Russians, and the school books lying about were used, according to Yavon, by the whole family.

Everyone was very congenial, and we were immediately served tea and cookies, as is customary in Russia. They made us feel welcome, and except for the language barrier we felt at ease with them. They told us that several languages are spoken in Dubossar, but primarily Russian and Romanian. I had noticed that some of the signs in store windows were printed in Romanian. Other than a few familiar words, my Russian had almost entirely been forgotten.

Finally, after two exhausting days of touring, we left Dubossar. Nearly everyone, both citizens and officials, had been cordial, and the journey back to Kishinev was more pleasant than the two days earlier, which had been filled with such black memories. Yet even now a few unpleasant things came back to me as we passed the horse drawn wagons and the trucks carrying workers home from the fields. I remembered the cold winters of my childhood, the deep snow, and the threat of starvation that was so real to so many. As I watched the faces of these Russian laborers flashing by, I wondered if they possessed the some competitive drive that American farmers have. I felt a certain kinship with them as I thought about what these people had endured—the Japanese-Russian war, the revolutions, and the two world wars. It was hard in Dubossar at best.

As we drove on, my thoughts returned to my relatives. "What has become of them?" I wondered. "How did they meet their fate?" All my inquiries had come to nothing. Finally, I had to admit the probability that they had either been killed during the Revolution or relocated as refugees.

I could only wonder, as we crossed the stark Dneister bridge, how a country which could build such bridges and power plants could remain so static in other respects. Our visit had been like turning back the clock. I wondered what my destiny might have been had I stayed in Dubossar, had my family not been forced to flee. As a child, I had regarded the flight as an adventure. And today, as I look back on the years since that time, I see that my entire life has been an adventure. I only hope that in some way I have done my share to show my appreciation to my adopted country.

We arrived back in Kishinev in the middle of the afternoon. Inez and I first planned to rest and then to dress for dinner with Anna Molotov, whom we were to meet in the hotel lobby at six o'clock.

But things did not quite work out that way.

As we entered our room I silently noted that the arrangement of magazines on my film valise had been disturbed. Although I immediately went through the contents of the valise, I could not be sure that anything was missing.

"I think we've had a snoopy maid in our room while we were gone," I said as nonchalantly as I could. "Do you notice anything disturbed?"

"My jewelry," my wife exclaimed, running to her cosmetic case. "I should say! It's been unlocked and opened." Hurriedly, she dug down through the contents, and there on the bottom, in a small, inconspicuous box, lay the jewelry. Apparently, whoever had looked in the case had overlooked the jewelry. I was still stewing about it when the telephone rang.

It was Yavon, but his voice had taken on an unfamiliar, harsh tone. The local head of Intourist, he snapped, wanted to see me immediately in the lobby.

Full of apprehension, I went down the stairs. Both Yavon and the official from Intourist, whom I had met before, assumed a solemn manner. They escorted me to a room on the mezzanine, where I was surprised to see the three policemen whom I had encountered three days before. My heart began thumping against my ribs, and my face flushed with anger. I now figured that they must have discovered the jewelry, and I resented the way they were trying to toy with me. I silently began to prepare myself to counter their interrogation.

But it was just as well that I kept my thoughts to myself, because I soon realized that they really had overlooked the jewelry. Instead, they began to question me about my photography. The driver, they said, had reported that I had taken pictures of the power plant and the bridges near Dubossar. They also wanted to know why I had been so curious about every nook and cranny in Dubossar and why I had asked so many questions of so many people.

They put it bluntly. "Who sent you?"

Stifling an impulse to tell them that the driver had not been sober long enough to know what I took pictures of, I instead went after Yavon, demanding that he explain to the police that he had given me permission to take the pictures. I could see that Yavon's instinct for survival would not allow him to relay my words to the police. They were becoming angry at his answers, however, whatever those answers were. The real trouble was manifest as the were becoming more angry with me.

"Why did you take pictures without permission?" they wanted to know.

"It is my custom in every country to take many pictures," I replied. "I photographed the bridge and power plant to show how my childhood home had changed."

"And why did you take so many pictures of the poorest parts of Russia?" they continued evidently referring to the many pictures I took of the poorer sections of Dubossar. "Look," I answered. "If you would visit our country, you would be free to take any pictures you wish, so I cannot see why I cannot do the same in your country."

"This is not every country! This is the Union of Soviet Socialist Republics! You must ask permission before taking pictures of anyone or anything!"

A policeman who had been silent until now asked, "Why are you only interested in taking pictures of our poorest parts if you do not intend to show Russia at its worst?"

I knew I must try to defuse this potentially explosive situation, so I replied as calmly as possible, "I cannot understand you people. What are you so disturbed about? Why are you so sensitive about your situation? If, as you say, you are ahead in progress, you are the first in inventions, and that your people are healthy, your crops are good, and everyone is working, then what is it that you fear? That we will tell lies about those pictures? We don't insult your people, yet you insult us."

They chose not to respond to my questions. Instead, one of them tapped a booklet that he held in his hand. It apparently explained how tourists should conduct themselves in the Soviet Union. "Have you read this?" he asked.

"I was never given one," I replied.

Yavon was taking no chances, so he refused to tell them that he had failed to give me the booklet. Eventually the argument reached a stalemate, so the police changed tactics.

"Where are your passports?"

I pulled my passport from my pocket and handed it to one of them.

"Where are your travel tickets?"

"In my room," I replied.

"Go up and get them," one ordered curtly.

I walked to my room, recalling that I had left the tickets, the only means we had of obtaining transportation in Russia, in the valise with the film. But when I opened the bag, I could not find them. A hasty search through the rest of our belongings failed to turn them up.

"What's happened?" Inez asked. "You look pale."

"Nothing," I mumbled as I went back out the door. "We're just making travel arrangements." I do not think I sounded very convincing.

When I returned to the mezzanine, I admitted that I did not have the tickets.

"I gave them to you just the other day," the man from Intourist fumed. "Don't you remember?"

I was rapidly losing patience. Their attempts to badger me were provoking. "The way you people are treating me," I snapped, "I don't remember anything anymore."

"You do remember," he insisted. "I gave them to you myself and you put them in your shirt pocket."

"I don't think so," I returned. "If you had given them to me, I would have left them in my room, and they would be there now."

For several minutes the four officials conferred among themselves. Then abruptly they were silent.

"May I leave now?" I inquired to break the silence. I had allowed my voice to show my disgust, so it was not without surprise that I watched them nod in assent.

"Before I go," I added, "can you tell me just where my travel tickets are?"

"We cannot," the Intourist official answered. Again we all stood in awkward silence. Our plans for Moscow, the balance of our trip, all depended on the travel tickets. Unsure of what to do, I simply turned around and walked out the door.

As I returned to our room, I was still nervous. I could not imagine them making such a fuss over the pictures. The jewelry, I once again reasoned, must have been discovered, and they were trying to find out what I intended to do with it. The effects of the confrontation must have been obvious as I reached the room, because my wife would not accept my story about the travel arrangements. I had just decided to tell her about both interrogations when a knock at the door interrupted me.

I opened the door, fearing the worst, but it was only Yavon. Silently he handed me the missing travel tickets and then walked away. I didn't know what to say. Whatever they might not be, I finally decided, the Russian police are certainly masters at the art of surprise.

Relieved of my most pressing problem, I brightened considerably and began to get ready for dinner. I was not pleased at the prospect of bringing an interpreter along, especially because that interpreter was Yavon, but as we entered the lobby I was in high spirits.

Shortly after six o'clock Mrs. Molotov arrived. A pounding rain, which had begun falling earlier that afternoon, was still drumming on the roofs. But even though our hostess was soaked, she presented the most welcome and happy smile. Anna was her name and I remembered how she impressed me as a sincere, generous, guileless young host, and it would be a pleasure to spend dinner time with her. Since Yavon had not yet arrived, she told us that she would go look for him.

It was a full hour before she returned with Yavon, and during the interval I concluded that she was probably being interviewed by the police, which seemed to be confirmed as she walked toward us. Her spontaneous, charming smile and natural, direct manner had been replaced with a gaiety that seemed false. The evening apparently, would be a cat-and-mouse game, and the mouse would have to be extremely careful indeed.

Although Kishinev is a large city, taxis are hard to come by, and Mrs. Molotov had to walk some distance in the rain to find one for us. As I watched, I saw her wade through a torrent of water that swirled along the gutter. Once in the taxi, we drove several miles through the downpour before halting at what looked like an alley. Mrs. Molotov explained that we would have to walk through several of these narrow passageways before reaching her house. I had some misgivings as we made our way along the dark corridors. The events of the day still weighed heavily on my consciousness.

Anna Molotov lived in a small, four-room cottage which we entered through a rear door. The front door, she told us, was seldom used, since it only opened into a small, common courtyard. She showed us the courtyard, a small area completely bare of any growth, although three other cottages also faced out onto it. I could not help but wondering why four Communists could not co-operate in creating a little garden for their mutual benefit.

Mrs. Molotov's cottage was, by American standards, humble. The rooms were small, and everything was put to double use. For example, the bathtub was covered by a board, which converted it into a work table. The dining table was in the living room. With the chairs placed around it, the arrangement nearly filled the room. On one side of the table was a bed, evidently part of the seating arrangements. Every room in the house had at least one bed in it, making it look as though part of her family had been dismissed for the evening so that six guests could be invited.

I could tell that the people already present had taken pains to dress up for the Americans, but something seemed awkward in their actions and their way of standing. They did not have the poise that we usually see in young Americans. Perhaps I only imagined it.

But the room itself took on a cheerful appearance because of the beautiful table setting, and it was apparent from the extravagant meal served that the hostess had gone to a great deal of personal sacrifice to make the evening enjoyable.

"It's too bad," I thought, "that she is being forced to participate in such a pathetic sham after she has gone to so much effort and expense to prepare for the evening."

Only one picture hung on the wall, a double frame with only one side filled. "I see you have a picture of Lenin," I commented, "but why is the other half vacant?"

"Stalin," she replied, implying that further comment was unnecessary.

The atmosphere during the first few courses of the dinner was unpleasant, because Yavon and Mrs. Molotov were obviously intent upon carrying out their assignment. Whatever their object, I was kept busy carefully tailoring my answers to their questions. But the caviar, vodka, wine, cheese, and roast goose soon had their effect. Eventually the conversation began to lag, and the other women guests saw their chance to change the direction of the talk. They began asking questions about American food and fashions. Yavon was reluctant to translate such foolish subjects.

But then Mrs. Molotov told a joke that included a rather obscure Moldavian colloquialism which oddly enough I remembered from my childhood. Yavon had, of course, been translating, but when I heard the colloquial expression, I repeated it enthusiastically. I was so delighted to have recognized it after so many years that I interrupted Yavon and nodded to Mrs. Molotov to show her that I understood her words.

"I thought you didn't understand Russian," Yavon said, looking at me with narrowed eyes.

"I don't," I replied, and I tried to explain how I happened to remember the words.

Yavon began asking me questions. We started to argue. Ignorant of the significance of our debate, my wife brought out a small bottle of perfume to show to Mrs. Molotov. Spraying some on her hostess's arm, she told her to keep the bottle as a remembrance. Mrs. Molotov answered with a squeal of delight and began chattering happily about things far removed from politics and ideological differences.

Although the other women had not been able to persuade Yavon to change the course of the conversation, Mrs. Molotov overwhelmed him with her questions. She insisted that he translate for her immediately. Looking totally disgusted, Yavon reluctantly relayed her request for a dress pattern to my wife.

Inez had brought along some earrings and a necklace and had been waiting for the right time to present them to Mrs. Molotov. Now she handed her hostess the gifts, which ended, once and for all, any would-be intrigue as far as Mrs. Molotov was concerned. Yavon was kept busy for a long time translating from one language to the other questions and answers about makeup and foundation garments.

Several women from the neighborhood dropped in later, and we presented them with nylons and American magazines. They immediately began leafing through the magazines and were especially intrigued by the advertisements, because Russian magazines contain no advertising. They loved the cosmetic ads and asked innumerable questions about mascara, false eyelashes, perfume, hair rinses and shampoo. Yavon was obviously embarrassed to translate such intimate things as questions about what kind of brassieres American women wore. But the women insisted, and everyone laughed hilariously except Yavon.

They pointed to advertisements of electric can openers, knife sharpeners and ice crushers and asked how these small electric appliances were used. They were like children in their wonderment and enthusiasm. They were astounded at the varieties of canned goods in our stores. They had never heard of grapefruit and pineapple. They wished they could buy ready-made clothing for their children.

Later in the evening, when all the magazines had been gone through, a few of the neighborhood children came in to recite poetry in English for us. The thought occurred to me that here we were communicating, and that the children who were learning English today in school would tomorrow be grown up. Then we will be more at ease with them. As today we are able to establish civil and perhaps even cordial relations with the Russian people, tomorrow perhaps we may become genuine friends. More communication still would be forthcoming if we would do more with foreign languages in our schools.

I had brought along some pictures of my drug stores and food markets, which I now showed to the group. They could not understand such abundance. But their reactions convinced me that if these people had enough money and the freedom to leave, they would all have joined us on our trip back to the United States. I enjoyed myself immensely, smiling smugly at Yavon, who returned a sour look and bore up under his task of translating comparisons of American and Russian marketing procedures.

Finally, it was time to leave, and Yavon went out to find a cab. When he returned we said our goodbyes and followed him down the narrow alleyways to the street. The alley seemed even longer and darker than it had before. When we reached the gate it wouldn't open.

"What does this mean?" I wondered. Finally, with a bit of fumbling and a push, it opened. In front of us stood the taxi, and I could make out two men sitting in the front seat beside the driver. My apprehension increased.

"Who are they?" I asked Yavon, who shook his head.

"Get in," he replied.

The four of us climbed into the back seat, and as we drove off in a new direction, I became certain that we were going to another police station. I wondered if I could take another hazing with good grace. Eventually we stopped in a darkened neighborhood, and one of the men got out. To my surprise, we drove on.

Our next stop was in front of the police station where I had been detained on my first morning in Kishinev. Here we stopped only long enough for the other passenger to leave us. Again I was relieved. And as we drove on to the hotel, I thought about the joy women are able to experience in such trivial things as lace and perfume.

"Never again," I silently vowed, "will I scoff at what I have always regarded as a mild form of lunacy."

Anna, Yavon, Inez and I were still crowded together in the back seat of the taxi when we finally arrived back at the hotel. Mrs. Molotov looked like a contented hostess. Her party, after all, had been a social success. Her guests would talk about us for months. She was the one who had discovered the two Americans, and she was the one who brought them home for her guests' entertainment. We warmly thanked her for her hospitality and said goodbye to her and to Yavon.

But my experiences with Yavon and the police had their effect on me. Even the next day on the flight from Kishinev to Moscow, I spoke to my wife cautiously, in whispers. Two Russians who had boarded the plane with us sat nearby, even though there were many other vacant seats. After Kishinev there seemed to be a shadow behind every bush, and it nearly ruined the rest of my trip.

We had heard a great deal from people who had toured in Russia. Some of them assured us that hotel rooms were routinely bugged.

"Anything you say in the room can be heard," they told us. Because of these warnings, Inez and I were very careful not to speak of the jewelry in our hotel room, fearing that there might be a listening device installed. Consequently, most of our conversations were conducted in whispers. And I changed our flight from Moscow to Paris from the Russian airline to Air France.

On the day of our departure, I re-marked the film, printing "Bucharest" on the films of Kishinev and labeling the other films "Kishinev." Once again Inez put the jewelry in a stocking and tied it around her waist. We went to the airport, bracing ourselves for the worst. After a long wait, we were ready to board the French airliner. We had, I thought, passed the inspections of all the various customs officials. But suddenly a uniformed guard appeared and ushered us to a room where a female attendant was standing.

"This is it," I told myself. "After all the trouble that blasted jewelry has caused, this woman will search my wife and find it." Cursing our bad luck, I entered the room with Inez, whispering to her that she could just as well begin untying the stocking, since she would be searched anyway. We sat down and waited. I realized that I should have told her about my visits with the police, an element of Russian society with which she had not become acquainted. At least she would have been prepared for what was about to happen. The woman walked toward us and introduced herself politely.

"I'm your Air France representative,'" she said.

I stifled an impulse to laugh.

Minutes later we were in the air on a nonstop flight to Paris.

"Tonight we're going to paint the town white - not red," I assured my wife.

"That sounds wonderful!" she laughed.

I leaned back in my seat and began to muse. Although the Russian people have a long history of endurance, they are not the only ones who have suffered hardships. My wife's mother, a convert to the Mormon religion, pushed a handcart through the American wilderness and withstood many trials. And many millions like her fought and worked to produce the America we have today.

For a long while I just sat looking out the window and trying to relax. Finally, I turned to Inez and told her a story I had once heard. As the story goes, a prominent American official and his wife were visiting Russia. They were informed that they must be very careful of what they said in their hotel suite because the Russians had nearly all the rooms wired and could hear everything that was said. After a few days of saying almost nothing to each other, the official became provoked and began to search the room, thinking that he would be able to find the listening device. At last, after a thorough search, he felt in the middle of the floor, under the carpet, a very thin, almost invisible square. Pulling back the carpet, he saw that the square was a metal plate fastened to the floorboards. He decided to pry up a corner of the plate and found it was attached to some wires. Angrily, he cut through all the wires with his pocket knife. Quickly he bent back the metal plate and covered it again with the rug. A few minutes later there was a loud knock on the door. When he opened it, he was pushed back into the room by several excited people, who loudly informed him that their chandelier had just fallen on them and would he please explain the hole in his floor. Of course, this is just a story, but seriously speaking, wasn't it unnecessary for the chandelier to fall?

Africa 1970

For our tour of Africa in behalf of UNICEF, KSL-TV in Salt Lake City sent along a photographer to film the trip.

Africa's peoples are nearly all emerging from colonialism, but they have not yet learned to govern themselves. Civil or tribal wars have been costly. Mismanagement of their resources and institutions since independence shows in the poor maintenance and going down hill of many buildings and lands.

Ethiopia is one of the poorest countries on earth. I could not understand the poverty. There is very little evidence of progress or even concern for the people.

I met many experts of various kinds trying to help the Africans, but many said they felt Africa would never progress. I do not believe that, but I can clearly see that it will take a long time. For one thing their lands are largely eroded or leached out, and they have a lot of debilitating diseases, both of which make it almost impossible to grow adequate crops without a great deal of technical assistance in soil conservation.

There is good work being done in Rehabilitating the Disabled, but it is extremely limited.

There are all kinds of church organizations and foundations such as Ford and Rockefeller lending African countries a hand in building colleges and hospitals. The United Nations agencies are trying hard to raise the standards of production for African farmers, but some of the best technical assistance projects are being conducted by Israeli experts. Coming from a newly independent country themselves that had many of the same problems at first, Israelis seem to understand what these people are up against. Their projects in raising cattle, poultry and fish are very successful.

Africa is a magnificent continent with wonderful people. I left wishing them well.

Russia 1970

In 1970, I made my fourth trip to Russia to look over their day care centers. When I arrived in Moscow I first went to the United States Embassy and from there, directly to the market place. It had always been my custom to scout around a city on my own to get a good look at the daily life of its people. It was November and all the fruit was gone except for some specked apples. Russia was always a country for garlic, and there were bins of it for sale along with cabbage, cauliflower and root vegetables such as potatoes and parsnips. I wondered how they ever got any variety in their meals or how they ever found enough food for their families to eat wholesomely. No one was losing any weight, though, and everyone seemed to be hale and hearty, yet food seemed to be rather scarce. I bought some prunes which the clerk put into a cone-shaped container fashioned out of newspaper. I also found some grapes which cost $6.50 per kilo (two-and-a-half pounds).

Later in the week I attended the theater with a group of Americans. It was a very cold evening, and as I stepped outside after the performance, I felt the chill. We had to walk many blocks back to our hotel, and when I finally entered my room I began to feel ill. Suddenly, I was seized with a heart spasm. A friend called an ambulance and I was rushed to the hospital. The spasm turned out to be inconsequential, but the Russians were taking no chances.

Four men carried me down fourteen flights of stairs on a stretcher, back out into the cold November air, and into the waiting ambulance. The ambulance was not equipped with blankets, and autumn can be very cold in Russia. They covered me with bedding from my room that one of the attendants thought to bring along.

The Russians have a world-wide reputation for medical progress, but from what I experienced in that hospital, that reputation seems ill-founded. There was only one telephone for the entire hospital of one thousand beds. The nurses' uniforms were limp and grey. I was given one towel during my nine day stay, which I also had to use as a wash rag and napkin. The bed sheets were not changed and there were no hospital gowns provided. A nurse finally smuggled in a pair of pajamas for me. The only thing they did furnish was a pair of old leather slippers, but when I went into the bathroom I could not help getting them wet in the water that always lay on the floor. The toilets never seemed to work right.

The multitude of shortages and inconveniences that I observed during my short hospitalization convinced me that socialized medicine left much to be desired, but the doctors, nurses and other patients were very friendly. I was a real curiosity to them during my stay. I showed them slides of my stores, which intrigued them. An interpreter would come down for three hours a day to interpret for us, and I enjoyed telling my fellow patients about how most of the working people in America owned their own homes and had cars to drive.

"If you are so well off, why do you have so much trouble in your country?" they asked. "If there is so much for each person, why is there so much crime?" was another typical query.

The Russian newspapers told them that Americans had everything they wanted and yet they were always full of dissension. It was often very hard for me to answer their questions. Still, we were all very friendly. When twenty-four candy bars were delivered from the American Embassy, I passed them out to the doctors, nurses, and other patients. I was the talk of the hospital.

Everybody loved to discuss Capitalism and Communism. They especially enjoyed emphasizing how wasteful our system was and how conservative theirs was. I was surprised to hear them claim that they had more freedom under their government that we did under ours. They talked about pollution, saying "at least we have good air and no smog," and would cite newspaper pictures of the pall that hung over New York and Los Angeles. They also loved to bait me with questions about the riots in Detroit and Watts.

But all our debates were carried out in the spirit of basic cordiality. My fellow patients were friendly. The doctors and nurses knocked themselves out attending to me. If Russia were to be judged solely from the atmosphere in the ward, it must be a wonderful, beautiful country.

None of the people in the hospital shied away from me. On the contrary, they wanted to help me turn out my light, cover me up, or share any fruit they happened to have. I was never treated better, not even in the United States. The nurses and doctors borrowed my magazines. A patient in the next bed gave me a piece of cake; another, some cookies. Still another one brought me a delicious apricot drink. One day my nurse brought me a plate of apples, the man next to me peeled them with his penknife, and we shared them with everyone. The patients were considerate not only of me, but of each other as well.

My birthday came around while I was still in the hospital. The patients presented me with a card they had signed. Each one also wrote a little note with his address on it so I could write to them. Every one of them managed to come over to my bed to shake hands and say "Rostia"—health and happiness. Someone had brought a birthday cake, so we cut it up and passed it around. I also received cookies, tomatoes, tangerines, and more apples. A friend of mine from the American Embassy brought a big can of orange juice. I filled all our glasses and someone proposed a toast.

I learned a lot about the Russian people during that hospitalization. They are not a people to cry. Instead, they try to cheer each other up with jokes and bright chatter. Their families visit them constantly, bringing them food and reading matter or games to while away the time. They sit and hold each others' hands, just like people all over the world.

After a few days, I was tired of lying about. I had a sore back and a sore shoulder, but apart from that I felt wonderful and I wanted to go home. The doctors refused to allow me to leave unless I promised to go home on a stretcher. If I didn't consent, I'd have to stay five days longer. I agreed immediately, so Pan Am arranged for a stretcher and removed several seats from one of their planes. Several people from the Embassy came to see me off.

I was taken to the airport by ambulance. As we rode along I watched the billboards from the window. There is no advertising in Russia so they were used for propaganda. Every billboard I saw was "hate America" oriented.

The first one was of a heavy booted police type person wearing a dollar sign patch on his sleeve and carrying a pistol holster labeled "Pentagon." He was stomping his way along a place labeled Cambodia. On one foot there stood a soldier with a helmet labeled "Saigon" while on the other foot there was a soldier labeled U.S. The caption read "One foot there, the other foot here." The message, of course was directed at labeling the U.S. aggressor nation in Southeast Asia.

A particularly vicious billboard showed the head of the Statue of Liberty. The points on the crown were in the form of missiles, rifles and a hangman's noose, behind which lurked a small Klu Klux Klan figure, and two other unsavory looking characters. The Statue of Liberty was shown wearing dark glasses with prison bar-like stripes. The caption read: Liberty, American Style."

I could only see the Statue of Liberty through the eyes of the immigrant, as I had that first day when I so joyously looked at her as she welcomed us to the land of freedom.

I looked at another billboard showing Uncle Sam facing a map upon which was written the word MIR (the three letter word in Russian meaning PEACE). An arrow was drawn from each letter of the word, with the labels "Attack on Laos," "Attack on Cambodia," and "Attack on Vietnam." The caption read "Peace Strategy of the U.S.A."

I grew weary of looking at billboards and closed my eyes. Could the friendly Russian people, such as I have just left at the hospital, be stirred up by this hate propaganda as they had been so long ago in Dubossar? First against the Jews and then against the State. The people had cried peace then too, but they could not tolerate the nothingness of a limbo under the complete subjection of the Monarchy. They rose in rebellion which resulted in communism. In the end they just traded the Czar for Stalin.

As I left Russia, which in all probability would be my last trip to my native land, I could only hope that the people of the Soviet Union and all people under such regimes would become sufficiently skeptical of any hate propaganda to ignore it.

I was going home now, and as we winged our way toward America my memory again wandered back to the past: to the time when we first came to the United States. From the beginning my father had loved America and could discern its brightness through the dark clouds of social and political unrest, even when its melting pot had bubbled with the ferment of terrible working conditions, low wages and strikes, creating hot disputes between capital and labor.

Yet the lesson taught me from living under a democracy is that man grows in freedom. When he is not bound or held down he begins to flourish and triumph over the conditions that beset him, and rises to create the reality of his dreams. His philanthropy can then increase to embrace the whole world.

I reflected back on the Jews through the centuries and how they had kept their government intact, even when, for them, there was a non-existent home-land, except in their hearts and minds. No matter where they were driven or in what country they lived, they governed themselves according to the ancient laws handed down by Moses. The strength of their government had been preserved in their traditions, and those traditions were a part of me .

Russian, Jew, American? I was part of all. This should have caused division within me; rather I have learned that if the brotherhood of man and the long hope for peace among the nations is to come, we are going to have to find a way to reconcile our differences in order to correlate our similarities.

Nature is diversified and so are peoples. If in nature we find harmony, then also should man be able to attain it.

It will remain for future generations to build a highway, broad and free towards peace. I leave this message to them and to my children and grandchildren.

I emphasize my gratefulness for life. How it came about I do not know but I do know that you can waste it away or use it in the service of others.

Death is not a fearful thing. It is natural. It comes to everyone. If there is more after this, I shall be grateful. Life cannot be a "Primrose path." Sometimes it is more like the refiner's fire that separates the precious metals from the base ones, but the answer has always been, and still is, the salvation of human dignity.

I know that life can be harsh, but it can also be fair. Even in its darkest moments the light is always discernible, just as the clouds part on a stormy night to reveal the stars.

Sometimes it is bitter and sometimes it is sweet, but we can always fined *Life more Sweet then Bitter.*

Observation:

Maurice left this world in 1979 only 9 years after his last visit to Russia. My Father Clarence and my mother Rhoda retired from service to Grand Central Stores after the loss of Maurice. My father died of cancer three years later in 1983. My mother Rhoda died in 1998. Keith Warshaw died in 2008, about 18 years after he closed Keith Warshaw and Company in 1979. When Keith was about to close, I left for California. The team was gone, but the vision will be in the memories for years to come. This second edition of the life of Maurice Nathan Warshaw is dedicated to his only son Keith Maurice Warshaw and a good friend to me.

Ronald Kelsch
Editor Vision Impact Publishing
Saint George, Utah
2015

Society for the relief of disabled children - Hong Kong

Medico - old Dooley operation - Hong Kong

Peace Corps in Chile

Training the young people in Israel to produce items
with the tool kits

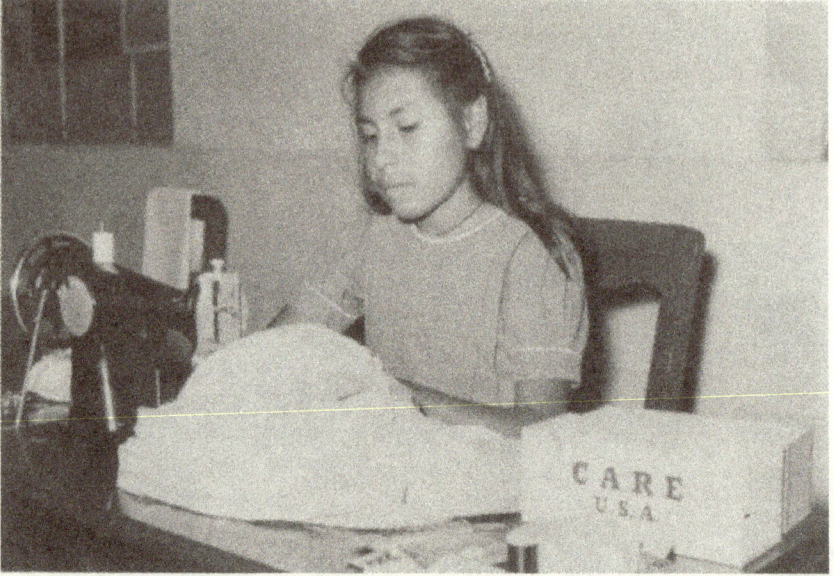

Young Honduran girl using equipment provided by CARE

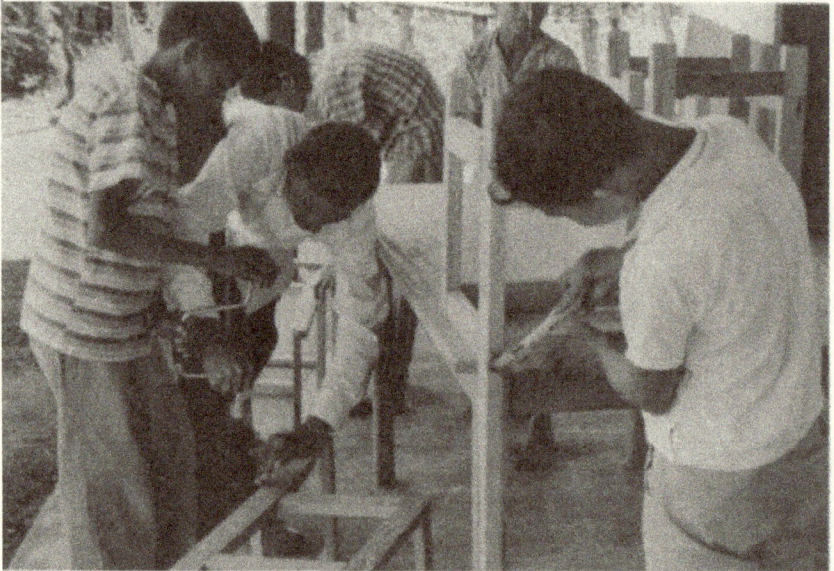

CARE carpenters' kits, donated by Four-H Clubs in the U.S. gives these Panamanian members the opportunity to build.

Using a wooden shovel in Mexico

*FOOD FROM AMERICA brings happy smiles to this widow
and her children in Bogola, Colombia*

A committee in Peru honoring the CARE committee with flowers

Peace Corps showing how to build in Honduras

CARE warehouse in Israel

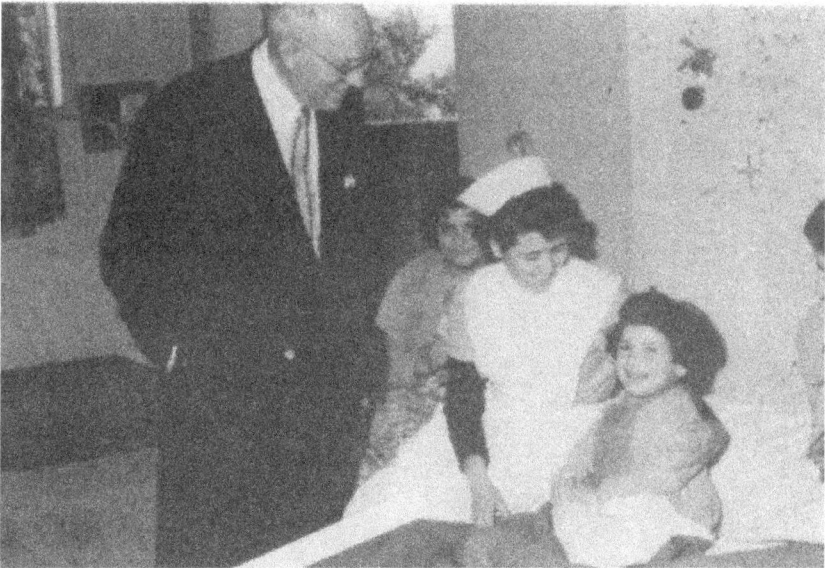

Children in Hong Kong Hospital

Teaching them how to dry fish in Hong Kong

Welfare program in Indian village in Guatemala

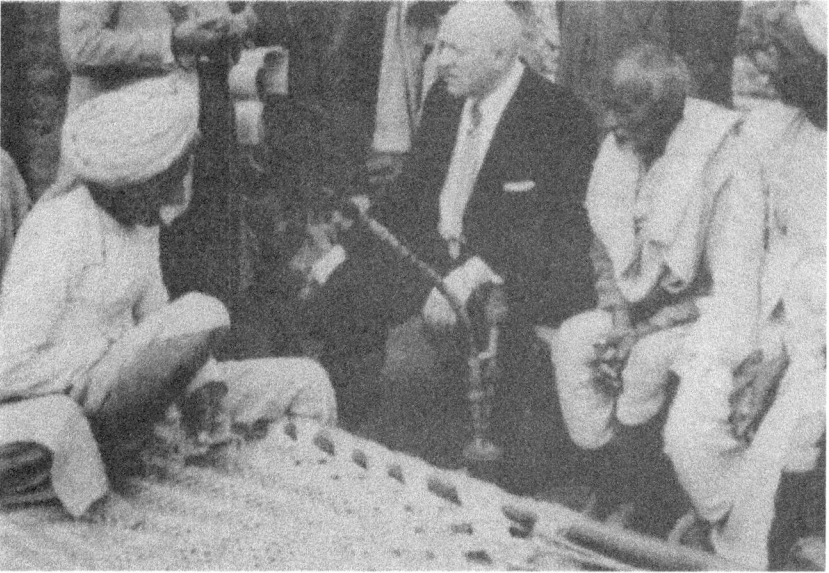

Smoking the Pipe of Peace, India - Unicef

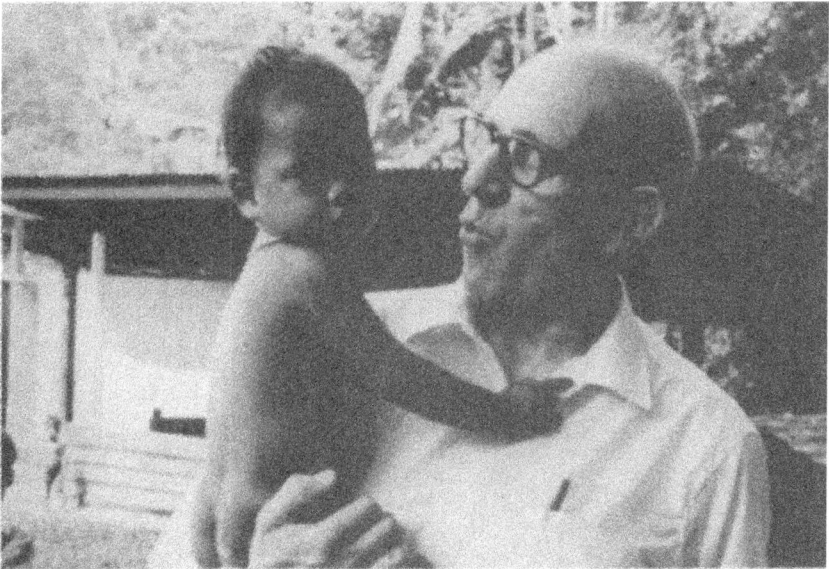

Aborigines in Kuala Lumpur Malaya - CARE

Meeting with the President on needs of the handicapped

Helping the Handicapped Award

The President's Committee on Employment of the Handicapped

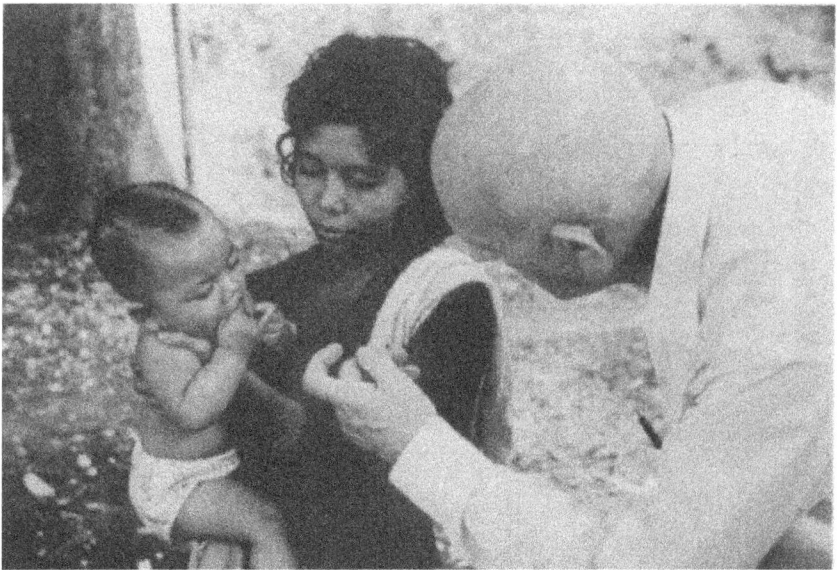

Aborigines in Kuala Lumpur Malaya - CARE

Representing CARE in Saigon, Vietnam - distributing goods to the war stricken

Overseeing CARE distribution of goods from the U.S. in Cambodia

A common experience for Maurice and Clarence

Loren D. Jensen, left, is congratu- | ence O. Kelsch, right, during award
lated by Maurice Warshaw and Clar- | ceremonies for handicapped employes.

Handicapped, Employers Get Awards

What Really Counts: Skill, Brains

"Society only pays for skill in your hands or knowledge in your head," the director of the Division of Physical Medicine and Rehabilitation, University of Utah Medical Center, said Friday at an employment of the handicapped awards luncheon.

Dr. James R. Swenson said that physical, psychological, social and vocational restoration at the center is possible in cases where the patient has a job to return to or a family or loved one that is interested in him.

Blinded in Combat

A former Marine who was blinded in combat during World War II — Loren D. Jensen, Tooele — was presented with an award by Gov. Calvin L. Rampton as Utah's "Handicapped Citizen of the Year."

A guided missile mechanic at Tooele Army Depot, Mr. Jensen was chosen "Zero Defects Employe" at the depot in 1965.

Clarence O. Kelsch, advertising director for Grand Central Drug Stores, received a citation for "Meritorious Service" at the program at Hotel Utah and Rex L. Campbell, master of ceremonies, said Mr. Kelsch has devoted much of his time to various areas of the employment of the handicapped movement.

Honor 5 Employers

Five Utah employers who have hired many handicapped workers and provided training for others were honored by the Governor's Committee on Employment of the Handicapped, headed by Maurice Warshaw.

Employers receiving merit awards were Hill Air Force Base, Tooele Army Depot, Litton Guidance and Control Systems, Ajax Presses and Quality Linen and Towel Supply Co.

Five high school students received first through fifth place awards for the written reports they submitted in this year's "Ability Counts" contest sponsored by the committee.

Contest Winners

They are Marilyn Syphus, Viewmont High School, Bountiful; James R. Howard, Granite High School; Maurine Jensen, Hillcrest High School; Mary Lee Memmott, Ogden High School, and Darrell F. Leo, Granite High School.

Miss Syphus will receive an expense-paid trip to Washington, D.C., by the Utah State AFL-CIO and all five students received savings bonds from Utah Disabled Americans.

Dr. Swenson described service available at the U. of U. Rehabilitation Center, the only facility of its type between Denver and the Pacific Coast, and said that each medical advance creates more work for rehabilitation services.

Disproves Old Myth

"The old myth of benefits of inactivity has been disproved," he said, pointing out that exercise, group activity and various types of motivation now are prescribed as early as possible.

"The team approach is utilized at the rehabilitation center," Dr. Swenson said, "and as soon as the stitches are taken out or the temperature is down, we try to get the patient back to work."

Clarence O Kelsch was at the side of Maurice his entire adult life. He was not only an employee that started setting up produce, he became a friend and confidant by using his talents as a commercial artist to give not only an image to Grand Central Stores, but he pioneered full color advertising for news print that could not be achieved by traditional color separation in which magazines used. He lettered the Grand Central logo with a few hand strokes. His favorite newspaper ads were the full color art of produce and color enhanced black and white photos of meat cuts. His greatest achievement was an award from McCall's Magazine advertising award in New York for his portrayal of Grand Central Stores from Push Cart to Supermarket. He worked along side Maurice in every effort to promote and advertise for the various needs of the handy-caped, March of Dimes, American Cancer Society, and many other organizations.

Rhoda Kelsch

A musical play of Life more Sweet the Bitter
Presented at the Promise Valley Playhouse
Music by K. Newell Dayley Lyrics by Pat Davis

Note:

Rhoda Kelsch was too modest to require her name with Maurice on the cover of the first printing. Clarence Kelsch designed the cover and titles. He also instigated the artwork, but he did not know how to list Rhoda Kelsch as a participating author. It has been corrected with this publication.

Maurice honored both Rhoda and Clarence for their work in publishing the Book and collaboration with the production. The LDS Church, who owns the rights to the music should receive ultimate appreciation for the musical. Both Newell Dayley and Pat Davis put together many productions for the Church. Ron Kelsch produce the album recoding.

www.ingramcontent.com/pod-product-compliance
Lightning Source LLC
Chambersburg PA
CBHW031944090426
42739CB00006B/79